ACTIVE TRAINING

ACTIVE TRAINING

A Handbook of Techniques,

Designs, Case Examples,

and Tips

Mel Silberman,

assisted by Carol Auerbach

An Imprint of
Pfeiffer Jossey-Bass Inc., Publishers

To my father, Jules Silberman.
May his memory be for a blessing.

Published by

An Imprint of Jossey-Bass Inc., Publishers
350 Sansome Street, 5th Floor
San Francisco, California 94104–1342
(415) 433–1740; Fax (415) 433–0499
(800) 274–4434; Fax (800) 569–0443

Pfeiffer

First published by Lexington Books.

Printed in the United States of America

ISBN 0–7879–0908–4

HB Printing 10 9 8

Library of Congress Cataloging-in-Publication Data

Silberman, Melvin L.
    Active training : a handbook of techniques, designs, case examples, and tips / Mel Silberman, Carol Auerbach.
        p.   cm.
    Includes bibliographical references (p.   ) and indexes.
    ISBN 0-7879-0908-4
    1. Employees — Training of — Handbooks, manuals, etc. I. Auerbach, Carol. II. Title.
HF5549.5.T7S555   1997
658.3'124 — DC20   96-41933
                                                                    CIP

Visit our website at: http://www.pfeiffer.com

Outside of the United States Pfeiffer products can be purchased from the following Simon & Schuster International Offices:

Prentice Hall Canada
PTR Division
1870 Birchmount Road
Scarborough, Ontario M1P 2J7
Canada
(800) 567–3800; Fax (800) 263–7733

Prentice Hall Professional
Locked Bag 531
Frenchs Forest PO NSW 2068
Australia
61 2 9907 5693; Fax 61 2 9905 7934

Prentice Hall/Pfeiffer
P.O. Box 1636
Randburg 2125
South Africa
27 11 781 0780; Fax 27 11 781 0781

Prentice Hall
Campus 400
Maylands Avenue
Hemel Hempstead
Hertfordshire HP2 7EZ
United Kingdom
44(0) 1442 881891; Fax 44(0) 1442 882288

Simon & Schuster (Asia) Pte Ltd
317 Alexandra Road
#04–01 IKEA Building
Singapore 159965
Asia
65 476 4688; Fax 65 378 0370

CONTENTS

FIGURES

CONTRIBUTORS

———

We wish to express our appreciation to the following training professionals from whom we have obtained tips, designs, and case examples for this book:

Jackie Agostini
Marie Anderson
Sharon Balaban
Jeff Brown
Marion Burns
Gretchen Castle
Claire Conway
Karen DiNunzio
Germaine Edwards
Chris Gillespie

Janis Heil
Alf Higginbotham
Serge Farmer
Steve Krupp
Jody Gandy
Allan Geller
Linda Guerra
Neal Goodman
Dan Harvey
Ann Houser

Cathleen Hulce

Linda Hyman

Maryann Keenan

Rosa Landes

Janice Engler Marks

Monica McGrath

Rick McKnight

Elaine Mendelow

Chrissa Merron

Lee Miller

Nasim Mohamed

Karla Nurcyzk

D. J. O'Loughlin

Cindy Perkiss

Bill Pinchuk

Whit Raymond

Sandy Saville

Milt Silver

Jane Silverman

George Spence

Bill Stieber

Fay Stokes

Maria Sudeck

Karon West

Susan Wheelan

Vicky Whiteling

Charlotte Zaback

Ruth Zasloff

INTRODUCTION

Training is one of the biggest growth industries today. The need for trainers is so great that line managers often are recruited to provide training within a corporate organization. Moreover, training professionals no longer reside solely in the private sector. Many public sector organizations now have a serious commitment to training their employees and the communities they serve. In addition, there is an increase in the number and size of human resource development programs at colleges and universities.

The active approach to training described in this book involves a commitment to **learning by doing.** Everything we know about adult learners suggests that participants must be actively engaged during a training program. Without group participation, they will forget or fail to apply what they are taught, as well as be bored by the material presented.

As *Active Training* promotes learning by doing, it will show you how to acquire these skills through **learning by example.** We will not only describe several active training techniques but also show how they have been applied in actual training situations. These designs and case examples drawn from private and public sector training professionals will give you ideas for your own situation, encouraging you to become an interactive reader.

One of the special features of *Active Training* is the wide variety of training topics covered in our examples. They include such diverse issues as:

team building	word processing
coaching and counseling skills	problem solving
project management	banking procedures
time management	claims adjustment
customer relations	performance appraisals
assertiveness training	real estate sales
meeting management	business writing
career development	creative thinking
stress management	cultural diversity
addictions	developmental disabilities
interviewing skills	employee motivation

We cannot promise to provide you at every point with the perfect example for your particular needs. Nonetheless, you should find that the examples are flexible enough for you to customize them to the topics and groups you may be training.

Unlike many training guides, *Active Training* emphasizes what you can do to *create* training designs, not just to deliver them. Some professional trainers are asked to teach a program straight from a published instructor's manual, with no opportunity to modify either the structure or the content of the course. *Active Training* is intended for those of you who have some freedom to modify how a course (or seminar, workshop, or program) is taught. Altering the sequence of course modules or changing, however slightly, the format and methods through which the course materials are delivered often can improve the learning experience dramatically for your participants. Further, you may have the opportunity to redesign a previously taught course, adding new approaches and ideas gained through the reading of *Active Training*. And, finally, you may find yourself in complete control over a course design. In this situation, when you must make the multiple design decisions that constitute a professional training program, the many techniques, designs, case examples and tips described within *Active Training* become especially useful.

If you are new to training, reading *Active Training* can help you to understand the reasons why trainers make specific design choices when creating an active training program.[a] In addition, you will learn a variety of facilitation techniques that can help you to conduct any training program professionally. The examples will help you to make sense of the components of a good active training program in a way that straight text never could.

It is our hope that *Active Training* will continually provide you with specific guidance as you refer to the text throughout your career, whether you work in a business, governmental, educational, or human service setting.

[a]A distinction is often made between a "course designer" and a "trainer" when the assumption is made that they are two separate people. We will use the term "trainer" throughout this book to designate a person who both designs and conducts training programs. This "trainer" will alternately be referred to in the singular as he or she (except when an actual person is being mentioned) since both sexes are well represented within training ranks.

ACTIVE TRAINING

DESIGNING AN ACTIVE TRAINING PROGRAM

I

Many training programs seem like an inert, gray mass. One part of the program blends into the rest. Even when intentions are sincere, the activities seem to progress like an endless freight train of content, going nowhere in particular. By contrast, an active training program is characterized by **activity, variety,** and **direction.** More specifically, eight qualities set it apart from other program designs.

- **Moderate level of content.** In designing training programs, the tendency too often is to cover the waterfront by throwing in everything possible about a given subject. After all, you only get one shot at these participants, so you'd better make sure you have covered it all. You may fail to realize, however, that participants will forget far more than they will ever learn. The best approach is to be selective, choosing the need to know before the nice to know. Training programs that promote active learning have a lean curriculum. They concentrate on the critical learning areas—those elements that provide the essential basis on which to build later. When the content level is kept moderate, the trainer has time to design activities that introduce, present, apply, and reflect upon what is being learned.

- **Balance between affective, behavioral, and cognitive learning.** Active training involves a three-pronged approach: fostering attitudes, developing and practicing skills, and promoting understanding of concepts and models behind the subject. Some training programs tend to focus on one of these areas to the exclusion of the others. But you want participants not only to know about something but also to be able to do it. Furthermore, you want them to look at themselves in relationship to what you are teaching and consider how it works for them.

- **Variety of learning approaches.** Active training employs a wide assortment of methods. A variety of learning approaches keeps interest alive and can help minimize the downtimes when energy levels are low. Another and even more important argument for variety is that adults learn in different ways. Using different learning approaches is likely to be more effective than a single approach that may work for some but not for others. Time allocations, group formats, and the physical setting can also be varied to heighten the training experience.

- **Opportunities for group participation.** Group participation has advantages in any active training program. Involving the group moves training from the passive to the active. Group activity engages participants in the learning process and makes them working partners with the trainer. Lecturing is held to a minimum as highly participatory methods such as role playing, simulated exercises, and case discussions are featured.

- **Utilization of participants' expertise.** Each participant in an active training program brings relevant experiences to the classroom. Some of these experiences will be directly applicable; others may involve analogies from previous jobs or situations. In either case, much of the active learning in a training program comes from one's peers. You can build into your design many opportunities for participants to learn from each other.

- **Recycling of earlier learned concepts and skills.** Programs that feature active training have designs that are continually referring back to and incorporating earlier skills and concepts. In effect, the curriculum spirals. Participants get the chance to review what they have already learned and apply it to more challenging tasks. What has previously been taught is rarely passed by, never to appear again. Instead, key concepts and skills get reintroduced as the program becomes more advanced.

- **Real-life problem solving.** Active training designs emphasize the real world. Opportunities are set up for participants to utilize course content to address and help solve actual problems that they are currently experiencing. Application is not just something that happens after training; it is a major focus during training. Participants learn best when they get to work on their own material, cases, and examples. This gives the information immediacy and enables participants to assess its utility on the spot.
- **Allowance for reentry planning.** At the conclusion of any training program, participants will naturally ask, "Now what?" The success of an active training program is really measured by how that question is answered—that is, how what has been learned in the course is transferred to the job or back home. An active training design ends with consideration of the next steps that participants will take and the obstacles that they will face as they implement new ideas and skills.

When you go about the task of designing a training program that reflects these eight qualities, you face a creative challenge not unlike an artist's. Many decisions are ahead, and there is no right way to make them all. And there are different ways to create the same effect. Consequently, there is no orderly way to proceed. Many instructional designers, in fact, don't always function best in a step-by-step progression. The following sequence of steps, however, should serve as a general guide to designing an active training program.

1. **Assess participants.** The first step in designing an active training program is to find out as much as possible about the participants. If this information cannot be collected prior to training, assessment activities should be incorporated into the beginning of the program. The more assessment data that you obtain, the better for planning, customizing, and modifying a design.
2. **Set general learning goals.** With the assessment data in mind, identify potential learning goals for participants. In general terms, describe their needs in the areas of affective awareness, cognitive understanding, behavioral skill building, real-life problem solving, and on-the-job (or back-home) application.
3. **Specify objectives.** Get specific about the kinds of learning you want the participants to experience and the results you want to achieve. Each general learning goal will have one or more objectives that, when met, will signal accomplishment of that goal. State these objectives in

a form that will make them effective tools for managing, monitoring, and evaluating the training.

4. **Design training activities.** Now that objectives have been clearly and explicitly stated, you must design training activities to achieve them. At this stage, it is sufficient to generate a broad outline (method and format) of all the activities that you think will be necessary to meet each objective in your program. List the possibilities in pencil, on index cards, on a personal computer, or using any other medium that is erasable or rearrangeable.

5. **Sequence training activities.** Play with the order of the activities until you obtain a sequence that has a good mixture. Consider which designs are needed for the beginning, middle, and end of your program. Adjust the order to improve the flow.

6. **Start detailed planning.** Now begin working on the details, specifying how to conduct each activity in the overall design. Decide on timing, introductory remarks, key points and instructions, materials, setting, and ways to end.

7. **Revise design details.** Mentally walk through the overall design, visualizing the participants' experience. Revise any details (particularly timing and instructions) so that each activity complements the ones that precede and/or follow it. Delete any designs that seem unnecessary, impractical, or ill conceived. Develop contingency plans in case time runs short, the group is more or less skilled than you thought, or any other turn of events you can imagine!

8. **Evaluate the total result.** Examine the program to see if it has the eight characteristics of an active training program. If you see flaws at this point, redesign to achieve a better result.

Of course, designing is never static. It's an ongoing process in which you try things out, perhaps even making revisions as you obtain feedback from participants and evaluate participant performance. The continuing challenges you'll face in designing an active training program are their own reward. The process is creative, exhilarating, and reinforcing, and the outcome is not only something in which you can take pride but also a real benefit to the people you are training.

The ten chapters that make up part 1 have been sequenced to assist you, step by step, in designing an active training program. As promised, the chapters will be filled with examples drawn from real-life training situations to illustrate every point made. Here is an overview of their contents.

Chapter 1 explains and illustrates how to assess a training group prior to the start of a program to help determine course content, obtain case material, and establish an early relationship with participants.

Chapter 2 tells how the development of training objectives drives the design of a training program and illustrates how objectives are specified, expressed, and presented to participants.

Chapter 3 shows how to create opening exercises that promote group building, on-the-spot assessment, and immediate learning involvement. It also suggests ten ways to obtain participation in the opening phase of a training program.

Chapter 4 describes ways to gain interest in a lecture, maximize understanding and retention, invite audience participation, and reinforce what has been presented.

Chapter 5 discusses and illustrates six strategies to avoid or reinforce a lecture presentation: demonstration, case study, guided teaching, group inquiry, read and discuss, and information search.

Chapter 6 shows how role playing, games and simulations, observation, mental imagery, writing tasks, and projects can be utilized to achieve affective and behavioral learning.

Chapter 7 demonstrates how training activities are formed around a purpose, method, and format. It further provides guidelines for detailed construction of active training activities and criteria for including those activities in an overall design.

Chapter 8 suggests ways to sequence training activities to achieve an effective mix and flow and illustrates in two examples how sequencing principles are applied.

Chapter 9 identifies strategies that can be employed prior to, during, and at the end of a training program to promote the transfer of learning.

Chapter 10 illustrates the overall structure and flavor of an active training program and outlines the steps you should take in planning one of your own.

As you navigate each chapter, avoid being a passive reader. Identify a design problem that you are facing currently or anticipate facing in the future and keep it in mind as you read. By maintaining a problem-solving mindset rather than an information-receiving one, you will be an active reader.

To encourage your participation further, we have provided a worksheet at the end of each chapter to give you an opportunity to apply what you have learned. From time to time, we will also surprise you with questions and brief exercises. That way, we know we're doing *our* job as active trainers.

ASSESSING THE TRAINING GROUP

1

The design of a training program is often approached in a hit-or-miss fashion. Many trainers decide what they want to teach without sufficient regard for what participants need to learn. If the training is a hit, that's great. *But,* if it's a miss (even a partial one), everyone suffers. You can avoid all this by making the effort to assess participants prior to training. Gathering information about your participants (actual or potential) is the first step in designing an active training program from scratch or tailoring an existing one to a specific group. Even before you begin to think about what material to include, you must learn as much as you can about the group you will be training.

Unfortunately, the opportunity to assess the training group is often limited by time constraints and the availability of data. Even in less than ideal circumstances, however, some assessment is necessary before finalizing the design. At the very least, you should try to answer as best you can the following questions about your proposed training group:

1. How many participants will there be?
2. What roles and tasks do the participants perform?
3. How familiar are the participants with the subject matter of the training program?
4. What are the ages, genders, and other important descriptive factors of the participants?
5. What are their attitudes and beliefs (relevant to the training topic)?
6. What successes and problems have the participants encountered?
7. What is the skill level of the participants?
8. Is the training voluntary or mandatory?
9. How well do the participants know one another?
10. What, if any, expectations do the participants' supervisors have with regard to the training program?

WHY DO ASSESSMENT?

When a problem exists within an organization or a need surfaces within a community, the first impulse often is to try to solve it with a training program. Yet other forms of intervention may be far more beneficial. Consequently, before even thinking about developing a training program, one should determine that training is the way to address the problem. When training makes sense, some form of assessment is necessary to **help determine the training content.** For instance, your group may need certain information or skills more than others. Perhaps the members have some prior exposure to the training topic and now require more advanced knowledge and skills. Or possibly the group faces certain problems that will affect how much they can apply what you are going to teach them. Without such assessment information, it will be difficult to gear your program to the participants' needs.

Here are some examples of how assessment work completed prior to the training program paid off.

- A bank manager felt that his platform service personnel needed further product knowledge training. An assessment survey revealed instead that what they needed more than additional product knowledge was training on how to sell the bank products to potential customers. The subsequent training was well received by the participants and led to increased sales figures for the branches.

- A trainer was designing a course on assertive communication for battered women. After consulting with experts in the field and learning that batterers often beg for forgiveness between episodes, she decided to include in the course a discussion of why these pleas occur and when they may be misleading.

There are other good reasons to do assessment prior to the training program. When designing training activities, it is extremely helpful to **obtain case material** directly from the workplace or personal situation of the participants. This way, you can base your designs on real issues that participants actually face rather than simulated or canned material. Here are two examples:

- For a sales training course in the office automation field, a trainer obtained examples of how area sales managers failed to solicit ongoing feedback from accounts who had made recent purchases. The examples were weaved into role-playing exercises that successfully engaged participants who previously had disliked the artificiality of role playing.
- Prior to a training program, Head Start teachers were asked to list the most common problem behaviors that they faced in their classrooms. The list was utilized in a course worksheet in which participants were asked to evaluate their consistency as classroom managers. The teachers reported that their evaluations were highly revealing because their own list had been used.

One further reason to conduct assessments is the opportunity it affords to **develop a relationship with participants** before meeting them at the training site. Sending a questionnaire to participants, for instance, can be an occasion to tell them about yourself and your plans for the upcoming program or to learn about their expectations. Phoning or visiting some or all of them for an assessment interview can give you a chance to get acquainted face to face. Having some prior contact with participants reduces the feeling of awkwardness when you meet in the classroom at the start of the program. Again, here are two examples:

- A training consultant was asked to conduct a course on organizational change for a management team of an insurance company. Upon learning that some members strongly opposed the course, a meeting was arranged prior to the start-up date to gain their trust and willingness to participate. The consultant clarified the agenda of the course and responded to the concerns of the group. At the conclusion of the meeting, he obtained not only their agreement to participate but also their commitment to play an active role in planning the course!

• A trainer decided to interview some of the participants who would attend her course on performance appraisals. Knowing that management had been unhappy about the quality of performance appraisals in their organization, the trainer began each interview with both frankness and reassurance: "I have been asked by management to develop a training program to improve the ways performance appraisals are conducted here. I said I wanted to talk to some of the participants first before I planned the program. I'd like to learn straight from the source what actually happens in conducting performance appraisals as they are set up now. That way I might learn more about the problems that are occurring." Word circulated about the interviews and helped to establish greater acceptance of the training program that followed.

To summarize, assessing participants prior to the beginning of a training program is important for three major reasons:

1. It helps you to determine the training content.
2. It allows you to obtain case material.
3. It permits you to develop a relationship with participants.

WHAT INFORMATION SHOULD BE COLLECTED?

As you think about the kinds of information that would be useful to you, consider first asking directly what **training needs participants have.** Going straight to the participants for their input gives them a hand in designing their own program. Moreover, involving them in this manner is usually well appreciated.

One simple way to do this for a public workshop is to send out a brief questionnaire similar to the one in figure 1–1. You can attach it to a course registration or confirmation form.

Figure 1–1. Parents' College Planning Workshop Participant Questionnaire

In order to make your College Planning Workshop productive for you, please take a few minutes to respond to the following:

1. My daughter/son is presently a ____ senior ____ junior ____ sophomore.
2. I have been through the college selection process as a parent
   ____ never ____ once before ____ twice before.
3. I would benefit by a general overview of the college selection process.
   (no need)   1   2   3   4   5   (strong need)
4. I need to learn more about the role of SATs in college planning.
   (no need)   1   2   3   4   5   (strong need)
5. I need to know what resources are available in the Guidance Office.
   (no need)   1   2   3   4   5   (strong need)
6. I need to know how to go about applying for colleges.
   (no need)   1   2   3   4   5   (strong need)
7. I need to know how to plan visitations and interviews.
   (no need)   1   2   3   4   5   (strong need)
8. I need to learn more about financial aid.
   (no need)   1   2   3   4   5   (strong need)
9. I plan to attend the College Planning Workshop ____ yes ____ no
10. List three specific questions that you hope this workshop will be able to answer for you.
    a. _____
    b. _____
    c. _____

Please mail this questionnaire in the enclosed envelope before September 25th. Thank you.

For an in-house program, consider sending a precourse questionnaire similar to the one described in the following case example.

- A training department instituted the practice of sending a precourse participant feedback form to all participants of upcoming courses. It asks three basic questions:
  (1) What are your expectations of the course you are about to take?
  (2) Based on the course description outlined in the catalog, how do you perceive this program helping you in your current position?
  (3) What additional objectives or needs would you like the course to address?

Such a form usually gains widespread acceptance because it is perceived as indicating a positive desire to meet the needs of company employees.

Besides participants' wishes, there are many other areas worth exploring, both with the participants and with others who know them. First and foremost is information concerning **the nature of the participants' work (or personal) situations.**

- What are the participants' responsibilities?
- Whom do they report to or relate to?
- In what aspects of their work or personal life will participants employ the skills and knowledge you will teach?

If you were asked to conduct a program on meeting management, for example, you would want to know to what extent the participants' work involved team meetings and what those meetings were like. If you were conducting a public workshop on conflict resolution, knowing whether or not most of your participants are usually the victims in conflict situations would make a big difference in your design.

Next in importance is information about **the knowledge, skills, and attitudes of the participants.**

- How familiar are participants with the content of your training program?
- How much opportunity have they had to practice or utilize skills that have been demonstrated to them previously?
- What are their views about the kind of training you are planning?

Suppose you were designing a program on coaching and counseling skills for managers. It would be useful to know what skills they already have acquired about coaching new employees or what attitudes they have held about the value of counseling troubled employees. Likewise, you would benefit from knowing how many participants in a weight control program have ever exercised seriously or what they feared about being thin.

Finally, it is helpful to find out any **conditions that will affect participant involvement** in the training program.

- What kind of support are participants likely to obtain in implementing the training they will receive?
- Are they worried about their level of competence relative to each other?
- Do they feel that they have been sent to the program because someone thinks they need to be fixed?

• Are they unaccustomed to the active learning methods you hope to employ?

Assume, for example, that you have been asked to conduct a program for employees with writing deficiencies. Naturally, it would be useful to know if these employees have merely been sent to the program as opposed to having been positively encouraged by their supervisors to improve their skills. Notice in the two questionnaires in figures 1–2 and 1–3 how several areas of assessment information are tapped.

Figure 1–2. Word Processing for Managers Participant Questionnaire

Please take a few moments to answer the questions below. Your response will be helpful in planning this course. Participation is voluntary, and your answers are confidential.

1. Rate your comfort level with using the following pieces of equipment:
   a. Typewriter   (low)   1   2   3   4   5   (high)
   b. IBM PC (or compatible)   (low)   1   2   3   4   5   (high)
   c. ITT Courier   (low)   1   2   3   4   5   (high)
   d. Apple/Macintosh   (low)   1   2   3   4   5   (high)
   e. IBM Displaywriter   (low)   1   2   3   4   5   (high)
   f. Wang Word Processor   (low)   1   2   3   4   5   (high)
2. Have you ever sent an E-Mail message before? ＿＿ yes ＿＿ no
3. Do you type your own letters and memos   ＿＿ usually?
                                                ＿＿ sometimes?
                                                ＿＿ rarely?
                                                ＿＿ never?
4. Explain why you have not used a Wang terminal previously:

5. Do you have access to a Wang terminal in your work area other than the one at the secretary's desk? ＿＿ yes ＿＿ no
6. Describe one skill that you would really like to learn during this class:

7. I learn new skills best by (select one in each column)
       ＿＿ step-by-step instruction   ＿＿ a quick paced course
       ＿＿ some guidance and some of   ＿＿ a leisurely paced course
          my own trial and error

Figure 1–3. Assertiveness Training Participant Questionnaire

Please take a few minutes to answer this brief questionnaire. The information we get from participants will help to determine the direction of our assertiveness training program. Your answers will not be revealed to anyone other than the program leaders.

1. Sex: M ____ F ____ Age: _____ Occupation: _____

2. The people with whom I feel a need to increase my level of assertiveness are (check as many as apply):

   _____ coworkers   _____ peers

   _____ immediate family   _____ extended family

   _____ supervisors   _____ subordinates

   _____ close friends   _____ strangers

   _____ other _____

3. Please rank the skills below in order of importance to you, with "1" indicating most important and "5" least important.

   _____ saying no without apologizing

   _____ initiating a conversation

   _____ stating feelings honestly

   _____ being persuasive

   _____ handling very difficult people

4. Indicate the degree of difficulty you have in the following situations:

	Easy	Somewhat difficult	Very difficult
talking with the opposite sex	____	____	____
disciplining children	____	____	____
talking on the telephone	____	____	____
asking for a raise	____	____	____
talking in a group	____	____	____
resisting salespeople	____	____	____
returning food in a restaurant	____	____	____

5. Briefly describe a recent situation in which you acted assertively:

6. Describe a recent situation in which you did not act assertively and regretted it:

Figure 1–3. continued

7. Who are the people in your life who will support you in becoming more assertive?

8. Who are the people in your life who will resist your new-found assertiveness?

9. Complete the two sentences below:
    a. One reason I sometimes don't like to assert myself is _____

    _____

    b. Sometimes, I feel I have the right to _____

    _____

10. Please circle any techniques below with which you are familiar:
    fogging   the broken record technique
    free information   empathic assertion
    "I" messages   negative inquiry

HOW CAN INFORMATION BE COLLECTED?

If you had unlimited time and resources, how would you ideally collect information for a training program you were designing? Would you only utilize a questionnaire? Give this question some thought and then compare your ideas to the chart in figure 1–4 on page 16.

As figure 1–4 indicates, you can choose among a wide variety of techniques to gather assessment information. In addition, you can easily combine some of them. Here is a case example:

• The president of a credit union contracted out for a team-building program for his senior management team. In preparation for the program, the trainer requested copies of the new business plan that this team had recently submitted to its board of directors and of the minutes of the team's weekly meetings over the last two months. He also interviewed the president and the three vice presidents of the credit

Figure 1–4. Advantages and Disadvantages of Nine Basic Needs Assessment Techniques

	Advantages	Disadvantages
Observation	• can be as technical as time-motion studies or as functionally or behaviorally specific as observing a new board or staff member interacting during a meeting. • may be as unstructured as walking through an agency's offices on the lookout for evidence of communication barriers. • can be used normatively to distinguish between effective and ineffective behaviors, organizational structures, and/or process.	• minimizes interruption of routine work flow or group activity. • generates in situ data, highly relevant to the situation where response to identified training needs/interests will impact. • (when combined with a feedback step) provides for important comparison checks between inferences of the observer and the respondent.	• requires a highly skilled observer with both process and content knowledge (unlike an interviewer who needs, for the most part, only process skill). • carries limitations that derive from being able to collect data only within the work setting (the other side of the first advantage listed in the preceding column). • holds potential for respondents to perceive the observation activity as "spying."
Questionnaires	• may be in the form of surveys or polls of a random or stratified sample of respondents, or an enumeration of an entire "population." • can use a variety of question formats: open-ended, projective, forced-choice, priority-ranking. • can take alternative forms such as Q-sorts, slip-sorts, or rating scales, either pre-designed or self-generated by respondent(s). • may be self-administered (by mail) under controlled or uncontrolled conditions, or may require the presence of an interpreter or assistant.	• can reach a large number of people in a short time. • are relatively inexpensive. • give opportunity of expression without fear of embarrassment. • yield data easily summarized and reported.	• make little provision for free expression of unanticipated responses. • require substantial time (and technical skills, especially in survey model) for development of effective instruments. • are of limited utility in getting at causes of problems or possible solutions. • suffer low return rates (mailed), grudging responses, or unintended and/or inappropriate respondents.

Key Consultation

- secures information from those persons who, by virtue of their formal or informal standing, are in a good position to know what the training needs of a particular group are:
  a. board chairman
  b. related service providers
  c. members of professional associations
  d. individuals from the service population
- once identified, data can be gathered from these consultants by using techniques such as interviews, group discussions, questionnaires.

- is relatively simple and inexpensive to conduct.
- permits input and interaction of a number of individuals, each with his or her own perspectives of the needs of the area, discipline, group, etc.
- establishes and strengthens lines of communication between participants in the process.
- carries a built-in bias, since it is based on views of those who tend to see training needs from their own individual or organizational perspective.
- may result in only a partial picture of training needs due to the typically non-representative nature (in a statistical sense) of a key informant group.

Print Media

- can include professional journals, legislative news/notes, industry "rags," trade magazines, in-house publications.

- is an excellent source of information for uncovering and clarifying normative needs.
- provides information that is current, if not forward-looking.
- is readily available and is apt to have already been reviewed by the client group.
- can be a problem when it comes to the data analysis and synthesis into a useable form (use of clipping service of key consultants can make this type of data more useable).

Figure 1–4. continued

Observation	Advantages	Disadvantages
Interviews		
• can be formal or casual, structured or unstructured, or somewhere in between.	• are adept at revealing feelings, causes of and possible solutions to problems which the client is facing (or anticipates); provide maximum opportunity for the client to represent himself spontaneously on his own terms (especially when conducted in an open-ended, non-directive manner).	• are usually time consuming.
• may be used with a sample of a particular group (board, staff, committee) or conducted with everyone concerned.		• can be difficult to analyze and quantify results (especially from unstructured formats).
• can be done in person, by phone, at the work site, or away from it.		• unless the interviewer is skilled, the client(s) can easily be made to feel self-conscious.
		• rely for success on a skillful interviewer who can generate data without making client(s) feel self-conscious, suspicious, etc.
Group Discussion		
• resembles face-to-face interview technique, e.g., structured or unstructured, formal or informal, or somewhere in between.	• permits on-the-spot synthesis of different viewpoints.	• is time consuming (therefore initially expensive) both for the consultant and the agency.
• can be focused on job (role) analysis, group problem analysis, group goal setting, or any number of group tasks or themes, e.g., "leadership training needs of the board."	• builds support for the particular service response that is ultimately decided on.	• can produce data that are difficult to synthesize and quantify (more a problem with the less structured techniques).
• uses one or several of the familiar group facilitating techniques: brainstorming, nominal group process, force-fields, consensus rankings, organizational mirroring, simulation, and sculpting.	• decreased client's "dependence response" toward the service provider since data analysis is (or can be) a shared function.	
	• helps participants to become better problem analysts, better listeners, etc.	

Tests

• are a hybridized form of questionnaire.	• can be especially helpful in determining whether the cause of a recognized problem is a deficiency in knowledge or skill or, by elimination, attitude.	• the availability of a relatively small number of tests that are validated for a specific situation.
• can be very functionally oriented (like observations) to test a board, staff, or committee member's proficiency.	• results are easily quantifiable and comparable.	• do not indicate if measured knowledge and skills are actually being used in the on-the-job or "back home group" situation.
• may be used to sample learned ideas and facts.		
• can be administered with or without the presence of an assistant.		

Records, Reports

• can consist of organizational charts, planning documents, policy manuals, audits and budget reports.	• provide excellent clues to trouble spots.	• causes of problems or possible solutions often do not show up.
• employee records (grievance, turnover, accidents, etc.)	• provide objective evidence of the results of problems within the agency or group.	• carries perspective that generally reflects the past situation rather than the current one (or recent changes).
• includes minutes of meetings, weekly, monthly program reports, memoranda, agency service records, program evaluation studies.	• can be collected with a minimum of effort and interruption of work flow since it already exists at the work site.	• need a skilled data analyst if clear patterns and trends are to emerge from such technical and diffuse raw data.

Work Samples

• are similar to observation but in written form.	• carry most of the advantages of records and reports data.	• case study method will take time away from actual work of the organization.
• can be products generated in the course of the organization's work, e.g., ad layouts, program proposals, market analyses, letters, training designs.	• are the organization's data (its own output).	• need specialized content analysts.
• Written responses to a hypothetical but relevant case study provided by the consultant.		• analyst's assessment of strengths/weaknesses disclosed by samples can be challenged as "too subjective."

Source: S. V. Steadham, "Learning to Select a Needs Assessment Strategy," *Training and Development Journal* 30 (January 1980): 56–61. Copyright 1980 by the American Society for Training and Development, Inc. Reprinted with permission. All rights reserved.

union. These interviews focused on the problems facing the entire team (twelve members). On the basis of the interviews, the trainer designed a questionnaire. Before all team members were sent the questionnaire, the interviewees were asked to evaluate and approve the first draft. Several items were reworded to use familiar language. Figure 1–5 reproduces the final questionnaire preceded by the cover letter that accompanied it.

As a result of the data obtained from the reports, interviews, and questionnaire, the trainer discovered that two problems significantly influenced the effectiveness of this team: (1) a lack of understanding of the needs of each work unit in the credit union and (2) poor team meetings. The standard course on team building offered by the trainer was redesigned in order to give significant attention to these two problem areas.

Figure 1–5. Senior Management Questionnaire, with Cover Letter

Dear (Team Member):

I am a team-building consultant who has been asked to conduct a special two-day course with the senior management staff of your credit union.

As your organization is making a clear commitment to its own professional growth and development, I hope that you will see these two days as a wonderful opportunity to communicate with each other without the constraints of daily deadlines and to build relationships with each other that will make you feel cohesive and united in purpose.

We will begin with some activities designed to "warm us up" and help us feel good about working together as a group. Following this, there will be some skill-building exercises to increase your group's effectiveness as a problem-solving team. The third phase of the course (and the longest) will be focused on identifying issues that need to be worked through in order to maximize your future effectiveness as a group.

An excellent way to begin doing some of this work is to collect information through a questionnaire and to feed back that information for group discussion during the course. I would like you to join with your colleagues in filling out the attached questionnaire. Your honest responses will enable the group to have a clear view of itself.

Your participation will be totally anonymous. My job will be to *summarize* the results and report them to you for your reactions.

Figure 1–5. continued

Thank you in advance for your cooperation and support. I look forward to working with you.

1. To what extent do you agree or disagree with the following statements?
    a. We avoid conflict among ourselves to keep things peaceful.
       (strongly disagree)   1   2   3   4   5   6   7   (strongly agree)
    b. We are dedicated to the credit union movement.
       1   2   3   4   5   6   7
    c. We speak up when we need to; there can be healthy disagreements among us.
       1   2   3   4   5   6   7
    d. We don't communicate frequently enough with each other.
       1   2   3   4   5   6   7
    e. It's not always clear who's responsible for a certain assignment or problem ("I thought you were going to do it").
       1   2   3   4   5   6   7
    f. Others don't understand my operation and its needs.
       1   2   3   4   5   6   7
    g. There's little backbiting around here.
       1   2   3   4   5   6   7
    h. We have a tendency to be unrealistic.
       1   2   3   4   5   6   7
    i. There are different beliefs among us about the way the credit union should conduct its business and relate to members.
       1   2   3   4   5   6   7
    j. Men and women in our group can work comfortably together.
       1   2   3   4   5   6   7
    k. We give each other recognition and words of appreciation.
       1   2   3   4   5   6   7
    l. It's hard to know what others think about the issues and problems around here.
       1   2   3   4   5   6   7
    m. We are well organized with clearly defined procedures. Things run smoothly here.
       1   2   3   4   5   6   7
    n. Decisions are controlled from the top.
       1   2   3   4   5   6   7
2. Because the president holds the key leadership role in this credit union, it would be helpful to provide him with some feedback. Please comment about the following:

Figure 1–5. continued

What are some things you would like the president to
a. continue doing?

b. stop doing?

c. start doing?

3. What suggestions do you have to maximize your team work and team effectiveness in the future?

One additional technique for assessing participants should be considered along with those already discussed. If conditions warrant, a trainer can give a **precourse assignment** to participants both to learn about their skills and to obtain case material for the course.

- A precourse assignment was used in a "train the trainer" program. The memorandum reproduced in figure 1–6 was sent to participants, and, when Part I of the assignment was returned, it was possible to assess how well participants were able to specify training objectives. Part I was also used as an exercise in the training program: When that portion of the program devoted to the skill of specifying objectives had been completed, participants were asked to rewrite their own statements of objectives. Part II of the assignment also served to provide course material for the program.

Figure 1–6. "Train the Trainer" Precourse Assignment

TO: Participant

FROM: Human Resources Department

SUBJECT: Administrative information and Preconference Assignment

We are pleased to confirm your enrollment in the Active Training program that is being conducted at the Federal Plaza Building on June 30 through July 2.

Figure 1–6. continued

As our organization changes, the ability to train and develop people on the job has become increasingly critical. Our main purpose in this seminar is to help managers and professional staff to share their expertise effectively and efficiently with others.

This seminar is designed to help you improve your effectiveness in any training you may be asked to do. Our goal is to help you with your specific training needs. To ensure that we can accomplish this, please complete Part I of the precourse assignment by Monday, June 22nd.

PART I

COMPLETE AND RETURN TO *(trainer)*
AT *(place)* BY *(date)*

Select a topic that you might be asked to teach over a two to three hour period. This topic could be something that you've already taught in a training program or a topic that you can imagine teaching in the future.

What are your objectives for this session? Outline them below.

PART II

COMPLETE AND BRING TO CLASS ON *(date)*

Choose a fifteen-minute segment from the training topic you described in Part I and follow the directions below.

• Specify your objectives for this fifteen-minute segment.
• Think about how you would present this fifteen-minute segment.
• Identify the instructional materials, if any, that you would use. *Please bring an example of these materials to class.*
• Develop an outline of your presentation.

NOTE: *On the second day of the program, you will be asked to present this material to four or five other participants. In this way, you will get some useful feedback on your presentation style.*

WHAT IF THERE IS NO TIME TO DO A PROPER ASSESSMENT?

The last question we will consider is a practical one. Not all situations are ideal; obstacles to collecting assessment data do arise. As long as there is significant lead time, you can utilize many of the techniques that we have just outlined. But you may easily face a situation in which a training program has to be designed and implemented hastily and/or the identity of the participants is largely unknown (this is particularly true for public workshops).

When these problems occur, try not to be discouraged. You will, of necessity, have to design the program using your best guesses about the nature of the participants and their needs. But there are still some opportunities to obtain quick information and adjust the design accordingly. Here are some recommendations:

1. Phone a contact person who may have some familiarity with the participants and ask her the basic questions listed at the beginning of this chapter.
2. Phone a few participants, introduce yourself, and ask them some key questions. Hope that their responses are representative and treat them as a sample of the larger group. Or ask a contact person to set up a phone interview schedule for you.
3. Have any relevant materials (e.g., surveys, meeting notes, or records) express mailed or faxed to you.
4. Contact other trainers who have worked with your training group to get their opinions and impressions.
5. Talk to participants who arrive early and obtain whatever information you can.
6. Design some activities to enable you to make some assessments of the group at the beginning of the program. (More information about this in chapter 3.)

If you have done some contingent planning in your overall design, you should still be able to make final adjustments before your class begins.

Worksheet

ASSESSING THE TRAINING GROUP

Before going on to the next chapter, try your hand at applying the ideas in this one. Use this worksheet to outline how you might assess participants for your next training program.

Information Desired:
(check as many as desired)

_____ participants' stated needs

_____ the nature of the participants' work or personal situations

_____ participants' knowledge

_____ participants' skills

_____ participants' attitudes

_____ conditions affecting participant involvement

Methods Desired:
(check as many as desired)

_____ observation	_____ print media	_____ tests
_____ questionnaire	_____ interview	_____ records, reports
_____ key consultation	_____ group discussion	_____ work samples

Assessment Outline:

_____

_____

_____

_____

_____

_____

_____

_____

_____

_____

DEVELOPING ACTIVE TRAINING OBJECTIVES

2

After assessing participants, you are in a position to start planning your training program. At this stage, it is not enough simply to list the topics you intend to cover. As Carl Rogers, the psychologist, once quipped: "To cover means to hide." An active training program is constructed in terms of the achievement of objectives. *The critical question, therefore, is not what topics to cover but what you want participants to value, understand, or do with those topics.* A clear sense of where you want to go and what you are trying to accomplish is the single most important ingredient for designing active training experiences.

Determining program objectives may take a lot of thinking up front, but it is worth it. When you are designing a training program, you are figuring out what steps will lead to the accomplishment of your objectives. If you are not clear about your objectives, you might overlook some of the learning experiences that your participants require. Here is a case in point:

- A trainer's assessment revealed that a group of real estate sales trainees knew little about the closing process in the sale of properties. Consequently, the trainer decided to cover this topic in his real estate course. He did a good job of explaining how a closing is done, but afterward participants still seemed hazy about how to conduct a closing themselves. Wanting to improve the situation, the trainer decided to ask experienced sales personnel to identify the specific on-the-job skills the trainees would need in order to deal with closings. Their responses enabled him to develop a clear set of objectives for the next time that he taught the course. Specifically, he concluded that trainees needed to be able to

- describe the closing costs for which the buyer would be responsible.
- clearly and concisely answer typical customer questions about closing costs.
- estimate closing costs for different types of properties.

With these objectives in mind, the program was redesigned to include experiences that not only taught the closing process but also tested the group's understanding of the process and allowed ample opportunities to practice how this knowledge would be applied on the job.

When you set training objectives, you also wind up setting appropriate limits on how much material you will cover. Active trainers keep their content level moderate because they are serious about achieving their objectives. They understand that covering too much material is a sure way to prevent real learning from taking place.

Clearly stated objectives also provide participants with a list of what is expected of them. Knowing what they are being held accountable for gives participants direction and responsibility. They can be **active partners** in your program rather than mere attendees.

SETTING LEARNING GOALS

Once you have decided on the basic subject matter for a training program, begin your planning by setting general learning goals. Learning goal statements articulate the outcomes you want to achieve. As you develop learning goals for your training program, keep in mind that some types of learning differ from others. The three major types of learning are easily remembered as "ABC":

- **Affective learning**
- **Behavioral learning**
- **Cognitive learning**

Affective learning involves the formation of attitudes, feelings, and preferences. For example, you may want participants to value a certain situation, procedure, or product. Or you may wish them to become more aware of their feelings and reactions to certain issues and new ideas. Here are some examples of affective learning:

- First-line supervisors in an engineering company explore their feelings about managing the work of employees who were previously their coworkers.
- Bank managers examine to what extent their orientation is inward looking or customer focused.
- New hires share reactions to their first weeks on the job, including feelings about corporate culture, new procedures, and relations with coworkers

Behavioral learning includes the development of competence in the actual performance of procedures, operations, methods, and techniques. For example, you may want participants to practice skills that you have demonstrated and to receive feedback on their performance. Here are examples of behavioral learning:

- Participants attending new employee orientation learn how to complete payroll time cards.
- Research-and-development personnel practice creative thinking techniques by applying them to problems back on the job.
- Staff nurses at a hospital practice how to effectively prepare pre-operative patients who are about to undergo surgery.

Cognitive learning includes the acquisition of information and concepts related to course content. You may want participants not only to comprehend the subject matter but also to analyze and apply it to new situations. Here are some examples of cognitive learning: *Judge*

- Participants in a training program called "The Law and the Workplace" learn the legal definition of sexual harassment and apply it to issues at their jobs.
- Spouses of alcoholics learn to identify common characteristics of codependency such as people pleasing, workaholism, and perfectionism.
- Managers with responsibility for hiring learn to identify unlawful questions that should not be asked in an interview.

Although it is possible to design your training program with only one of these types of learning in mind, a design that incorporates all three is more likely to result in lasting change. Even a relatively short program can include affective, behavioral, and cognitive learning goals, as represented in the following examples.

- A trainer accepted an assignment to teach managers how to use a new purchasing system. She decided that her overall learning goals were to have participants
  - value the benefits of the new system (affective learning).
  - complete and process the forms (behavioral learning).
  - determine the correct forms to use (cognitive learning).

- For a course on understanding group dynamics, the trainer chose to devote one session to the task and maintenance roles that members need to play in groups. He designed the session so that participants would be able to:
  - identify their current and future preferences for task or maintenance roles in a group (affective learning).
  - utilize new task and maintenance behaviors when conducting meetings (behavioral learning).
  - differentiate between task and maintenance behaviors exhibited by colleagues at a group meeting (cognitive learning).

Of course, your training program may be a response to a specific organizational program. In such an instance, you can focus on the learning goal dictated by the problem.

1. **Cognitive goals** are the priority when there is a **lack of knowledge.** This is often referred to as a "don't know" situation.
2. **Behavioral goals** are the priority when there is a **lack of skill.** This is often referred to as a "can't do" situation.
3. **Affective goals** are the priority when there is a **lack of desire** to use new knowledge or skills. This is often referred to as a "won't do" situation.

SELECTING OBJECTIVES

Once you have established a set of learning goals, the next step is to break those goals down into specific training objectives (or outcomes).

These should represent the concrete accomplishments to be attained in the training. Each learning goal will have one or more objectives that, when met, will identify accomplishment of that goal. Here is a case example:

■ A trainer in a term lending seminar for bankers set a **cognitive** learning goal that participants would become familiar with the key business and legal considerations in structuring a team lending agreement that would meet both the bank's and the customer's needs. The results he wanted to achieve included the ability to analyze complex corporate organizations and financial statements and to understand how complex credit facilities are structured. The training objectives that he selected were that, at the completion of the seminar, participants would be able to

- identify the key credit risks in a range of complex lending situations.
- analyze the corporate structure of an organization with multiple subsidiaries, with emphasis on the appropriate lending entity.
- identify key management issues for at least three companies seeking term lending facilities.

For the **behavioral** learning goal of applying term lending strategies on the job, the results he wanted to achieve included the drafting of a term lending agreement for review by a more experienced bank officer. The objectives that he developed were that, at the completion of the term lending seminar, participants would be able to

- draft a proposed structure for term credits for the three companies previously analyzed.
- draft terms for each of the credits and discuss these with the appropriate bank attorneys.
- monitor at least two ongoing term credit facilities and write waivers and amendments as appropriate.

Finally, the trainer wanted to include as an **affective** learning goal that participants would learn to value the interests of both the borrower and the lender in a term loan. The objectives developed were that, at the completion of the term lending seminar, participants would be able to

- identify their own feelings about business risk and protection.
- support the goals of each party to a term lending agreement, unless the goals are mutually exclusive.

Sometimes trainers have too many objectives crammed into one program. To avoid this, be careful to distinguish between objectives that would be nice to achieve and those that are necessary. For example, it may be critical for insurance claims adjusters to know how to access medical reference books in their offices when evaluating injury claims; it would be less important for them also to learn prefixes and suffixes common in medical terminology.

Whether something is required training or not can be determined through a thorough analysis of the tasks involved in a job. Mayo and DuBois (1987) cite eight criteria for including a task in a training course (see figure 2–1). Think about how you would apply these criteria to a task area that you teach (e.g., performance appraisals, word processing, project management, etc.).

Figure 2–1. Criteria for Selecting a Training Task

1. The percentage of job incumbents who actually perform the task.
2. The percentage of total work time that job incumbents spend on the task.
3. How critical the task is.
4. The amount of delay that can be tolerated between the time when the need for performance of the task becomes evident and the time when actual performance must begin.
5. The frequency with which the task is performed.
6. The difficulty or complexity of the task.
7. The probability of deficient performance of the task on the part of job incumbents.
8. How soon the task must be performed after a person is assigned to a job that involves it.

Finally, the selection of training objectives may hinge on one's understanding of adult learning needs. In what has become a classic article, Ron and Susan Zemke (1981) describe "30 Things We Know For Sure About Adult Learning." Many items from their list have strong implications for choosing some training objectives and rejecting others. Consider a few of them:

- Adult learners tend to be less interested in survey courses. They tend to prefer single-concept, single-theory courses that focus heavily on the application of the concept to relevant problems.
- Adults need to be able to integrate new ideas with what they already know if they are going to keep—and use—the new information.

- The curriculum designer must know whether the concepts and ideas will be in concert or in conflict with learner and organizational values.
- Programs need to be designed to accept viewpoints from people in different life stages and with different sets of values.
- Adults prefer self-directed and self-designed learning projects seven to one over group learning experiences led by a professional. (Self-direction does not mean isolation. In fact, studies of self-directed learning show that self-directed projects involve an average of ten other people as resources, guides, encouragers, and the like.)[1]

SPECIFYING OBJECTIVES

When you have selected your objectives, state them in a form that will make them effective tools for managing, monitoring, and evaluating the training. Typically, training objectives use a format such as: "By the completion of the program, participants will be able to" . . . (the specific objectives would then be listed).

This written format will give you specific criteria to determine if the course design is appropriate. For example, if your objective is that participants will be able to utilize a skill in a job-related situation, you might ask if sufficient time to practice that skill has been built into the course.

When training objectives are more technical in nature, some trainers make it a practice to state not only what participants should be able to do after training but also under what **conditions** and according to what **standards.** Conditions involve such things as the availability of information aids or the allowance for performance simplifications. Standards relate to the level of performance being sought in terms of perfection, time utilization, output, and so on. Here are two examples:

- At the end of this training session, employees will be able to process lockbox items through the TRP at a rate of 500 per hour with no more than two errors per 1,000 items.

- When practicing in skits on telephone interruptions, participants will deal with five phone call interruptions in ten minutes with no quantitative decrease in work completed.

[1]Adapted with permission from the June 1981 issue of *TRAINING: The Magazine of Human Resources Development.* Copyright 1981, Lakewood Publications Inc., Minneapolis, MN (612) 333–0471. All rights reserved.

If objectives are in the right format, the development of training evaluations can be very straightforward. A comparison of the written objectives to the participants' experiences provides a direct means of evaluating the success of your training program.

You should be careful, however, to avoid overspecifying your training objectives, particularly in nontechnical training programs. When teaching management skills, for instance, overly precise objectives can lead to mechanistic training. No one wants managers to do everything precisely by the book, with little room to exercise their personal style and their own sense of the right way to do things. Often, your job is not to train but to educate—to expose participants to new ways of thinking, feeling, and acting and to allow them to integrate these ways into their being. You may be advocating a five-step procedure for counseling troubled employees, but your participants may willingly accept and adopt only some of the steps. Or they may decide that they need to figure out an entirely different first step to make the rest of the procedure work for them. The better you educate participants concerning your subject matter, the less likely they are to leave the program as mindless clones.

EXPRESSING OBJECTIVES

With the above caution in mind, it is still important that the training objectives you do specify be written in a style that is easy to understand and straight to the point. Avoid commonly misinterpreted terms such as those in figure 2–2. Additionally, use specific action verbs to assist both the group members and the sponsor of your training program to evaluate your program. Figure 2–3 lists action verbs that are frequently used when writing training objectives.

Figure 2–2. Tips for Writing Objectives

Skill	Commonly misinterpreted terms	Behavior terms
Knowledge	To know, learn	To write, define, repeat, name, list
Comprehension	To understand, appreciate	To restate, discuss, describe, explain, review, translate, locate
Application	To show, apply a thorough knowledge of	To operate, illustrate, use, employ, sketch

Figure 2–2. continued

Skill	Commonly misinterpreted terms	Behavior terms
Analysis	To analyze	To differentiate between/among, appraise, calculate, test compare, contrast, solve, criticize
Synthesis	To establish creativity	To compose, propose, plan, design, manage, collect, construct, organize, prepare
Evaluation	To show good judgment	To evaluate, rate, select, estimate, measure

Figure 2–3. Action Verbs Frequently Used in Writing Training Objectives

administer	consolidate	expedite	proceed
adopt	consult	formulate	process
advise	control	furnish	promote
analyze	coordinate	implement	propose
anticipate	correlate	improve	provide
appraise	correspond	initiate	recommend
approve	delegate	inspect	report
arrange	design	instruct	represent
assemble	determine	interpret	research
assign	develop	investigate	resolve
assist	devise	issue	review
assume	direct	maintain	revise
assure	discuss	monitor	schedule
authorize	dispose	negotiate	secure
calculate	disseminate	notify	select
circulate	distribute	obtain	sign
clear	draft	operate	specify
collaborate	endorse	participate	stimulate
collect	establish	perform	submit
compile	estimate	place	supervise
concur	evaluate	plan	train
conduct	execute	practice	transcribe
confer	exercise	prepare	verify

COMMUNICATING TRAINING OBJECTIVES TO OTHERS

Communicating your objectives effectively to others is an important skill to develop. You may submit your training plans to management for approval only to discover that they are confused by your language or put off by the format of your objectives. In addition, participants can feel overwhelmed by laundry lists of objectives like those sometimes presented in course catalogs or by language that is laden with jargon.

Compare the lists of stated objectives for two very different types of training programs presented in figures 2–4 and 2–5. The more technical of the two programs, "Shelter Products," is described in clear sets of objectives that help to make sense of difficult subject matter. The less technical program, "Management Skills," has a lengthy list of objectives that is difficult to read and comprehend in one glance.

Figure 2–4. Shelter Products: Training Objectives

At the end of this course, you will be able to

A. Define mortgage terms
   1. Define the following:
      a. Mortgage
      b. Condominium
      c. Co-op/co-op loan
      d. Second mortgage
      e. Equity source account
      f. Refinancing
      g. Bridge loan
      h. Real estate loan

B. Perform calculations
   1. Demonstrate use of an amortization table
   2. Show how you determine monthly payments of principal and interest for fixed and ARM loans
   3. Explain origination fees and the annual percentage rate

C. Describe mortgage finance
   1. Explain the role of the secondary market for mortgage funds
   2. Identify FNMA requirements and their relationship to the NYBD RAAC

Figure 2–5. Management Skills: Training Objectives

When you complete this course, you will be able to

- define and identify what affects motivation.
- discuss the impact of leadership style on motivation.
- identify your leadership style.
- identify and determine different leadership strategies.
- explain the impact of effective communication on motivation/leadership.
- demonstrate effective verbal and nonverbal communication skills.
- use positive reinforcement and coaching skills.
- give corrective/negative feedback to keep motivation intact and maximize workers' productivity.
- use effectively the performance appraisal process.
- recognize the benefits of teamwork and win/win situations.
- describe the difference between compromise and collaboration.
- assess the impact of your style on team development.
- remove barriers to teamwork and overcome resistance to change.
- develop a strategy to promote and build teams.
- discuss how to maximize individual workers' learning.
- identify common pitfalls made in on-the-job training and how to avoid them.
- systematically plan, implement, and follow up with on-the-job training skills.
- explain your role in customer service and in the overall company image.
- use effective communication skills with customers to build relationships and establish a rapport.
- demonstrate effective conflict resolution techniques.
- develop personal action plans for improvement.

Worksheet
DEVELOPING TRAINING OBJECTIVES

Try your hand at specifying objectives. Take the content of a program you are presently conducting or hope to teach in the near future and state your objectives for the program on this worksheet.

Upon completion of this module/course, participants will be able to:

_____

_____

_____

_____

_____

_____

_____

_____

_____

_____

_____

_____

_____

_____

_____

_____

_____

_____

_____

_____

_____

_____

CREATING OPENING EXERCISES

3

Once you have gathered information about your participants and selected your training objectives, you start planning your program. Opening exercises are an important element in an active training program. Like the appetizers to the full meal, they allow participants to get a taste of what is to follow. Although some trainers choose to begin a course with only a short introduction, including at least one opening exercise in your design is a first step that has many benefits. Let us explore why.

WHAT OPENING EXERCISES ACCOMPLISH

In the first moments of an active training program, three goals are important to accomplish, even if the program is to be short or an assessment has preceded the course:

1. **Group building**—helping participants to become acquainted with each other and creating a spirit of cooperation and interdependence

2. **On-the-spot assessment**—learning about the attitudes, knowledge, and experience of the participants

3. **Immediate learning involvement**—creating initial interest in the training topic

All three of these goals, accomplished singly or in combination, help to develop a training environment that engages the participants, stimulates their willingness to take part in some active learning, and creates positive training norms. Whether you devote as little as five minutes or up to as much as two hours to opening activities (depending on the overall length of your program), the time will be well spent.

GROUP BUILDING

Group-building exercises foster positive group attitudes by asking participants to learn each other's names and to get to know each other. If the members have already met, opening exercises can help them to become reacquainted after a period of separation. Either way, an opening design that stresses group building can develop a feeling of spirit and pride among the members of your program.

There are numerous getting-acquainted exercises that give participants an opportunity to introduce themselves to the other members of the group in an interesting and nonthreatening manner. One of the most widely used involves asking participants to pair off and get acquainted. Each participant then introduces his partner to the full group. This is a perfectly fine opener *as long as the group is not too large* (would you like to be the twentieth person introduced to the group?). A less time-consuming exercise is Name Bingo, the instructions for which appear in figure 3–1.

Almost all opening exercises can be varied to produce different effects. For example, Name Bingo can be modified to increase self-disclosure. Besides names, participants can be asked to obtain and record on the bingo form one fact about each person they meet. *Each time a person is asked for a fact about himself, he is required to share one different from those given to other participants.* In step 7, all the participants share the many facts they have learned about the person whose name is picked. This change lengthens the exercise, however, so it's best to use it only when the group is small.

Figure 3–1. Name Bingo

1. Participants mill around the room and meet each other.
2. Each time a participant exchanges names with someone, she writes the new name anywhere on a Bingo form.
3. After all participants have met, each one places an *O* in any unused box.
4. The trainer then places a copy of everyone's name in a hat.
5. The hat is passed around the group, one participant at a time. Each participant picks a name out of the hat. Everyone places an *X* on the box on their cards containing the name picked.
6. Whenever any player obtains a full row of 5 *X*s (horizontally, vertically, or diagonally), he or she yells "Bingo!" (Everyone eventually will get Bingo several times.)
7. As each name is picked, that participant should introduce him/herself to the group and share three facts about him/herself.

NOTE: Use a three-by-three format if the group includes fewer than ten people or a four-by-four format if the group has numbers between ten and sixteen.

A fun way to do group building once participants have become acquainted is a takeoff on the game show "To Tell the Truth" (see figure 3–2 for instructions.)

Figure 3–2. To Tell the Truth

1. Ask each participant to write down (legibly!) on a card three personal facts not previously shared with the group.
2. Mix up the cards and distribute a card to each participant. (Be sure no one receives her own card.)
3. Have each participant read the card she has been dealt, then ask for three guesses as to whose card was read. Prior to the guesses, request that the writer of the card not reveal her identity even if it is guessed.
4. Ask: "Will the real writer of this card please stand up?"
5. Allow for surprise or self-congratulatory applause.

A more self-disclosing yet still fun-filled way to accomplish the same purpose is Predictions, a guessing game based on first impressions. Participants are formed into small groups to do the activity, which is described in figure 3–3.

Figure 3–3. Predictions

Your job is to predict how each person in your group would answer the following questions. (Try to be as specific as possible. Don't be afraid of bold guesses!) When you finish your predictions, the participant should then respond to each question about him- or herself.

1. Where did you grow up?
2. What were you like as a child? A student?
3. Were your parents strict or lenient?
4. What type of music do you enjoy?
5. What are some of your favorite leisure activities?
6. How many hours do you usually sleep nightly?

Note: Other questions can be added or substituted.

Other group-building activities are especially appropriate for a group where members already know each other well. Often they involve some way for the group to produce something they can take pride in. One activity that can be used in a longer training program is called TV Commercial (see figure 3–4).

Figure 3–4. TV Commercial

1. Divide participants into teams of no more than six members.
2. Ask each team to create a thirty-second TV commercial that advertises the group or the organization they work for. The commercial should contain a slogan (e.g., "Coke's the real thing") and visuals.
3. Explain that the general concept and an outline of the commercial are sufficient. But, if a team wants to act out its commercial, let it.
4. Before the teams begin planning their commercials, discuss the characteristics of well-known commercials to stimulate creativity (e.g., use of a well-known personality, humor, comparison to competition, sex appeal).
5. Ask each team to present its ideas. Praise everyone's creativity.

A second activity is called Group Resume (see figure 3–5).

Figure 3–5. Group Resume

1. Divide participants into groups of at least six members.
2. Tell the groups that within each one is an incredible array of talents and experiences.
3. Suggest that one way to identify and publicize the group's resources is to compose a group resume. (You may want to suggest a job or contract they could be bidding for.)
4. Give the groups markers and newsprint on which to display their resume. It should include any data that sells the group as a whole, such as information about

    educational background, schools attended

    total years of professional experience

    positions held

    professional skills

    hobbies, talents, travel, family

    major accomplishments

    publications

5. Invite each group to present its resume and then celebrate the total resources contained within the entire group.

Yet another way to promote group cohesion is to invite participants who already work with each other to share new information with each other. The following self-disclosure exercise was designed for the staff of a real estate office.

- Each salesperson in the group was asked to give a three-minute presentation entitled "Anatomy of a Salesperson." Participants were given five minutes to prepare written notes. It was suggested that the presentation respond to the following questions:
  1. What motivated you to go into real estate sales?
  2. What were you doing in your life before entering real estate sales?
  3. What do you like about this career?
  4. If you could change anything about the work of a real estate salesperson, what would it be?

ON-THE-SPOT ASSESSMENT

On-the-spot assessment exercises ask participants to do such things as

- share their learning goals or expectations.
- raise questions or concerns they may have about the course.
- relate their knowledge and experience to the course topics.
- list successes and problems they have experienced that are relevant to the course.
- explore their opinions and attitudes about the course topic.

Such exercises elicit information that will help you to gauge the expertise of the group while giving participants a sense of immediate participation. Often, you can request the information you want in a spontaneous manner by asking **general** questions in the opening minutes of the training program—for example, "What motivated you to come here today?" or "Are there any concerns you may have about today's program or what you may be asked to do?" Or you can ask **training-specific** questions such as these used in a time management seminar: "Who uses a 'to do' list on a daily basis?" "How does it help you to organize your day?" You can also use structured exercises to gain on-the-spot assessment information, as the following examples illustrate.

1. Managers participating in a mandatory workshop on new corrective action policies are asked to discuss the following questions with their seat partner:
   a. From your experience, what constitutes a "problem behavior"?
   b. How do you feel when you have to confront a problem employee?
   c. What actions have you taken in the past to discipline employees?

After each question, the trainer asks two or three participants to share their answers with the whole group. As group members have an opportunity to explore their own perspectives on handling problem situations previous to learning new corrective action procedures, the trainer gains valuable information about the training group.

2. Child-care workers in group homes are formed into a rotating group of panelists. Each panel is asked to discuss its responses to one of the questions below:

   a. What do you like about the kids you work with?

   b. What turns you off about the kids you work with?

   c. What do the kids do to "push your buttons"?

   d. What advice do you think you will get in this training program?

   As panelists respond in front of their coworkers, the trainer learns about their willingness to self-disclose, their feelings about the children they care for, and their understanding of the course content.

3. Family therapy trainees are asked to form trios. Each trio is asked to generate two questions, one concerning the theory of family therapy and the other concerning its practice. The questions should relate to topics about which the participants hope to learn during the training program. Some of the questions that emerge are:

   - (Theoretical) What is the role of interpretation in family therapy?

   - (Practical) Do you have to see the entire family to do family therapy properly?

   - (Theoretical) Are the various models of family therapy really different from each other?

   - (Practical) Is a fifty-minute hour enough for most family sessions?

   The trainer gains two insights from these questions. Not only does he learn some of the issues that participants want to discuss, but he also finds out about their knowledge regarding the program content and their expectations regarding its level of sophistication.

An interesting way to gather on-the-spot assessment information is recommended by Thiagarajan (1989). He suggests letting the participants collect the data as a kind of icebreaker. Here are six design steps he offers:

1. Figure out assessment questions you want to ask.

2. Divide the participants into as many teams as you have questions.

3. Ask the teams to spend a few minutes devising a strategy for efficiently collecting information about their assigned questions.

4. Ask the teams to collect the data simultaneously, using whatever strategies they devised earlier.
5. Call time and ask the teams to meet in corners of the training room to prepare summaries of their data.
6. Have each team make a presentation.

Another design to consider, outlined in figure 3–6, focuses on the concerns of the training group.

Figure 3–6. Concerns of a Training Group

1. Hand out a blank index card to each participant.
2. Ask each participant to write down any concern she has about the nature of the training program (names should be withheld).
3. Request participants to pass the cards clockwise around the group. Each time a participant receives a card, he should read it and place a checkmark on it if it contains a statement that is also of concern to the reader.
4. By the time all of the participants have gotten back their own cards, each person will have reviewed the concerns of the entire group. At this point, hold an open discussion of the concerns that have emerged.

Variation: Instead of holding a discussion, identify the top four concerns in the group by establishing which cards contain the most checkmarks. Break the class into four groups and invite each group to elaborate on the concern written on one of the four index cards. Ask each group to summarize its discussion for the whole class.

IMMEDIATE LEARNING INVOLVEMENT

Immediate learning involvement exercises ask participants to respond to initial questions about the course content, to try out learning activities related to the course content without previous instruction, or to view presentations or demonstrations that give an initial description of the skills to be learned within the program. These activities help to introduce the course in a dramatic, active manner that draws the participants into the training program right from the session's beginning.

One of the simplest ways to get started is to display an interesting proverb or slogan relevant to the training topic and then ask each participant to introduce himself and share how the statement applies to his personal or professional life. (Divide into small groups if the total group size is too large.) Here is a sample of sayings that could be used for common topics:

1. Why put off until tomorrow what you can do today? (Time management)
2. It's not what you say but how you say it. (Communication)
3. You can't sell a product until you understand how it works. (Sales)
4. We cannot fully understand the beginning of anything until we understand the end. (Planning)
5. I hear and I forget; I see and I remember; I do and I understand. (Coaching)
6. A company is known by the people it keeps. (Customer service)
7. Children are afraid of the dark; adults are afraid of the light. (Self-awareness)
8. Yesterday's home runs don't win tomorrow's ball games (Product improvement)
9. Managers do things right; leaders do the right things. (Leadership)
10. The only person who likes change is a wet baby. (Organizational development)

Often giving participants the big picture of what they will learn is an excellent technique for obtaining immediate learning involvement. Here is a representative example:

- A trainer began a seminar on word processing software by demonstrating how a document is composed. She printed the document, edited it slightly, and printed it again. Some participants were invited to enter a few of the commands. She then asked for questions from the participants as they watched the document change. By demonstrating how a document is composed, she gave participants a vision of what they would be learning without resorting to detailed lectures and lists of objectives. Seeing a document created and edited also helped immediately to hook participants' interest in the training content.

Another type of involvement exercise has the participants fill out a questionnaire concerning the course content. Figure 3–7 reproduces an attitude questionnaire that is given as an opening activity to new staff members in a human service agency that serves disabled clients. All the items should be answered "false." As each myth is highlighted, the trainer and/or participants introduce further information to clarify any misconceptions. The course then begins with a discussion of the implications of these myths of disabled populations commonly held by society and their impacts on lifestyles, opportunities, and values.

Figure 3–7. Beliefs about Disabled People

Please answer *true* or *false* for each statement:

_____ 1. Mental retardation can be cured.

_____ 2. Deaf people cannot speak.

_____ 3. People with disabilities live very differently than others.

_____ 4. Blind people prefer other blind people for romantic relationships.

_____ 5. Most people with cerebral palsy are less intelligent than the general population.

_____ 6. Blind people have exceptional hearing.

_____ 7. During an epileptic seizure, the person tends to be violent against him/herself and others.

_____ 8. Wheelchair users have limited sex lives.

_____ 9. Adults with mental retardation should not carry valuables because they might lose them.

_____ 10. Persons with mental retardation have a stronger sex drive than other people.

_____ 11. Adults with mental retardation should never have children.

_____ 12. Tranquilizers are the best way to control problem behaviors.

_____ 13. Persons with mental retardation stop learning in adulthood.

_____ 14. Disabled people are more likely to have accidents than others.

_____ 15. Multiple sclerosis is a virus that can be transferred from person to person.

Source: Rosa Landes, Center for Human Development and Education, Temple University. Reprinted with permission.

MULTIPURPOSE EXERCISES

While it is possible to design one of each kind of exercise as part of your course introduction, too much time spent on opening exercises may require you to skimp on the meat of the training program. Another approach is to design one opening exercise that simultaneously accomplishes **group building, on-the-spot assessment,** and **immediate learning involvement.** An example is an opening exercise called Trio Exchange, described in figure 3–8.

An opening exercise that both fosters group building and provides assessment information is based on a scavenger hunt. Participants receive a set of questions that must be answered with the names of other group

Figure 3–8. Trio Exchange

Participants are asked to discuss within trios a variety of questions that help them get to know each other, learn about their attitudes, knowledge, and experience, and begin discussion of the course content. For example, a new group of trainers could be divided into groups of three and asked such questions as: "How do you learn best?" "What works well in your current training programs?" "What advice would you give yourself to be more effective as an trainer?" Similar questions could be developed for other subject matter areas. In a course on stress management, for example, participants could be asked questions such as: "What are some of the causes of stress in your job?" "At home?" "How do you currently try to deal with stress in your life?" With each question posed by the trainer, new groups are formed by rotating two members, thereby increasing the number of participants who become acquainted with each other.

members. Use a wide variety of questions that touch upon both personal information and course content. (This activity is extremely flexible as you can easily adapt the questions to fit any type of group.) You might want to offer a token prize to the participant who finishes first. When a winner has been declared, reassemble the participants and survey the entire group about each of the items. Promote short discussions of some items. A sample People Scavenger Hunt for real estate sales representatives is given in the next figure.

Figure 3–9. People Scavenger Hunt

Read the following items, then, for each item, find someone in the group who fits the description. Write his/her first name in the space under the item. You may not use any person's name more than once.

Find Someone . . .

1. . . . who has the same first initial as you.
2. . . . who has explained an Adjustable Rate Mortgage to a customer within the last two weeks.
3. . . . who is the newest hire/transfer.
4. . . . who was born in the same month as you.
5. . . . who likes the pace of her work.
6. . . . who specializes in commercial real estate sales.
7. . . . who thinks that a portion of commissions should be pooled.

WHAT TO KEEP IN MIND WHEN CREATING OPENING EXERCISES

As you design your active training program, take the time to consider carefully what initial objectives you wish to accomplish in the opening moments of your session. Your goals might include any combination of group-building, assessment, or involvement exercises. In addition, you should be aware of other considerations as they relate to the particular group you will be training.

1. Level of Threat. Is the group that you will be training open to new ideas and activities or do you anticipate hesitation and reservation from the participants as you begin your session? Opening with an exercise that exposes participants' lack of knowledge or skill can be risky; group members may not yet be ready to reveal their limitations. Alternatively, an activity that asks participants to comment on something familiar eases them into the course content.

2. Appropriateness to Group Norms. A group of executive managers may initially be less open to playing games than would a group of students. Health care professionals and therapists might feel more comfortable sharing their feelings in a "Trio Exchange" exercise than would a group of research scientists. You are setting the stage for the entire course as you plan an opening activity; consider your audience and design appropriately.

3. Relevance to Training Content. Unless you are interested in only a simple exchange of names, an initial design offers an excellent opportunity for participants to begin learning course material. Adapt one of the icebreakers suggested here to reflect the material that you are planning to teach in your course. The closer your exercise ties in to the course content, the easier the transition to your next design.

The design considerations mentioned above have relevance for every aspect of your training program but are especially important in the opening stages. A successful opening exercise sets the course toward a successful program; conversely, one that seems threatening, silly, or unrelated to the rest of your course can create an awkward atmosphere that will be difficult for you to overcome.

TEN WAYS TO OBTAIN PARTICIPATION

No matter how creatively you design your opening exercises, they may still fall flat if the training group is reluctant to participate. A wide range of methods can be used to obtain active participation in the opening phase of a training program. Here are ten possibilities, one or many of which likely will suit the opening exercise you have in mind. You can also use these methods when designing activities for other portions of an active training program.

1. **Open sharing:** Ask a question and open it up to the entire group without any further structuring.
   - Use open sharing when you are certain that several group members want to participate. Its straightforward quality is appealing. If you are worried that the discussion might be too lengthy, say beforehand: "I'd like to ask four or five participants to share . . ."

2. **Anonymous cards:** Pass out index cards and request anonymous answers to your questions. Have the completed cards passed around the group or otherwise distributed.
   - Use anonymous cards to save time or to provide anonymity for personally threatening self-disclosures. The concise expression necessitated by the use of cards is another advantage of this method.

3. **Questionnaires:** Design a short questionnaire to be filled out and tallied on the spot.
   - Use questionnaires to obtain data quickly and in quantifiable form. Feeding back the results immediately can be appealing to participants. You can verbally poll the group instead of using written questions.

4. **Subgroup discussion:** Break participants into subgroups to share (and record) information.
   - Use subgroup discussion when you have sufficient time to process questions and issues. This is the best method for obtaining everyone's participation.

5. **Seat partners:** Have participants work on tasks or discuss key questions with a participant seated next to them.
   - Use seat partners when you want to involve everybody but don't have enough time for small group discussion. A dyad is a good configuration for developing a supportive relationship and/or work-

ing on complex activities that would not lend themselves to large group configurations.

6. **Whips:** Go around the group and obtain short responses to key questions.

   • Use whips when you want to obtain something quickly from each participant. Sentence stems (e.g., "one thing that makes a manager effective is . . .") are useful in conducting whips. Invite participants to pass when they wish. Avoid repetition, if you want, by asking each participant for a new contribution to the process.

7. **Panels:** Invite a small number of participants to present their views to the entire group.

   • Use panels, when time permits, to gain a focused, serious response to your questions. Rotate panelists to increase participation.

8. **Fishbowl:** Ask a portion of the group to form a discussion circle and have the remaining participants form a listening circle around them. Bring new groups into the inner circle to continue the discussion.

   • Use fishbowls to help bring focus to large group discussions. Although time consuming, this is the best method for combining the virtues of large and small group discussion. As a variation, you can have everyone remain seated and invite different participants to be the discussants as the others listen.

9. **Games:** Use quiz game formats and the like to elicit participants' ideas or knowledge.

   • Use games to pick up energy and involvement. Games are also helpful to make dramatic points that participants will seldom forget.

10. **Calling on the next speaker:** Ask participants to raise their hands when they want to share their views and request that the present speaker call on the next speaker (rather than performing this role yourself).

    • Use calling on the next speaker when you are sure that there is a lot of interest in the discussion/activity and you wish to promote participant interaction. When you are ready to resume your role as moderator, inform the group that you are changing back to the regular format.

Worksheet

CREATING OPENING EXERCISES

This worksheet can help you to plan an opening exercise for your next training program. Modify one of the sample exercises from this chapter or go ahead and create your own.

Goal(s) Desired:
(check as many as desired)

    ____ Group building

    ____ On-the-spot assessment

    ____ Immediate learning involvement

Method Selected:
(check as many as desired)

____ Open sharing	____ Whips
____ Anonymous cards	____ Panels
____ Questionnaires	____ Fishbowl
____ Subgroup discussion	____ Games
____ Seat partners	____ Calling on the next speaker

Activity Outline:

_____

_____

_____

_____

_____

_____

_____

_____

_____

_____

PREPARING EFFECTIVE LECTURES

4

As you move from designing the opening exercises to the more central portion of your training program, you will almost certainly decide to present some of the information you wish to cover in a lecture-type format. Lecturing is the most efficient and low-cost method to transmit information in a classroom setting, useful for conveying information to a large group, especially when you need to get across general knowledge. The lecture is a standard tool, which remains in use in most training environments.

If you are committed to active training, however, you face a potential problem: *Lectures put participants in a position of sustained, passive listening.* Learning, unfortunately, is not an automatic consequence of pouring information into another person's head. It requires the person's own mental processing. Therefore, lecturing by itself will never lead to real learning.

Nonetheless, a lecture still can hold an important place in an active training program if you work to involve participants and maximize understanding and retention through participative techniques. To accomplish these ends, a lecture has to be as carefully designed as any other training activity.

FIVE WAYS TO GAIN YOUR AUDIENCE'S INTEREST

The first design element you should consider if you want a lecture to be effective is a method to grab hold of your listeners' attention. Instead of diving right into your course content, try building your participants' interest and involvement in the subject matter. Here are five techniques (with examples) to help you do just that.

INTRODUCTORY EXERCISE

Begin with a game or fun-filled activity that dramatically introduces the main points of the lecture.

1. A lecture on the merits of one-way versus two-way communication is about to begin. Before plunging in, the trainer utilized the short activity described in figure 4–1 to build interest in the lecture.

Figure 4–1. Paper-Tearing Exercise

Time Allocation: 5 minutes

Materials: Blank 8½-by-11-inch sheets of paper for each participant

Instructions:

1. Tell the participants the following: "We are going to play a game that will show us some important things about communication. Pick up your sheet of paper and hold it in front of you. Now, close your eyes and follow the directions I will give you—*and no peeking!*

2. Give the following directions, carrying them out yourself with your own sheet of paper and pausing after each instruction to give the group time to comply:

   "The first thing I want you to do is to fold your sheet of paper in half."

   "Now tear off the upper right-hand corner."

   "Fold it in half again and tear off the upper left-hand corner of the sheet."

   "Fold it in half again. Now tear off the lower right-hand corner of the sheet."

3. After the tearing is complete, say something like "Now open your eyes, and let's see what you have. If I did a good job of communicating and you did a good job of listening, all of our sheets should look the same!" Hold

Figure 4–1. continued

your sheet up for them to see. It is highly unlikely that any sheet will match yours exactly.

4. Observe the differences. There will probably be much laughter.

5. Ask the group why no one's paper matched yours. (You will probably get responses like "You didn't let us ask questions!" or "Your directions could be interpreted in different ways.") Then, lead into a presentation on the need for two-way communication in the workplace.

2. A trainer is about to give a presentation about techniques for obtaining volunteers to serve in community service organizations. Before the presentation, the trainer guided participants through this mental imagery exercise: "Close your eyes. Imagine who you would consider to be a typical volunteer. What age and gender is this volunteer? What kind of clothes does he or she wear? What are his interests and skills? What career is she involved in? How does he act? Is she dependable? Likable? Why does he volunteer? What is her motivation? Get a good picture in your mind. Now, open your eyes, turn to your partner, and share your description of a typical volunteer." After the dyadic sharing, the trainer began her presentation with a portrait of the broad range of people who might volunteer and urged participants to remove any preconceptions from their minds.

LEAD-OFF STORY OR INTERESTING VISUAL

Begin with a work-related anecdote, fictional story, cartoon, or graphic that focuses the audience's attention on the subject of your lecture.

1. A trainer accepted an assignment to deliver time management training to a group of hospital administrators. Instead of jumping into a lecture on organization and time-wasters, she began her presentation with the well-known **lead-off story** recounted in figure 4–2.

Figure 4–2. A Story about Time Management

The utility of planning the day's work is seen clearly in a well-known story concerning Charles Schwab. When he was president of Bethlehem Steel, he presented Ivy Lee, a consultant, with an unusual challenge. "Show me a way to get more things done with my time," he said, "and I'll pay you any fee within reason."

Handing Schwab a sheet of paper, Lee said, "Write down the most important tasks you have to do tomorrow and number them in order of importance. When

Figure 4–2. continued

you arrive in the morning, begin at once on No. 1 and stay on it till it's completed. Recheck your priorities; then begin with No. 2. If any task takes all day, never mind. Stick with it as long as it's the most important one. If you don't finish them all, you probably couldn't do so with any other method, and without some system you'd probably not even decide which one was most important. Make this a habit every working day. When it works for you, give it to your men. Try it as long as you like. Then send me your check for what you think it's worth."

Some weeks later, Schwab sent Lee a check for $25,000, with a note saying that the lesson was the most profitable he had ever learned. In five years, this plan was largely responsible for turning Bethlehem Steel Corporation into the biggest independent steel producer in the world.

Schwab's friends asked him later about the payment of so high a fee for such a simple idea. Schwab responded by asking, what ideas are not basically simple? He reminded them that, for the first time, not only he but his entire team were getting first things done first. On reflection, Schwab observed that perhaps the expenditure was the most valuable investment Bethlehem Steel had made all year.

Source: R. Alec MacKenzie. 1972. *The Time Trap*. New York: AMACOM. Used with permission.

2. During a course on training evaluation, a trainer was about to lecture on four ways that psychological tests are validated (predictive validity, concurrent validity, construct validity, and content validity). Before the start of his presentation, he displayed a list of the vocabulary words on the Wechsler Adult Intelligence Scale. He then asked participants if they thought the use of such vocabulary words was a valid way to test intelligence. After receiving a variety of opinions (mostly dissenting), he proceeded to explain how psychometricians make positive claims about the validity of using vocabulary words to test intelligence and how these procedures can be used for all psychological tests.

INITIAL CASE PROBLEM

Present a short problem around which the lecture will be structured.

1. Figure 4–3 outlines a brief case problem that was used to introduce a lecture given to claims adjusters on what constitutes a "work-related" injury.

Figure 4–3. Case Problem 1: Claims Adjustment

Sarah Secretary drives to work each day. Her route takes her past the post office. Each day she stops and picks up the mail for the office, and on her way home each afternoon she drops off the outgoing mail. One day on her way home, she is involved in a two-car accident and is injured.

Is the injury compensable? As I discuss the factors defining a work-related injury, try to answer this question for yourself.

2. The case problem in figure 4–4 was used to introduce a lecture on resume writing.

Figure 4–4. Case Problem 2: Resume Writing

Joan has been an employee of a national pharmaceutical company for the last seven years. She began her work at the company as a secretary in the human resources department and after four years moved into an entry-level position as a benefits administrator. Her job responsibilities included answering employees' benefit questions, handling the enrollment of new employees into one of the company's medical plans, and researching any problems that employees had as they filed insurance claims with the medical plan providers.

Yesterday, Joan found out that her job had been eliminated. All responsibility for benefits administration henceforward would be handled out of corporate headquarters in New York. Joan and three other coworkers have been told that they will be let go at the end of the month. Once they have left the company, they will each receive three months of job severance pay.

Joan is terrified of looking for a new job. She enjoyed working at the company very much and hates to think of starting all over again somewhere else. Moreover, she has not written a resume since the last time that she had to look for a job, seven years ago. This old resume identified only her skills as a secretary, yet Joan is certain that she would like to continue her career in benefits and not return to a secretarial position.

What advice could you give Joan as she writes her new resume? As I present some tips on resume writing, think through how Joan could best present her last seven years of work at the pharmaceutical company.

TEST QUESTIONS

Ask participants questions related to the lecture topic (even if they have little prior knowledge) so that they will be motivated to listen to your lecture for the answers.

1. Most people might think that the purchase of a co-op is financed by a mortgage; in fact co-ops are financed with loans because co-op owners do not actually own their apartments but, rather, share in a corporation. Thus, a lender cannot repossess an apartment in the event of foreclosure since it does not hold title to the property. A $1 mortgage is a way for a bank to establish title when a home equity loan is taken on a co-op. Such a loan is generally a second mortgage, so this device gives the lender some security.

   Before presenting the above information in a lecture on the nature of co-op loans in a course for loan officers, the trainer asked this simple question: "Why would anyone want a $1 mortgage?" He invited several responses by urging participants to speculate. After they had responded, the trainer proceeded with his lecture, explaining to participants that the answer to the question would be clear at the end of the presentation.

2. A trainer was preparing a lecture presentation on techniques for managing meetings effectively. Concerned that participants would find the lecture boring, he decided to introduce it with a true/false test (see figure 4–5). Instead of going over the answers immediately, the trainer promised participants that the correct answers would become evident during his presentation. The group was all ears.

Figure 4–5. Meetings!

True or false?

_____ 1. Preparing an agenda in advance tends to promote meeting efficiency.

_____ 2. Distributing an agenda to members in advance generally does not affect the efficiency of meetings.

_____ 3. Starting meetings on time is inconsiderate to latecomers; wait until everyone is present before starting the meeting.

_____ 4. Begin to wind meetings down five to ten minutes before the meeting is scheduled to end.

_____ 5. Brief meetings (e.g., fifteen minutes or shorter) can be efficiently held standing.

_____ 6. Experts consider the ideal meeting length to be two to two-and-a-half hours.

_____ 7. Most experts advise holding meetings even if the agenda does not justify the expenditure of time and money.

Figure 4–5. continued

_____ 8. Reading something out loud at a meeting when a printed version has been distributed is generally considered to be a waste of time.

_____ 9. Meetings are the most efficient forums in which to make general announcements.

_____ 10. Don't hold a large meeting to deal with a problem that affects only a few people.

PREVIEW OF CONTENT

Give highlights or "coming attractions" of the lecture in an enthusiastic manner to entice interest and involvement.

1. A trainer was about to give a lengthy presentation on a new automated purchasing system. To build interest in the lecture, she stated:

   "You have been asked to come here today for an explanation of our company's new automated purchasing system. Before I go into the details of how the system operates, I want each one of you to realize that, when you leave this room today, you will know how to spend approximately two hours a week less on ordering forms and supplies than you do currently. You will also know how to use the system effectively to monitor items that are on back order and to anticipate when items will arrive. Finally, by the end of this presentation, you will know how to receive your purchased items two weeks sooner than you have been with the old paper-based system of ordering supplies."

2. A trainer introduced a lecture on the history of leadership theory with the following remarks:

   "For the next twenty minutes, we are going to explore how our thinking about the nature of leadership has changed dramatically over the last thirty-five years. In that span of time, we have gone from rather simple notions of what makes a good leader to highly complicated models of leadership behavior. You be the judge! Are we any better off today than we were back in the fifties? My opinion is that we are, but I don't know if you'll be convinced."

   These few remarks immediately hooked the group's active attention to a presentation that might otherwise have met with resistance because of the tedium of the subject matter.

FIVE WAYS TO MAXIMIZE UNDERSTANDING AND RETENTION

After engaging the interest of your audience with one or more of these five interest-building techniques, it is time to begin the actual lecture. As you design your presentation, remember that your instructional goal is to maximize the participants' understanding and retention of the subject matter. Ultimately, the participants will learn more if they can focus their attention on the subject matter and make the ideas relevant to themselves. Five ways to maximize understanding and retention follow; try to use some or all of them as you present your lecture.

OPENING SUMMARY

At the beginning of the lecture, state (or summarize in writing) its major points and conclusions to help participants organize their listening.

1. A trainer was about to give a lengthy presentation on business writing styles. He asked participants to read the handout reproduced in figure 4–6 so that they would have an overview of the presentation before he began.

Figure 4–6. Opening Summary

To achieve an effective style for a specific writing occasion in business, you must speak to the reader in an appropriate way. It is particularly important to sequence information in a way that helps readers more readily understand what you have to say.

"Most important to least important" order is preferred by most business readers and writers because it is easy to read. The most important points are clearly stated at the beginning, and less important evidence or arguments are relegated to minor positions in the body.

"Most important to least important" order is generally used for

- summaries
- memoranda
- letters requesting information
- letters replying to requests for information.

Another common pattern of organization requires the reader to follow a trail of logic and analysis leading to the bottom-line message at the end of the report. This inductive pattern is most often used for

Figure 4–6. continued

- research reports
- letters or reports that must say no or contain a message the reader will perceive as negative
- reports written to a *hostile audience*, where the writer must explain his reasoning process first to enable the reader to understand the bottom-line message and accept an unwelcome idea.

2. A trainer began a lecture on PERT (Program/Project Evaluation and Review Technique) with the following opening summary: "I'm going to give you a thumbnail sketch of PERT before we look at it in detail. PERT was developed by the Navy Department for the Polaris missile. It is useful in the *planning, scheduling,* and *monitoring* and *control* aspects of project management. In the *planning* phase, it requires you to list the tasks entailed by the project, calculate the gross requirements for resources, and make time/cost estimates. In the *scheduling* phase, it involves laying out the tasks in a time sequence and detailing schedule or resource requirements. In the *monitoring* and *control* phase, it entails reviewing the schedule and actual performance, revising the schedule if necessary, and assessing the likelihood of jeopardy and cost escalation. PERT can be employed in such applications as building construction, installing a computer system, or the end-of-month closing of accounting records. Now, let's take a closer look at the process and examine when and how it works.

KEY TERMS

Reduce the major points in the lecture to key words that act as verbal subheadings or memory aids.

1. A trainer was giving a presentation on supervisory styles. She decided to use these three catchy terms to describe alternatives open to supervisors:

    Tell & Sell: In this mode, the supervisor explains to employees what is expected of them and why their cooperation is needed.

    Tell & Listen: In this mode, too, the supervisor initially explains to employees what is expected but then asks for *(and listens to)* their feedback to his requests.

    Listen & Tell: In this mode, the supervisor asks his employees to comment on the work they are doing, listens to their responses, and then tells them what he feels and wants.

2. To convey five factors that customers use to rate the quality of service their receive, a trainer used a mnemonic aid with key terms (see figure 4–7).

Figure 4–7. RATER: A Mnemonic Aid

Reliability:	You don't make mistakes (too often).
Assurance:	You assure customers that they are valued.
Tangibles:	You convey a positive image [through] tangible evidence such as being neat and organized.
Empathy:	You express understanding of the customer's situation.
Responsiveness:	You deal with the customer's needs in a timely manner.

Source: Creating Customer Focus. The Forum Corporation, St. Davids Center, 150 Radnor-Chenter Rd., St. Davids, Penna. 19087.

EXAMPLES

As much as possible, provide real-life illustrations of the ideas in the lecture.

1. In a course on alcoholism and the family, the trainer was explaining how family members may not be the cause of a parent's alcoholism, but may play a role in keeping the problem alive. He then gave the following example of enabling an alcoholic.

"Consider the family of George, a retired mechanical engineer and an alcoholic. George began as a social drinker and eventually stepped over the invisible line into alcoholism. His wife, Joann, a registered nurse, played a key role in enabling George to remain an alcoholic. By taking on many of George's responsibilities, including budgeting, providing additional income, and handling the physical maintenance of the home, Joann was able to ensure that the household ran smoothly. In the process, of course, George did not have to confront his alcoholism. George's eldest children, Bill and Cathy, also contributed to the enabling process. Successes outside the family, both projected appearances of 'having it together' but, in truth, were often depressed. A younger sister, Laura, did her share by becoming a difficult teenager, refocusing family anger away from father to her. All members of the family adopted three rules that helped to maintain the status quo: (1) keep negative feelings to yourself; (2) don't talk about Dad's drinking with other family members; and (3) don't let outsiders know what happens in the family."

2. In a course called "Selling to Your Client's Style," the trainer was teaching the personality types described in the Myers-Briggs Type Indicator (MBTI), an instrument used widely to help people understand their personal style and the styles of others with whom they work. She was discussing the differences between a "Thinker" (T) type and a "Feeler" (F) type and illustrated the distinction with the following example: "A prospect who is a T will probably speak in a concise fashion, will appear to be firm and tough minded, likes to argue, and is focused on the bottom line. To be effective with a T, don't ramble, be logical, and address objections head on. A prospect who is an F, on the other hand, will appear personable and friendly, takes time to get to know you, seems to like harmony, and is more interested in process than outcome. With such a person, it's best to spend time getting to know the person, to be friendly and warm, to be affirming, and to understand that the prospect may have difficulty being critical and not reveal true feelings about your product or service."

ANALOGIES

If possible, make a comparison between your material and the knowledge or experience the participants already have.

1. An instructor in an adult education class on auto mechanics realized how frustrating it must be for people to understand how a car works. He found an interesting way to explain the sequence of events in, of all places, a children's book. The instructional approach is performed entirely through analogies.

   - The **gasoline tank** is like an *oil can*. The gasoline goes from here to the fuel pump.
   - The **fuel pump,** which is like a *water pump,* pumps the gasoline to the carburetor.
   - The **carburetor,** which is like a perfume *atomizer,* changes the liquid gasoline into a gasoline-and-air vapor, which goes to the cylinder.
   - The **cylinder** is like a *cannon* with a piston in it.
   - The **spark plug,** which is like a *lighter,* ignites the vapor in the cylinder. The vapor burns and expands quickly, pushing the piston down.

- The **crankshaft** is like the *handle of a hand drill.* The piston going down in the cylinder turns it.
- The **driveshaft** is turned by the crankshaft, like a *drill bit* is turned by the drill handle.
- The driveshaft and axle are connected by **ring gears,** like those of an *egg beater.* The driveshaft turns the ring gears, which turn the axle, which turns the rear wheels. The turning wheels make the car go.

2. Many well-known concepts are effectively explained by way of analogy. Here are a few:

- A person cannot adjust his behavior to meet your needs unless you give him sufficient feedback. You are like a *thermostat,* and the other person is like a *heating/cooling unit.* A thermostat reflects the temperature in a room for the heating/cooling unit. When the temperature is too hot or too cold, the heating/cooling unit can adjust its behavior, relying upon the thermostat for the feedback that indicates when to do so.
- A database will hold and organize information for you just as an *office file cabinet* does. Your information is stored in files like the folders in your office file cabinet.
- When your selling style is very different from your client's, think of your client as *an AM transmitter* sending out waves when you have only *an FM receiver.*
- If you don't take the time to save information, you'll lose it. It's like *being introduced to somebody* and doing nothing to retain the name. Within seconds, you'll forget the name.
- A body's ability to contain stress is much like a *rain barrel* that overflows when the water reaches the top. We all have rain barrels to contain our stress. As they begin to fill, we start to experience stress-related symptoms. When they reach the point of overflowing, we may have serious illnesses.

VISUAL BACKUP

Use flip charts, transparencies, brief handouts, and demonstrations that enable participants to see as well as hear what you are saying.

1. One of the best-known visuals in the training field is the Johari Window (see figure 4–8), which describes how we give and receive information about ourselves and others. The window has four "panes":

Figure 4–8. The Johari Window

Public knowledge	Blind spots
Secrets	Unknown

- *public knowledge,* thoughts and feelings that have already been openly expressed in a relationship
- *blind spots,* thoughts and feelings of others that have not been told to you
- *secrets,* thoughts and feelings that you have kept to yourself
- the *unknown,* thoughts and feelings of which neither you nor others are consciously aware

By depicting communication as a window, the developers of the model, Joseph Luft and Harry Ingram, are able to make an interesting point— for public knowledge to increase in a relationship, blind spots and secrets must decrease. This can only happen if you reveal some of your secrets and others let you know about your blind spots. This process is achieved by giving and receiving feedback. A by-product of such communication is the likelihood that previously unknown information will be uncovered.

2. Windows can have not only panes but also shades. An effective way to conceptualize the control of upper levels of management in some organizations is to compare their decision-making power to a window shade. Initiative at lower levels of management is often inhibited when the shade is drawn too far down. Even worse is when the level of the window shade is different every day. In this latter instance, initiative is further inhibited because middle managers and supervisors are continually confused about the boundaries of their areas of responsibility.

Figure 4–9. The Window Shade Model of Power

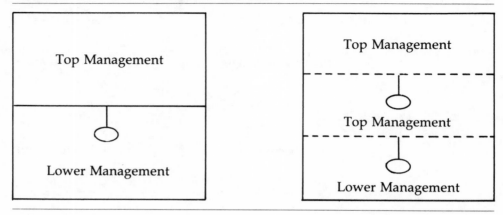

FIVE WAYS TO INVOLVE PARTICIPANTS DURING A LECTURE

No matter how scintillating your presentation, the participants are still placed in a passive role. Fortunately, steps can be taken to enlist group participation right during the lecture. Here are five suggestions.

LISTENER ROLES

Assign participants the responsibility to listen actively to the lecture so that, when it is over, they are able to produce points they agree or disagree with, questions to clarify the lecture, a summary of its contents, or quiz questions for other participants. Assignments can be given to the group as a whole, to subgroups, or to specific individuals.

1. Before a short lecture on six strategies for organizing and communicating information (definition, classification, example, process analysis, comparison/contrast, and cause/effect), a business writing trainer asked participants to listen carefully to the description of each strategy so that at the end of the lecture they would be able to provide a summary to their seat partners.

2. A trainer was about to give what might ordinarily have been a boring presentation on statistics concerning the current job market, turnover rates, and the cost of replacing an employee. Before starting, she distributed a list of questions for participants to answer as she lectured on the changing job market. By directing participants to search for

information in the lecture, the trainer was able to capture her audience's active attention.

GUIDED NOTE TAKING

Provide instructions or a form indicating how participants should take notes during the lecture. Stop at intervals so that participants can write down reactions or ideas that go beyond what you have presented.

1. In a project management seminar, the trainer was lecturing about the cost management process, including the financial planning of a project and the subsequent collection, organization, and analysis of actual cost data to attain the project cost objective. Participants had a worksheet listing in the following terms: *input, process, output,* and *feedback.* After the trainer discussed each element in the process, participants were asked to recall his remarks in the appropriate section of the worksheet and write down any questions they might have.

2. A time management trainer was about to give a lecture on timesaving tips. Before starting, she gave participants a handout on which to record "any information you find useful." She urged them to not write down every idea, explaining that, of all the information she was about to offer, probably 20% would be truly useful to any one person. She connected this suggestion to the Pareto Principle, which states that 20% of an effort produces 80% of the result. The key, she pointed out, was to focus on the critical 20% and not to allow the 80% to get in the way.

SPOT CHALLENGES

Interrupt the lecture periodically and challenge participants to give examples of the concepts presented thus far or answer spot quiz questions.

1. Before a lecture on delegation, a trainer explained to his audience that he would stop periodically to obtain audience responses. He proceeded to discuss a four-pronged analysis that managers might perform to identify new delegation opportunities—*things I have already delegated, things I could delegate, things I am uncertain about delegating,* and *things I cannot delegate*—and provided a case illustration as he presented each category. Participants were challenged to predict how the managers in the case illustrations would identify items for each category.

2. A trainer was lecturing on three homeostatic mechanisms in families (rules, roles, and symptoms). After each section of the lecture, he gave a multiple-choice quiz to participants to test their understanding of the material. Before continuing the lecture, he would review the answers to each quiz question.

SYNERGETIC LEARNING

Provide different information to different participants. Allow them to compare notes and briefly teach each other.

1. In a course on group process, the trainer divided the training group in half. One group was sent to another room to read information about the maintenance roles performed in effective groups. During this time, the other group heard a lecture on the task roles performed in effective groups. Then, the first group returned to hear a lecture designed to reinforce what they had read, while the second group was sent out to read information that reinforced the lecture they had just heard. Members from each group were then paired up to teach each other what they had learned.

2. A trainer was using overhead transparencies to present guidelines for writing job aids. At one point in the rather lengthy presentation, she asked half of the participants to close their eyes and listen to the next portion of the lecture and half to cover their ears for the same period of time and read the transparencies. After the lecture was completed, the trainer asked the two groups to compare notes about what they had heard or seen.

ILLUMINATING EXERCISES

Throughout the presentation, intersperse brief activities that illuminate the information, ideas, and skills being presented.

1. A trainer gave a brief lecture summarizing the problems that managers face today, including low productivity, poor quality of service, high stress, and low morale. She also noted that traditional management solutions often tend, like the mythological hydra, to generate two new problems for every one solved. She remarked on the need for a different approach, which she called "creating the ideal." At this point, the trainer interrupted the lecture with an exercise. She asked each participant to find a partner of approximately equal weight and strength.

One of the pair was asked to hold out his or her arm horizontally and to resist the partner's attempts to bend it. Most arms were easily bent. The trainer then requested the individual to imagine his or her arm as a steel rod before the partner attempted to bend it and to sustain the vision during the process. In most pairs, arms remained straight despite increased effort from the partners. The lecturer then continued: "Better results are obtained with less effort. The key is what one focuses on. In the first case, the individual tried to achieve contradictory results: keeping his or her arm straight and resisting having it bent. In the second case, he or she focused solely on the desired result." The trainer then presented four key elements that go into a visionary approach to problem-solving work.

2. In a workshop on preventing burnout, a trainer gave a brief overview of the three primary psychological motives discovered by David McClelland to drive behavior: (1) N-Ach—Need for Achievement; (2) N-Aff—Need for Affiliation; and (3) N-Pow—Need for Power. Before launching into a more discursive discussion of each need, the trainer posed the following question: "If I were to give you one thousand dollars to spend any way you wanted, how would you spent it?" After the participants wrote down their responses, the trainer asked them to examine their decisions in light of the three primary motives to determine which one predominated.

FIVE WAYS TO REINFORCE LECTURES

At the completion of the lecture, the conventional behavior is to wrap it up with a recap of the major points and a question-and-answer period. Although these conventions have merit and should not be overlooked in your planning, there are some more exciting and active ways to debrief and reinforce what has been presented. Consider these five methods.

PRESS CONFERENCE

Invite participants to prepare questions to submit for the trainer's response. Or provide a list of questions from which participants select.

1. During a seminar on a new statistical software package, the trainer periodically gave participants three questions that had emerged from the material he had just covered. Participants were asked to vote for one question to be reviewed before the trainer continued with the

seminar. By doing this, the trainer helped the participants to review what they were learning throughout the day.

2. At the conclusion of a lecture on reserving factors in an accident claim, participants were formed into quartets. Each quartet was asked to pose a question to the trainer that would help to clarify the lecture presentation. Participants were urged to incorporate hypothetical cases into their questions.

GROUP PROCESSING

Ask participants to reflect on the lecture's implications for them. Utilize any group format that you feel will maximize the quality of the processing.

1. A training group had just heard a lecture on five steps to effective meeting management. The participants were asked to break into small groups to discuss the following two questions: (1) "Which ideas were new for you and which were not?" and (2) "Which ideas do you think apply to your situation back home?"

2. A trainer completed a lecture on ten key points to remember when conducting a hiring interview:

   a. Build rapport.

   b. Describe the job and the organization to the candidate.

   c. Be aware of your body language.

   d. Review the candidate's resume.

   e. Ask as much as possible about the candidate's past behavior.

   f. Allow for silence.

   g. Maintain control.

   h. Seek contrary evidence.

   i. Answer the candidate's questions.

   j. Make important notes during the interview.

   She then asked participants to discuss the following questions with a seat partner:

   • Which of these behaviors comes easily to you? Which are difficult?

   • Which do you want to practice more?

   • What would help you to remember these key points the next time you conduct an interview?

POST-LECTURE CASE PROBLEM

Pose a case problem for participants to solve based on the information given in the lecture.

1. In a training program on mortgage product sales, the trainer gave a lecture on the ingredients of a mortgage commitment. When the presentation was completed, the following short case problem was presented to participants:

    A customer has received a good-faith estimate and believes this is a mortgage commitment. Confused, the customer makes an appointment with you for an explanation.

    In trios, participants were asked what they would explain to the customer.

2. At the conclusion of a presentation on bank products, the participants were formed into two groups and given the following case problem:

    A customer's daughter has just been accepted at a college with very high tuition. Unfortunately, she does not qualify for a state-guaranteed loan. She has come to you for alternatives. What would you recommend?

    After small group discussion, individuals from each group were matched with each other to compare notes on the case problem.

PARTICIPANT REVIEW

Ask participants to review the contents of the lecture with each other (in any group configuration) and commit the major points to memory. Or give them a self-scoring review test.

1. A trainer gave a presentation on six job-centered motivators that Herzberg believes have long-term effects on employee's attitudes:
    a. achievement
    b. recognition for achievement
    c. the work itself
    d. responsibility
    e. growth
    f. advancement

    When he finished, he asked participants to put away their notes and write down the six motivators from memory, providing an example of each. He then allowed participants to check their answers against their notes.

2. In a stress management seminar, the trainer explained and demonstrated over twenty stretching and relaxation exercises one can do while seated in an office. Participants were given a brief opportunity to practice each of the exercises. Assuming that participants could easily forget many of the exercises (even with a summary handout), the trainer divided participants into pairs and asked them to remember as many of the exercises as possible. Pairs were then allowed to check with each other to identify most of the twenty exercises. After working this hard to recall the exercises, the trainer hypothesized, individual participants likely would recall many of them for future use, without prompts and aids.

EXPERIENTIAL ACTIVITY

Design an activity that dramatically summarizes or illustrates the lecture you have given. Utilize any of the experiential learning approaches presented in chapter 6 (role playing, games/simulations, observation, mental imagery, writing tasks, and projects).

1. A trainer gave a lecture on family systems to drug and alcohol counselors who were learning to use a family treatment approach in their work. In particular, the lecture examined issues of proximity in families—how some family members are closely connected and how others become disengaged. At the conclusion, the trainer asked participants to join him in forming a circle, holding hands. He then released himself from the person to his right and began to lead the person to his left (and, consequently, all the participants who were connected to her) over and under the clasped hands of other participants. The result was a human knot, with some participants facing others and some facing no one. In addition, some participants emerged in comfortable body positions while others were in awkward positions. With the participants thus entangled, the trainer (who managed to end up in a comfortable position facing several other participants) began a discussion of a recent, controversial film. The discussion continued for several minutes, with some participants contributing easily and others showing little desire to become involved. The knot was then untangled, and participants returned to their seats. The trainer asked the participants to discuss their experiences in the knot and to relate them to the lecture he had just presented. It was a dramatic demonstration

of the varied degrees of involvement and detachment possible within a group or human system.

2. A trainer had just finished a lecture entitled "How Brain Dominance Affects Teaching/Learning Style." She wanted to reinforce the lecture with a demonstration showing that, if we teach only from our preferred mode, frustration will result for both teacher and student. She asked participants to pair off and for each pair to decide who would be the student and who would be the teacher. "Students" then were asked to write out their responses to this question: "What are the first two steps you would like your teacher to take in order to help you learn how to drive a car most effectively?" "Teachers" were asked to respond in writing to a comparable question: "What are the two first steps you would take in order to teach someone how to drive a car most effectively?" Each pair was then asked to compare responses and discuss any discrepancies and/or similarities between the steps proposed by the "teacher" and those desired by the "student." Pairs were also asked to compare their scores on the Hermann Brain Dominance Inventory, which had previously been completed and profiled for each participant, and to try to draw some conclusions about the impact of their learning styles on their approaches to teaching.

Worksheet

DESIGNING A LECTURE

Use this worksheet to assist you in the design of a well-organized lecture that will initiate participant interest in your subject matter, retain that interest throughout the presentation, enlist direct participation, and reinforce what has been presented.

Interest-Building Strategy(ies):
(check as many as desired)

_____ Introductory exercise
_____ Lead-off story or interesting visual
_____ Initial case problem
_____ Test questions
_____ Preview of content

Strategy Outline:

_____
_____
_____
_____

Understanding- and Retention-maximizing Techniques:
(check as many as desired)

_____ Opening summary
_____ Key terms
_____ Examples
_____ Analogies
_____ Visual backup

Notes on Techniques:

_____
_____
_____
_____

Participant Involvement:
(check as many as desired)

_____ Listener roles
_____ Guided note taking
_____ Spot challenges
_____ Synergetic learning
_____ Illuminating exercises

Notes on Techniques:

_____

_____

_____

_____

Lecture Reinforcing:
(check as many as desired)

_____ Press conference
_____ Group processing
_____ Post-lecture case problem
_____ Participant review
_____ Experiential activity

Notes on Techniques:

_____

_____

_____

_____

FINDING ALTERNATIVE METHODS

TO LECTURING

5

While a well-designed lecture can be an effective training method, over-reliance on lecturing usually leads to boredom, lack of involvement, or limited learning for the participants. A different method can often take the place of a particular lecture entirely. A lecture can also be reinforced by utilizing another method. In this chapter, we will examine six alternatives to lecturing that you can use even if your participants have little prior knowledge of the subject being taught. These methods are

1. **Demonstration**
2. **Case study**
3. **Guided teaching**
4. **Group inquiry**
5. **Read and discuss**
6. **Information search**

DEMONSTRATION

Instead of talking about a concept, procedure, or set of facts, you may be able to walk through a demonstration of the information in action. Involving participants in the demonstration, if possible, is important so that they can actually hear, see, and touch the relevant learning materials. The advantage to a demonstration is that it adds showing to merely telling. Here are two examples:

1. On the third afternoon of a five-day course on family process, a trainer began a module on family permeability—how a family relates to the outside world. He began by explaining that no family is self-sufficient; all need the stimulation and support of others. However, a family needs to rely on itself as well, since always turning to outsiders, he suggested, robs a family of its integrity. At this point, the trainer thought about continuing his presentation, raising specific issues that families face in considering how open they want to be. Fearing that he had already lectured too much in the afternoon session, however, he decided instead to invite one of the participants to be interviewed about her family. By discussing a number of specific questions with the participant (e.g., how much time did she spend with family and with friends? is religious and sex education left up to professionals? did she tell others about any problems occurring in the family? how much contact did the family have with people of other races, religions, or cultures?), the trainer provided a stunning demonstration of how a family negotiates issues of permeability.

2. In a communications course, a trainer was about to present a model by Jack Gibb on defensive versus nondefensive communication. According to Gibb, people become defensive when others are evaluative, controlling, strategizing, neutral, superior, and overly certain. They become less defensive when others are descriptive, problem oriented, spontaneous, empathetic, egalitarian, and provisional. Rather than defining and illustrating each of these twelve qualities, the trainer chose instead to create a live demonstration. He enlisted four participants to hold a discussion on the rights of smokers and nonsmokers in the workplace. The twelve categories were prominently displayed on newsprint off to the side of the discussion group. As the trainer heard an example of one of the communication categories emerging from the group discussion, he pointed to the category that was being demonstrated. In ten minutes, all the defensive communication categories had been illustrated, but few of the nondefensive ones had

been utilized. To demonstrate the remaining nondefensive behaviors, the trainer joined the discussion group and showed how the communication of one member could induce lowered defensiveness in others. He then encouraged others to try out the newly demonstrated behaviors.

CASE STUDY

A case study can be likened to a written demonstration. You are providing an account of a real or fictitious situation, including sufficient detail to make it possible for groups to analyze the problems involved. You can also embed in a case study information that is normally presented in lecture format. The major benefit of a case study is that abstract information is presented concretely. Notice in the two case examples that follow how the participants learn what the trainers want to teach without the trainers having to give to them in a lecture.

1. In a course on coaching and counseling skills for managers, the trainer normally used a lecture format to present a five-step interview process. He decided instead to give out the case example in figure 5–1 and to ask the participants, working in trios, to identify five steps that the supervisor took in counseling the employee. Answers were combined across the trios and compared to the trainer's lecture notes. To the trainer's delight, the participants hit on every one of the points that he had planned to cover in the lecture.

Figure 5–1. Counseling an Employee

The following exchange took place between Suzanne Smith, a manager, and her employee, David White, who had been "called on the carpet."

SMITH: Come in, David. Have a seat. I suppose you're wondering why I want to talk to you.

WHITE: Yes, I guess I am.

SMITH: Well, David, recently a little thing has come up that I want to know your feelings about. Remember the Adamson report?

WHITE: What about it?

SMITH: To be frank with you, there was a lot of disagreement on the figures that were used, and the boss wants the whole thing done over. It wasn't up to the level of the reports you've been turning out in the past. I have to admit that myself. But I want to hear your views about it.

Figure 5–1. continued

WHITE: Well, there isn't much to say. I sort of figured it would get rejected anyway. I wasn't happy about the damn thing either. *(Getting a little emotional.)*

SMITH: You weren't pleased with it either?

WHITE: Heck, no, I wasn't. Look, it takes about twenty-five to thirty hours, at least, for me to write up a report like that even when I've already worked up the figures! You know how long I spent on that report? About five hours! And I wasn't as sure on the figures as I should have been either.

SMITH: You didn't get to put in much time on the report, is that it?

WHITE: No, I didn't. In fact, I don't blame them for rejecting it at all. Like I said, it was a lousy job. But it won't be the last lousy job they get from me unless I get some help down here. There's no way I can run a research department and do the odds and ends that get sent in my direction. When we were a smaller outfit, it was possible, but not now. What the heck does everybody expect from me anyway?

SMITH: You're saying that you have too many assignments then?

WHITE: Yes, that's exactly what I'm saying! *(Getting more upset.)* I'm expected to do everybody's odds and ends. Production wants this, marketing wants that, cost accounting wants something else. Then along comes the Control Committee and their report. They give me a week's notice to get it out. I know I'm running a staff department, but there's no way one person can handle it all. And this was a sloppy report, I know. But it won't be the last.

SMITH: David, you know how we've counted on you in the past for these reports. Frankly, they're very important, and you've been doing such a great job on them. Is there any way we might be able to work out this problem?

WHITE: How we might work it out? Yeah, give me three new people. *(Only half joking.)*

SMITH: You think extra help would do it?

WHITE: Oh, I don't know. I guess we could handle it all if production would get off my back. Whenever they want something, they get the VP to call me and tell me how badly they need it in short order. That's what happened on the Adamson report. I had to finish it in three days. Millican [VP for Production] called with a rush job to be done and said that Henderly would be up to see me with the details. I guess I'm too meek to say "No, I can't do it on such short notice." But what do I say to a VP?

SMITH: It's hard to turn down a VP. Do you feel that I could help in any way?

WHITE: Well, you have a lot more say with Millican than I do. But he's sure a bull-headed type.

SMITH: Well, let me worry about that. I'll have a talk with him. And if he comes up with another of these "emergencies" that you honestly can't handle,

Figure 5–1. continued

explain to him as best you can that you can't get it out that fast. But offer to talk with me about it. If he still insists, then let me know and I'll talk with him. David, it is my job to help.

WHITE: Well, I feel a lot better getting this thing out. I was really getting in a rut.

SMITH: Well, I'm also glad that we were able to work this out.

Source: Donald C. Mosley, Leon C. Megginson, and Paul H. Pietri, Jr. *Supervisory Management* (Cincinnati: South-Western Publishing Co., 1985). Reprinted with permission.

2. In a workshop for counselors who provide support for parents who have suffered the death of an infant, the trainer provided the participants with the case example presented in figure 5–2 and asked them to identify (1) the issues faced by the parents and (2) the concepts of death held by their three children. With this case study approach, participants developed a much richer understanding of the issues and concepts than they could have gained from a lecture.

Figure 5–2. The Death of a Child

Lisa and Ron had been married for fifteen years when their child Nicole was born prematurely at twenty-eight weeks. They had three older children, Stevie (age eleven), Robbie (age seven), and Jen (age four).

After Lisa was discharged from the hospital, she and Ron rushed to the hospital each day to see Nicole. They felt very close to one another and had deep talks during the one-hour trip back and forth from the hospital. They knew that they had developed a lot of strength together as a couple over the years and could cope with any adversity. Twice a week they would bring their three children with them to the hospital to see Nicole. The children would bring toys and drawings to their baby sister. The children didn't seem frightened by all the tubes and wires attached to Nicole in the isolette.

Nicole had many ups and downs in the neonatal intensive care unit. Then, at four weeks of age, she faced a serious setback, from which she was unable to rally. Despite the intense efforts of doctors and nurses, at thirty days old, she died as a result of complications of prematurity, having never left the hospital. Lisa and Ron held her in their arms as she died.

At a time when they expected to be making plans for a christening, they found themselves planning a funeral. It was the first time they had ever had to do such a thing, since no one really close to them in their families had died.

Figure 5–2. continued

The first week or so after Nicole died, Lisa and Ron cried together often. Ron stayed out of work for a week. Lisa's mother looked after the children and took care of the house. Friends and relatives sent cards and flowers, and many attended the funeral. Ron and Lisa felt surrounded by love at the funeral. All three children attended, despite the advice of some friends that it would be too much for Jen, the four-year-old, to handle.

People (close friends and relatives) said a lot of things that were meant to comfort, such as, "Well, it's good you never got to bring the baby home from the hospital, because then you would have gotten attached and it would be harder now." And, "Now you have an angel in heaven." And, "It's best to put it all behind you." They also heard, "You can have another baby," as well as "You're not going to have another baby, are you?"

Lisa and Ron found that the children had many feelings about the death of their sister. Jen would ask her mother question after question: "Is Nicole with God?" "Is she cold under the ground?" "Will I die?" "When is Nicole coming back?" Sometimes she would pretend her dolly was dead. Lisa would just freeze and try to hold her tears in until Jen left the room.

Robbie, the seven-year-old, talked a lot about the funeral. He wondered if Nicole could see them from heaven. He explained to his parents, as he said his prayers, that her soul was with God on a cloud. If he saw his mother crying, he would say, "Are you crying about Nicole?"

Stevie, age eleven, asked why God let Nicole die. He expressed a lot of anger. His school work began to suffer, and he started having nightmares.

Lisa and Ron tried to listen to their children and comfort them, but they felt so consumed with their own grief that it was often very difficult for them to do. They felt helpless. When Stevie asked why God let Nicole die, it keyed into their own frustration and unanswered questions.

Lisa loved her children beyond words, but she was also frightened by some of her feelings. She sometimes wanted to be left alone to cry and think about Nicole, and the demands of her children to be fed, readied for school, and cared for seemed overwhelming. She hated herself when she found herself resenting them and their intrusions on her grief. Ron found himself short-tempered with them, yelling about things that never would have bothered him before.

Over the following weeks, back at work, Ron found a lot of people asking him, "How's Lisa doing?" Rarely did they ask about his well-being. Lisa found that friends and family seemed to be avoiding her. Three weeks after Nicole died, her mother said, "You need to get on with your life. You have people who are

Figure 5–2. continued

depending on you." Ron found it harder and harder to cry, and Lisa began to complain that he was withdrawing from her. Ron expressed his concern because she was staying in her bathrobe all day, saying that he was afraid things would never be the same again.

Lisa and Ron realized how their relationship was changing. Lisa resented Ron because his grief seemed to be so much less of a burden to him than hers was to her, as evidenced by his lack of tears and his seeming desire not to talk about Nicole. Ron knew how much he hurt and felt that his pain was not being acknowledged by society, let alone by his wife.

A month after Nicole died, they felt distant from one another and all alone in their grief. Lisa became particularly alarmed when a friend told her that she had read that 90% of all couples who lose a child split up. Both Lisa and Ron secretly worried, "Is there any hope that we can survive this together?"

Source: Janis Heil, M.Ed., United Inc., 7600 Central Ave., Philadelphia, Penna. 19111. Used with permission.

GUIDED TEACHING

Instead of presenting a lecture, ask a series of questions to tap the knowledge of the group or obtain their hypotheses or conclusions. Record their ideas, if possible, and compare them to the lecture points you have in mind. The guided teaching method is a nice break from straight lecturing and allows you to learn what participants already know and understand before making instructional points. Because it utilizes a Socratic-type teaching technique, this method encourages self-discovery. Here are two examples:

1. In a basic management skills course, the trainer wanted to broaden participants' thinking about motivation. She posted on a flipchart the following question: *Why does an employee quit?* Numerous and varied responses were given: money, limited opportunity, lack of recognition or appreciation, conflicts with supervisor, career change, and so on. Participants were then asked to categorize their answers into like groups. By interspersing her own ideas, probing, and prompting, the trainer guided the group into identifying three categories: employee factors (e.g., career change), management factors (e.g., conflicts, recognition), and organization or system factors (reward systems, culture).

2. While training nurses how to develop a plan for teaching patients to prepare for surgery, a trainer decided to refrain from lecturing and

instead to use a guided teaching approach. She began by asking the participants what they would want to know before they began guiding the patient (e.g., the patient's fears and concerns, the patient's understanding of the surgery, etc.). She then led the group into identifying the deviations in anatomy and physiology and the corrective effects of surgery to be addressed in the teaching plan. From anatomy and physiology issues, the trainer moved to what elements of the preoperative waiting period the group felt were important to include in the plan (e.g., diagnostic studies, dietary and activity restrictions, etc.). This discussion flowed into an examination of the components of the postoperative period (e.g., recovery room, pain management, exercises, etc.) needed to be presented. Whenever possible, the trainer asked other questions based on participants' responses (e.g., "Yes, mentioning the equipment that the patient can expect to see surrounding him/her postoperatively is an important item. What would you say if you were unsure what equipment would be used?").

GROUP INQUIRY

Instead of asking questions, the trainer could challenge participants to devise their own questions to further their understanding of a topic. If participants have little prior knowledge of the material, they should be presented with relevant instructional materials first (work examples, handouts, etc.) to arouse their curiosity and interest and to stimulate questions. Posing a problem that the group must solve might also encourage questions. Allow sufficient time for the group to form some questions, then field the questions one at a time or as a whole group. This method allows you to gear your teaching to participant needs. Notice how participants' questions are sparked in these two examples.

1. For a course entitled "Cross-Cultural Issues for an International Assignment," the trainer handed out a description of a series of interactions between Indonesians and Americans. One such incident is described in figure 5–3.

Figure 5–3. The Quiet Participant

Machmud had recently been promoted to a position of authority and was asked to represent his company and Indonesia's needs at the head office in Butte, Montana.

Relationships with fellow workers seemed cordial but rather formal from his perspective. He was invited to attend many policy and planning sessions with

Figure 5–3. continued

other company officials where he often sat, rather quietly, as others generated ideas and engaged in conversation.

The time finally came when the direction the company was to take in Indonesia was to be discussed. A meeting was called to which Machmud was invited to attend. As the meeting was drawing to a close after almost two hours of discussion, Machmud, almost apologetically, offered his first contribution to the meeting. Almost immediately, John Stewart, a local vice president, said, "Why did you wait so long to contribute? We needed your comments all along." Machmud felt that John Stewart's reply was harsh.

Source: Richard Brislin, *Intercultural Interactions,* (Beverly Hills: Sage Publications, 1986).

Rather than explaining the specific cultural differences involved in each incident, the trainer invited the group to ask him questions, based on the descriptions, about Indonesians, their behavior, and their culture. Some of their questions were immediately relevant to the assigned incidents, while other questions were helpful in understanding a wide range of events that the participants might experience when working with Indonesians. It was unlikely that the group would have developed as many insightful questions without the stimulus of the critical incidents.

2. A trainer wanted a group to be informed about the kinds of organizations and activities helpful to people in abusive relationships. She first gave participants a brief list to review. Instead of explaining each entry in detail, she asked participants to hold a discussion, using a call-on-the-next-speaker format, in order to share what they knew about the items on the list. During this time, the trainer was quiet. At the end of the discussion, she invited participants to ask questions about any organization or activity that they felt was not sufficiently explained in the group. This design provided a welcome break from the usual teacher-lecturing/teacher-questioning format.

READ AND DISCUSS

Ask participants to read a short, well-formatted handout covering lecture material and then to continue with small group discussion to clarify its contents. Individuals can also be assigned different materials to read and then instructed to teach what they have just read to the rest of the group.

Or participants can read aloud and discuss brief handouts within small group settings. Read and discuss is an excellent way to cover new material without lecturing. Here are examples.

1. In a stress management program, a trainer formed five groups of five members each. A member from each group selected a stress management strategy by picking one from a hat. The five strategies focused on relaxation, nutrition, delegation, assertiveness, and exercise. Each group received handouts on the strategy it had picked; these were read and discussed within the group. Then five new groups, each containing one representative from the read-and-discuss groups, were formed. In each group, each member explained his strategy to the others. By taking part in this process, every participant was responsible for teaching some of the information to other participants.

2. In a course on group process, a trainer gave participants a handout that charted the differences between effective and ineffective groups along eight dimensions. He then formed read-and-discuss groups, urging them to conduct themselves like Bible study groups, and asked participants to take turns reading aloud each of the eight sets of statements on the chart (e.g., "controversy and conflict are seen as positive keys to members' involvement" versus "controversy and conflict are ignored, denied, avoided, or suppressed"). After reading, the reader was told to ask the other group members:

    Do you want the statements clarified?

    How do you interpret the statements?

    Can you give an example from your experience that is related to the statements?

    Do you agree with the statements?

    Then the groups were reassembled, and participants discussed the chart as a whole using a fishbowl format.

INFORMATION SEARCH

This method can be likened to an open book test. Hand out worksheets containing questions about the topic. Have the group search for the information—which you would normally cover in a lecture—in a source book or collection of handouts. The search can be performed by small teams or by individuals. A friendly competition can even be set up to encourage full participation. Notice how an information search method serves to liven up dry material in these two examples.

1. For a mortgage product sales/marketing program, a trainer devised a worksheet containing fill-in-the-blank items, true/false items, and a matching test. (See figure 5–4 for some sample questions.) Participants were organized into teams and told to gather information from a variety of sources in the training room; each team also received a calculator. For the most part, participants did not know the information previously. When a team completed all items to the satisfaction of all its members, it brought the results to the trainer for scoring. Teams were given points on how quickly they finished. A penalty of sixty seconds per incorrect answer was assessed before the final results were tallied.

Figure 5–4. Information Search

Your mortgage applicant has indicated that a deposit of $10,000 has been made. What follow-up steps must be taken to account for this earnest money?

To be eligible for a mortgage from our bank, second homes must be family and owner-occupied.

True _____   False _____

In the space to the left of each number, write the letter corresponding to the correct definition.

_____ 1. Principal

A. A conveyance of interest in real property as security for payment of a debt.

_____ 2. Amortization

B. The amount of the loan outstanding at a particular point.

_____ 3. Mortgage

C. The process of paying down principal through the life of the loan.

2. A different information search approach was employed by a trainer in a course on diversity in the workplace. She presented participants with four articles discussing the topic (the articles focused on gender, race, ethnicity, and age). Their job was to research the topic as thoroughly as possible in order to participate in a panel discussion on how best to manage a diverse work force. The participants were urged to gather whatever facts, concepts, and opinions they could to enhance the quality of the discussion. In order to give every participant an opportunity to take part in discussion, the membership of the panel

changed every ten minutes. By the end of the segment, participants were very well informed about the topic.

APPLYING THE ALTERNATIVES TO A COMMON TOPIC

In order to help you consider how the six alternatives might be applied to a common topic, take a look at the memo in figure 5–5. If you received such a memo, how would you respond? Some suggestions follow:

Figure 5–5. Memorandum

TO: John Trainer, Assistant Vice President
FROM: Philip Doe, Senior Vice President
RE: Training

I have noticed that some of the people in our current credit training class still have a poor understanding of some basic accounting principles. I think we should start with the difference between a balance sheet and an income statement. Here are some points to stress:

- The balance sheet provides a capsule view of the financial status of an enterprise at a particular date. It helps external users assess the financial relationship of the assets, liabilities, and owner's equity. Trainees should understand

  the difference between current and long-term assets

  the difference between current and long-term liabilities

  the difference between liabilities and owner's equity as a claim against assets

  the difference between capital stock and retained earnings

  how to use the previous year's financial information for comparison purposes

- The income statement provides a measure of the success of an enterprise over a specific period of time. It shows the major sources of revenues generated and the expenses associated with these revenues. The income statement helps external users evaluate the earnings potential of the company. Trainees should understand

  what gross margin measures and how it is derived

  how operating income is determined

  how the bottom line is arrived at

  how to compute earnings per share

Figure 5–5. continued

I know I don't have to tell you how important it is for future credit analysts to have a clear understanding of these two key financial statements. I know that this material is being taught now, but it's not sinking in. Maybe it's the method. Can you think of any better alternatives to just lecturing on this material? Let's brainstorm. I'd like to see your ideas.

1. Demonstration: Illustrate the preparation of both an income statement and a balance sheet by walking through the process in a hypothetical situation. Involve participants in some of the steps such as separating the income statement accounts from the balance sheet accounts and performing the basic calculations.

2. Case Study: Prepare a written case description of an owner of a business seeking help in preparing an income statement and a balance sheet for the year ending December 31. Describe in detail the date provided by the owner and how it was organized by the accountant in order to prepare the two statements. Have the participants complete the income statement and balance sheet, then hold a discussion to review the two processes and how they differ.

3. Guided Teaching: Provide the participants with a list of account balances of a real or fictitious company. Ask them to select accounts that should be reported on the income statement and accounts that would appear on the balance sheet. If no one in the group knows the answers, encourage speculation. Present the correct lists. Ask participants if they can figure out the basis for the two lists (i.e., revenue and expense accounts belong on the income statement, while accounts showing the company's financial position belong on the balance sheet). After the group understands the basis for separating the accounts, discuss a proper format for preparing the income statement and the balance sheet. Ask as many questions as you can to push the participants into their own inferences and deductions.

4. Group Inquiry: Provide examples of an income statement and a balance sheet for a company. Ask participants to study the examples in order to figure out how the two processes differ. Volunteer no further information but encourage participants to ask you as many questions as they like. Using their own powers of inquiry and discovery, participants should be able to understand the concept being taught.

5. Read and Discuss: Give participants a short reading assignment that effectively describes and illustrates the two processes. Then form small groups so that participants can clarify with each other the contents of the reading assignment. Reconvene the full group and answer any questions. Make *brief* lecture points where necessary.

6. Information Search: Create quiz questions on the difference between a balance sheet and an income statement. Give out the reading assignment described in the previous suggestion, and have the participants, individually or in small teams, search the material for the answers to the questions in the quiz.

Now consider a very different challenge. Imagine that you want participants to have a solid grasp of the twelve ways to improve meetings listed in figure 5–6. Instead of lecturing, what alternative(s) would you select to teach this material? Compare your thoughts with the following suggestions.

Figure 5–6. Twelve Ways to Improve Your Meetings

1. Send out agendas in advance.
2. Be prepared with supporting facts and opinions.
3. Select problems that can be managed and solved.
4. Don't waste time. Stick to the issues at hand.
5. Agree on a definition of the problem before moving to solutions.
6. Allow adequate time for each problem-solving step.
7. Encourage positive confrontation.
8. Focus on the issues, not the people.
9. Take turns chairing long meetings.
10. Vary the pace of the meeting between reporting and discussion.
11. Rank alternative solutions before deciding on the best one(s).
12. Determine a date on which to check decision implementation.

1. Demonstration: Illustrate the twelve ways to improve meetings by simulating a meeting with your participants. Use such topics as summer party planning or monthly budget evaluations. Give participants a checklist (such as a copy of the twelve suggestions) to guide their observations of your techniques.

2. Case Study: Hand out a case description of two meetings held one week apart: one that was ineffective and one that was productive from beginning to end. Ask participants to figure out how the improvement might have been achieved.

3. Guided Teaching: Put up on the wall two sheets of flipchart paper that are blank except for the titles "Good Meetings" and "Bad Meetings." Ask participants to recall their own experiences in meetings and volunteer suggestions as to what made the meetings positive or negative. List suggestions on the charts, then compare them to the lecture points you have in mind.

4. Group Inquiry: Hand out a copy of the twelve ways to improve meetings. Divide the participants into small groups. Ask each group to come up with three questions that they would like you to answer concerning the information on the handout. Answer the questions in a large group format.

5. Read and Discuss: Divide participants into small groups and ask each group to study the twelve ways to improve meetings, clarifying each point and discussing their opinions of its worth.

6. Information Search: Provide brief examples of the twelve ways to improve meetings, without identifying which illustrates which suggestion. Have pairs work together to match examples to the suggestions on the list.

Now consider a topic from your own training situation. How could you avoid lecturing about it? As you think about this, remember that the methods can also be combined. For example, group inquiry can almost always follow one of the other alternatives. Used in this way, it serves as a means to debrief the training activity. Likewise, read and discuss can precede many of the other methods in order to provide a knowledge base for later application.

Worksheet

DESIGNING AN ALTERNATIVE TO A LECTURE

Use the worksheet below to design an alternative to the lecture presentation you selected in the previous chapter.

Topic:
(check one)

_____ Demonstration
_____ Case study
_____ Guided teaching
_____ Group inquiry
_____ Read and discuss
_____ Information search

Design Outline:

_____

_____

_____

_____

_____

_____

_____

_____

_____

_____

_____

_____

_____

_____

_____

_____

_____

USING EXPERIENTIAL LEARNING

APPROACHES

6

Active training promotes learning by doing. As we have indicated, even a lecture has to be designed to involve the participation of the learner and, at times, can be replaced by one of several methods that facilitate more direct acquisition of information. Still other methods place an even greater premium on active, participatory learning.

Experiential learning approaches are particularly suited for affective and behavioral training goals. They help participants to become more aware of their feelings and reactions to certain issues and new ideas. In addition, they allow participants to practice and refine new skills and procedures. In this chapter, we will examine and illustrate six major experiential learning approaches:

1. **Role playing**
2. **Games and simulations**
3. **Observation**

4. **Mental imagery**
5. **Writing tasks**
6. **Projects**

ROLE PLAYING

Role playing is a staple in any active trainer's repertoire. It is the best-known way to help participants both experience certain feelings and practice certain skills. Let's say, for example, that your training objective is to have participants get in touch with their feelings about confronting others (something many supervisors and, indeed, people in general avoid). You can set up a dramatic situation in which participants are required to confront someone else and then discuss the feelings generated by the role-playing experience. In addition, you can design a role-playing exercise to enable participants to practice constructive methods of confrontation.

SCRIPTING

You have many choices when designing role-play exercises. One set of choices has to do with the **scripting** of the drama.

PARTICIPANTS CAN BE GIVEN A GENERAL SCENARIO AND ASKED TO FILL IN THE DETAILS THEMSELVES.
EXAMPLE: "Let's imagine that you are at a restaurant and your order is overcooked. Let's have Mary be the customer and request that the order be redone. How about if Frank is the waiter and he gives the customer a hard time. Mary, you will try to persuade the waiter to redo the order. I'd like to see you both use all the skills we've been practicing so far."

PARTICIPANTS CAN BE GIVEN A WELL-PREPARED SET OF INSTRUCTIONS THAT STATES THE FACTS ABOUT THE ROLES THEY ARE PORTRAYING AND HOW THEY ARE TO BEHAVE.
EXAMPLE: "You are an accountant for an insurance company. You have been with the company since your graduation from college three years ago. You really like the company, feel you are doing well, and are looking forward to a promotion. You like your work except for writing letters, memos, and notes on your accounting reports. You've never admitted it to anyone, but you've always had difficulty in English. Your manager has just called you in. You're afraid it might be about your writing. You

will admit your deficiency only if your manager seems genuinely interested and concerned; otherwise, you will make up excuses."

PARTICIPANTS CAN BE GIVEN EXTENSIVE INFORMATION ABOUT THE SITUATION AND THE CHARACTERS TO BE PORTRAYED BUT NOT TOLD HOW TO HANDLE THE SITUATION.

EXAMPLE: "You are a recently appointed supervisor of a support engineering group that has overall responsibility for maintaining and improving test equipment hardware and software at its repair centers. In your group, there are twenty engineers differing widely in age and experience with the company. Each engineer is responsible for a specific list of test equipment. Up until now, staff members have not been called upon to work on test equipment that is not on their designated lists. This has meant that when one of them is sick or on vacation or has a priority assignment, it is difficult for anyone else to take up the slack.

You have decided to assemble a small team within the group to develop Support Test Equipment Protocols (STEPS) that will provide the information necessary to support the various pieces of test equipment. With these STEPS, you will be able to establish a rotation system within the group. The people you have invited to be on the team include two senior project engineers and two hardware and software technicians.

This is the first meeting of the group. Begin the meeting."

PARTICIPANTS CAN PORTRAY THEMSELVES IN SITUATIONS THEY HAVE ACTUALLY FACED.

EXAMPLE: "I'd like each of you to think about the last time you gave a performance appraisal. Tell your role-playing partner what generally happened and reenact the situation, the first time keeping to the approach you took when you actually gave the appraisal and the second time altering your approach to include the suggestions I have demonstrated."

PARTICIPANTS CAN BE ASKED TO DEVELOP A ROLE-PLAYING VIGNETTE OF THEIR OWN.

EXAMPLE: "I'd like for you and your partner to take the three management styles we've just discussed and create a skit that shows a manager using each of the styles while giving project instructions to an employee. Take about ten minutes to prepare your skits. When you're ready, let me know, and we will take a look at what you've come up with.

PARTICIPANTS CAN BE GIVEN A PREVIOUSLY PREPARED SCRIPT TO ACT OUT.
EXAMPLE. "Here is a script of an exit interview. It demonstrates very effectively some of the problems and some of the solutions we've been examining. In your pairs, one will be the interviewer and the other will be the employee who is leaving the company. Read your parts aloud to get a feel for the tension and relief experienced in the situation."

FORMATTING

Another set of choices has to do with **format.**

THE ROLE PLAY CAN EVOLVE INFORMALLY FROM A GROUP DISCUSSION.
EXAMPLE: A participant says, "I can't get any cooperation from my boss." Wanting to understand the situation better, the trainer spontaneously responds, "In order for me to have a clearer picture of what usually transpires between you and your boss, let me pretend to be him and you ask me for something you need from me. I'll respond the way I think your boss typically does but if I'm off base, let me know. We don't have to set this up in any formal way. Stay seated where you are and just start off the conversation."

ALL PARTICIPANTS CAN BE FORMED INTO PAIRS FOR A TWO-PERSON DRAMA, TRIOS FOR A THREE-PERSON DRAMA, AND SO ON, AND SIMULTANEOUSLY UNDERTAKE THEIR ROLE PLAYS.
EXAMPLE: "I'd like you to pair up with the person seated next to you and turn your chairs around to face each other. You should move away from the other pairs so that you have some privacy. One of you needs to volunteer first to be the client; the other will be the salesperson. Each of you will then get to practice how to close a sale."

ONE PAIR, TRIO, OR THE LIKE CAN ROLE-PLAY IN FRONT OF THE GROUP, WHICH WILL OBSERVE AND OFFER FEEDBACK.
EXAMPLE: "I need three volunteers who will portray for the rest of us a family discussing the college choices of their high school junior. Would someone agree to be the father, someone the mother, and someone the student?"

ACTORS IN FRONT OF THE GROUP CAN BE ROTATED, USUALLY BY INTER-RUPTING THE ROLE PLAY IN PROGRESS AND REPLACING ONE OR MORE OF THE ACTORS.
EXAMPLE: "I'd like to set up a scene in which an irate customer is calling to complain that her claim check has not yet arrived and the claims

adjuster somehow needs to remain courteous under great pressure. This time we'll do something a little differently. After every thirty seconds of the conversation, I'll tap out the role players, and their parts will be picked up by the next people in line."

MORE THAN ONE ACTOR CAN BE RECRUITED TO ROLE-PLAY THE SAME SITUATION, ALLOWING THE GROUP TO OBSERVE MORE THAN ONE STYLE.
EXAMPLE: "I need three brave souls who will agree to handle, one at a time, a disruptive junior high school class. These volunteers will be asked to leave the room and decide who will do the role play first, second, and third. While they're gone, the rest of us will set up the scene and then ask the first "teacher" to come in the room and manage the situation. The other two volunteers will stay outside until their turns arrive. This way none of the "teachers" will have seen either of the others role-play the situation before his or her turn. I realize that volunteering means taking a big risk but the rest of the group and I would really appreciate the chance to see three different people handling the same problem."

THE ROLE PLAY CAN BE REENACTED.
EXAMPLE: "Now that you've had a chance to try out this problem situation once, I'd like you to try it a second time. This time make any changes you'd like to improve upon your performance. Think of it as a dress rehearsal before going out to the real world and actually doing it. Good luck!"

PROCESSING

A final set of choices has to do with **processing** the role play.

ONE OR MORE OBSERVERS CAN BE ADDED TO EACH ROLE-PLAYING GROUP.

EXAMPLE: "In your trio, each of you will take a turn observing the other two. When role play is finished, share with the actors the nonverbal behaviors you saw that didn't seem to match what was being said."

THE ROLE PLAYERS THEMSELVES CAN DISCUSS THEIR REACTIONS TO THE EXPERIENCE.
EXAMPLE: "Take a few minutes as a group and share how you felt about the role play. When did you feel effective and when did you feel others were effective? What felt uncomfortable? What would you like to do better the next time?"

INVITE THE GROUP AS A WHOLE TO GIVE REACTIONS AND FEEDBACK TO A ROLE PLAY.
EXAMPLE: "Now that we've seen how Brad handled the customer's complaint, I'd like you first to comment on the good points and then to suggest how Brad could do things differently."

ASSIGN A SMALL GROUP FROM THE AUDIENCE TO EACH ONE OF THE ROLE PLAYERS AND ASK THE MEMBERS TO DISCUSS WHAT THEY SAW HAPPENING.
EXAMPLE: "Since we had three characters in this role play, I will ask the audience to count off by threes. The ones will go off with Joan and discuss her reactions to the role play and their reactions to her performance. The twos will go off with Don and do the same. The threes will go off with Lee."

THE TRAINER CAN GIVE HER REACTIONS TO THE ROLE PLAY FOR EVERYONE TO HEAR.
EXAMPLE: "This was terrific. I'm really impressed by the number of techniques you wove into your performance. I especially liked the way you handled his resistance. Your empathy really disarmed him. You might consider, for fine-tuning purposes, pausing a little more to emphasize what you're saying. Is this feedback helpful?"

THE ROLE PLAYERS AND OBSERVERS CAN COMPARE THE PERFORMANCE TO AN IDEAL SCRIPT.
EXAMPLE: "Let's take a look at a textbook example of this sales presentation. Look over this script and find things in it that you wish you had done. But also identify what you don't like. We'll get back together in fifteen minutes, after you've had a chance to read the script and discuss it with your seat partners."

GAMES AND SIMULATIONS

Some trainers are hesitant to use games and simulations in their programs, fearing that participants will find them too contrived and/or dismiss them as mere entertainment. And, certainly, like any other training method, games and simulations are not without risk. Used in the wrong way at the wrong time, they may do little good. Used appropriately, however, they can be an enjoyable and effective way to advance training objectives.

One of the advantages of games and simulations is the extent to which they encourage participants to confront their own attitudes and values. An excellent example is the Prisoner's Dilemma Game. This well-known game is set up in such a way that participants make a choice, often without realizing it, to compete rather than to cooperate. The effects of the choice become evident as the game proceeds. It's a terrific way to help participants become aware of their competitiveness. Many other games perform similar self-revelatory functions.

Games and simulations can also help participants grasp the total course content. An advantage of using a game at the beginning section of a program is that it can give participants a chance to experience the whole before discussing the parts. For example, starting a cross-cultural training program with a simulation game such as Bafa' Bafa' is a great way to prepare people being transferred abroad for the frustrations, joys, and insights that come from contact with a foreign culture. In Bafa' Bafa', participants are separated into two groups. Each group becomes a culture and is instructed in the culture's values and traditions. The two groups then exchange "ambassadors" who observe the other group and return to report on what they have learned about its culture. After consultation time, a different set of ambassadors is exchanged with the charge of interacting with the culture being visited. The game provides an excellent chance for participants to focus on what they consider normal, how they act within their own inner circle, and how they interact with strangers. They usually spend an hour playing the game and then up to five hours discussing how stereotypes are formed and perpetuated.

Games and simulations can also help test the behavioral style and performance of participants. Playing a game at the beginning of a course allows the trainer to identify the styles and skills that already exist and to note which need to be strengthened. Playing a game at the end of a course enables the trainer to assess the instructional experience. Take, for example, a simulation exercise called Desert Survival. Players are told that their plane has crashed in the desert, that their only priority is to survive, and that only certain items are available to them. In the first part of the game, players must decide how to survive individually. Then the game is replayed with groups working toward team consensus. A trainer could include this simulation exercise at the beginning of a course on team building to assess how well teams work toward consensus. Near the end of the course, a similar exercise, such as Winter Survival, could be employed to measure progress in team work.

DESIGNING

When designing games and simulations, there are several things to keep in mind.

THE GAME OR SIMULATION NEEDS TO BE RELEVANT TO THE PARTICIPANTS. EXAMPLE: A module on project planning methods began with a game called 64 Squares. On a flipchart, the trainer drew a large square, then divided it into sixty-four smaller squares (see figure 6–1). The trainer then selected a square, wrote its letter and number on a piece of paper, and did not reveal its contents to the group. The participants were chal-

Figure 6–1. Sixty-four Squares

	1	2	3	4	5	6	7	8
A								
B								
C								
D								
E								
F								
G								
H								

lenged to find the "secret square" by asking only six questions. These questions were to be answered by a yes or a no. Calling out questions without a plan, it took the group twelve questions to find the secret square. The trainer then commented that the most efficient path to the answer was a binary approach in which each question reduced the number of eligible squares by 50%. For example, if participants had asked first whether the secret square was in rows 1 to 4, they could have ascertained in which half of the matrix the square lay. The trainer pointed out that there is also a critical path to follow when it comes to managing a project; the challenge is to find it. All the participants were impressed by the experience, in large part because the game drove home a lesson that was highly relevant to their work situations.

THE EASIEST WAY TO CREATE GAMES AND SIMULATIONS IS TO MIMIC THE FORMAT AND CHARACTER OF WELL-KNOWN ONES.
EXAMPLE: Technical information is often dry stuff to learn. Television quiz games can easily be adapted for training groups. Probably the most widely copied ones are "Jeopardy!," "Wheel of Fortune," and "Family Feud." Board games often work, too. Trivial Pursuit is perhaps the most popular choice, since merely playing the game and learning the correct answers is a satisfying way to pick up information. A clerical staff trainer went one step further. She divided participants into teams and gave them an opportunity to teach each other as much information as possible. Then team members were pitted against members of other teams in a head-to-head individual competition of Trivial Pursuit using questions from the information the participants had just learned. Thus, both cooperative and competitive methods were used in a gaming approach to learning technical information.

WELL-KNOWN GAMES AND SIMULATIONS CAN BE MODIFIED TO SUIT YOUR NEEDS.
EXAMPLE: A story called "Alligator River" (see figure 6–2) is the basis for a well-known values clarification exercise. After reading the story, participants are asked to rank the four characters from most to least objectionable. Typically, groups are then formed to seek consensus. In the process of the discussion, participants are forced to clarify their values. A trainer in a course on listening skills decided to use this exercise for a different purpose. She dropped the consensus-seeking assignment and instead asked participants to do everything they could to force the group to accept their own opinions. When strong differences of opinion emerged, she instructed participants to assume the point of view of another person

Figure 6–2. Alligator River

Once upon a time there was a woman named Abigail who was in love with a man named Gregory. Gregory lived on the shore of the river. Abigail lived on the opposite shore of the river. The river which separated the two lovers was teeming with man-eating alligators. Abigail wanted to cross the river to be with Gregory. Unfortunately, the bridge had been washed out. So she went to ask Sinbad, a riverboat captain, to take her across. He said he would be glad to if she would consent to go to bed with him preceding the voyage. She promptly refused and went to a friend named Ivan to explain her plight. Ivan did not want to be involved at all in the situation. Abigail felt her only alternative was to accept Sinbad's terms. Sinbad fulfilled his promise to Abigail and delivered her into the arms of Gregory.

When she told Gregory about her amorous escapade in order to cross the river, Gregory cast her aside with disdain.

Source: Sidney B. Simon, Leland W. Howe, and Howard Kirschenbaum. 1978. *Values Clarification*, New York: Dodd, Mead & Co., pp. 291–92.

in their group. Often, this became impossible because people had barely listened to their antagonists. The trainer used the experience to reinforce an important lesson—listening is poorest when communication is competitive. In this instance, both the purpose of the game and the instructions were changed to suit the trainer's objective.

FUNLIKE, CONTRIVED GAMES CAN BE FOLLOWED BY MORE SERIOUS, LESS CONTRIVED ONES.
EXAMPLE: The trainer of a course on creative thinking designed for the marketing department of a large training vendor wanted participants to learn and value the process called group brainstorming. He began with a zany exercise in which teams were asked to brainstorm as many uses for dirty undershirts as they could think of. Afterward, they were asked to select their two most original ideas. The group had a ball, easily generating several ideas and quickly choosing their two best. Next, the teams were given a simulation exercise in which they were to generate new ways to market their training services. As each idea surfaced, the only response allowed was a single question to clarify each contribution.

The trainer then noted that it would be impossible in this brainstorming assignment to select the best ideas as quickly as in the previous one. Instead of a process in which individuals argued for the ideas they thought were best, the teams were asked first to develop a set of criteria by which to judge the proposals and then to evaluate each one against the criteria they had developed. The last step was either to choose the best marketing plans from the original list or somehow to combine the best ideas. Because the second brainstorming exercise was not contrived, as the first had been, it had a greater impact on the participants. Nonetheless, the first exercise served the purpose of warming the group up and setting the stage for the second and more important exercise.

INSTRUCTIONS FOR GAMES AND SIMULATIONS NEED TO BE CAREFULLY THOUGHT OUT.

EXAMPLE: A simulation called Instant Aging is designed to sensitize participants to sensory deprivation and the normal process of aging. Participants are given eyeglasses smeared with vaseline, dried peas to put in their shoes, cotton for both ears, and latex gloves for their hands. They are then asked to take out a pencil and paper and write down their names, addresses, telephone numbers, any medication currently being taken, and any known allergies. Next, they are told to take a walk outside the training room, opening the door and finding their way around. The simulation involves a number of directions concerning the order of applying the props, the specific details of the tasks that participants are asked to perform, and the manner in which they are to take turns assisting each other. When all goes well, the experience has a tremendous impact on the participants.

GAMES AND SIMULATIONS ALMOST ALWAYS NEED TO BE DISCUSSED AFTERWARD FOR THE EXPERIENCE TO BE AN EFFECTIVE TEACHER.

EXAMPLE: Talking about what has just happened is important not only to bring the learning into focus but also to take advantage of peer pressure toward positive change. In the middle of a week-long course for new managers at a manufacturing company, the trainer placed a box of Tinker Toys in front of the participants, who were seated in pairs. One member of each pair was to assume the role of a supervisor while the other was to be his employee. The supervisor's job was to assign the employee the task of building a four-sided object with 'something hanging in the middle' and to instruct the employee to accomplish the task in only a few minutes. After the allotted time, each supervisor was asked to seek feedback from his employee about his assignment methods and general leadership style. This exchange set the stage for a discussion about appropriate supervisory behavior and direction giving. Many participants enjoyed the experience and felt they would remember the point of it back on the job. A few participants complained, however, that the exercise was merely a game and that it revealed little about their real work situations. The trainer admitted that the exercise was contrived but then asked others how they found it applied to their company. Many examples streamed forth from the group, and a lively discussion ensued. The resisters, impressed by their peers' insights, were won over.

OBSERVATION

Watching others, without directly participating, can be an effective way to experience learning. Although it is worthwhile for participants actually to practice something, observation by itself can play an important part in a training design. The key is for the observation experience to be **active** rather than **passive.**

DESIGNING

There are several ways to design observation activities so that participants are actively involved.

GIVE AIDS TO HELP PARTICIPANTS ATTEND TO AND RETAIN PERTINENT ASPECTS OF A DEMONSTRATION THEY ARE WATCHING. When modeling how to conduct an exit interview, for example, make sure that participants take notice of its critical features by giving an overview of the demonstration and providing a visual display of a few key terms to describe the specific behaviors to be modeled. It may be helpful to point to these descriptions as they are being enacted. After the demonstration is over, you can help participants retain the observation points by asking them to recall them from memory. You may even want to challenge them to write out an imaginary exit interview that includes all the steps. A pocket-size card summarizing the features of an exit interview can also be given to the participants for future use as a job aid.

WHEN PARTICIPANTS ARE OBSERVING A ROLE PLAY OR GROUP EXERCISE, PROVIDE EASY-TO-USE OBSERVATION FORMS CONTAINING SUGGESTIONS, QUESTIONS, AND CHECKLISTS. Having concrete guidelines helps participants get the most out of the observation experience. Give them a chance to study the form before the actual observation. You may even want to provide a brief practice exercise. In addition, you can assign specific participants to observe specific behaviors. For example, while some are observing the verbal techniques employed in a sales presentation, others can watch the body language of the presenter.

PROVIDE KEY QUESTIONS TO HELP OBSERVERS FOCUS THEIR ATTENTION. When you find observation forms too specific for your purposes, a few questions can still help to guide observers. For example, observing group process can be enriched by asking observers to consider (1) who they are most aware of; (2) what that person is doing; (3) what her impact is on the group; and (4) how others are reacting to her.

EXPECTING OBSERVERS TO GIVE CONSTRUCTIVE FEEDBACK CHALLENGES THEM TO OBSERVE CAREFULLY AND APPLY WHAT THEY HAVE PREVIOUSLY LEARNED. In a longer training program, for instance, you can include several opportunities for observers to provide feedback to each other. At first, these exchanges should be kept short and focused on the positive behaviors displayed. As trust develops in the group, the feedback can be more extensive and more critical. Giving this responsibility to participants pushes them to review what they have been taught and to use it as the basis for their feedback.

OBSERVERS CAN HAVE STRONG VICARIOUS EXPERIENCES IF WHAT THEY ARE OBSERVING HAS PERSONAL IMPACT. Watching role plays that hit home, for example, often produces a kind of Greek chorus effect. Observers are moved to comment when they can readily identify with the role players. You can facilitate matters by asking observers to disclose the feelings they experienced while watching the drama and to lend emotional support to the role players. Vicarious participation can also be catalyzed by interviews or experiential exercises.

FORMATTING

Three formats are commonly used in the design of observation activities.

THE SIMPLEST IS TO USE OBSERVERS AS THE AUDIENCE WATCHING A DEMONSTRATION, VIDEO, ROLE PLAY, AND THE LIKE "ON STAGE".
EXAMPLE: Participants in a course on employee discipline watched a video that showed how a supervisor of an accounts payable department confronted one of his bookkeepers. The bookkeeper had been thirty to forty-five minutes late for work at least seven times in the last three weeks, had come back late from lunch on five occasions, and had made personal calls several times. Prior to the video presentation, the participants were given the observation checklist reproduced in figure 6–3 for their review. When the video had ended, the participants wrote their responses on the checklist and compared notes with seat partners. They then reassembled to poll results of their collective observations.

Figure 6–3. Observation Checklist

1. What did the manager do to let the employee know he was listening?
   Maintained good eye contact _____
   Nodded head _____
   Leaned forward _____
   Rephrased well _____
   Other (explain) _____

2. Jot down an example(s) of the manager rephrasing what the employee had told him. (i.e., "So, let me make sure I understand . . .")

3. Did you notice the manager using any specific rephrasing techniques?
   Verbatim repeating _____
   Paraphrasing _____
   Partial restating _____

4. In general, how did the manager deal with the employee's emotion?
   Addressed it directly _____
   Ignored it _____
   Danced around the edges _____
   Other (explain) _____

5. Overall, do you think the manager fully understood the employee's viewpoint before responding? What else might you have asked or clarified?

OBSERVERS CAN ALSO BE ASSIGNED TO SMALL GROUPS TO PROVIDE FEEDBACK AFTER THE SMALL GROUP PERFORMS.
EXAMPLE: On the morning of a three-day course for novice trainers, fifteen participants were divided into three groups. Each participant then gave a ten-minute lecture she had prepared the night before; the other four members acted as a training audience. After the presentation, audience observers gave the lecturer feedback on: (1) things that she did well; (2) skills and techniques she used that were previously demonstrated in the course; and (3) suggestions for improvement. Later in the day, participants were asked to reconvene in the same groups. One participant was asked to leave each group for a short time. These people were told,

upon their return, to deliver the opening segment of the lectures they had given in the morning. The rest of the members of each group were instructed to select one member each who would act as a troublemaker when the person returned to give her lecture. Other members would then observe and give feedback on how she handled the troublemaker. Finally, observers were asked to identify with the feelings of the beleaguered lecturer.

FINALLY, PARTICIPANTS CAN BE ARRANGED IN A FISHBOWL FORMAT, WHERE OBSERVERS FORM A CIRCLE AROUND THE INDIVIDUALS THEY ARE OBSERVING.

EXAMPLE: Employees of a major defense contractor were taking a course on work team effectiveness. Midway through the course, after learning several work team skills, participants were divided into two equal-sized groups. The members of Group A sat around a long conference table, and a member of Group B sat directly behind each one of them. Group A was asked to hold a meeting for the purpose of targeting "the most important changes your work teams should make in the way they operate." Each Group B member was to observe the task and maintenance behaviors of the person in Group A seated directly in front of him. After ten minutes, the meeting was interrupted by the trainer who asked each Group B observer to meet with his Group A observee and give him feedback. Then, Group B was asked to sit at the conference table and conduct the same meeting with Group A observing. Again, after ten minutes, a feedback round occurred. This back-and-forth process was repeated two more times, with the net effect that each group had thirty minutes to complete its task and to watch another group undertake the same task. In addition, each participant received feedback three times.

MENTAL IMAGERY

Mental imagery is the ability to visualize an object, person, place, or action not actually present. Trainers can design six kinds of imagery experiences:

1. **Visual imagery:** For example, various colored shapes—a golden triangle, a violet circle.
2. **Tactile imagery:** For example, shaking someone's hand, feeling its surface and temperature.
3. **Olfactory imagery:** For example, smelling the clean mountain air in a pine forest.

4. **Kinesthetic imagery:** For example, driving a car, sensing each turn of the wheel.

5. **Taste imagery:** For example, attending to the taste and texture of your favorite food.

6. **Auditory imagery:** For example, listening to the sound of a voice calling your name.

Being able to design activities that help participants visualize adds a powerful component to your experiential learning repertoire. While it can be utilized to help participants retain cognitive information, imagery has special value as a way to help them mentally rehearse putting skills into action and to bring feelings and events into focus.

Mental imagery exercises can be used to replace role playing. Since they are internal, they cause less anxiety to those participants who are shy about performing before other people. Skills such as speaking before a group or acting assertively, for example, can be practiced successfully through mental imagery—although a minimal amount of role-playing practice must also be interspersed.

Mental imagery exercises also stimulate discussion. Often it is hard for a discussion on a particular topic to get off the ground without a boost. When participants are guided to visualize a real or fantasized experience, thoughts and feelings relevant to a particular topic can be activated. For example, in a workshop on interfaith relations, participants were asked to imagine walking invisibly into the homes of people of different religious faiths and watching how they celebrate different holidays. A discussion followed on the norms of different groups. It was a lively and honest exploration of religious differences.

GUIDELINES

When conducting mental imagery exercises, certain guidelines are important.

HELP PARTICIPANTS TO CLEAR THEIR MINDS BY ENCOURAGING THEM TO RELAX. Use background music, dimmed lights, and breathing exercises to achieve results.

CONDUCT WARM UP EXERCISES TO OPEN THE MIND'S EYE. Ask participants, with their eyes closed, to try to visualize sights and sounds such as a rosebud, their bedrooms, a changing traffic light, or the patter of rain.

ASSURE PARTICIPANTS THAT IT'S OKAY IF THEY EXPERIENCE DIFFICULTY VISUALIZING WHAT YOU DESCRIBE. Some participants initially block before they are relaxed enough to visualize. Tell them to be patient with themselves. All participants find that other thoughts drift into their minds at times. When this occurs, suggest that they simply bring themselves gently back to the subject being described.

GIVE IMAGERY INSTRUCTIONS SLOWLY AND WITH ENOUGH PAUSES TO ALLOW IMAGES TO DEVELOP. If you use imagery scripts written by others, practice reading them in advance so that your delivery is smooth and well paced. Keep your voice soft enough to be soothing but loud enough to be heard clearly.

INVITE PARTICIPANTS TO SHARE THEIR IMAGERY. Sharing should always be voluntary. Also, keep the reports brief (lengthy disclosures can be boring to the other participants). Participants can also recount their imagery experiences in a journal.

EXAMPLES OF MENTAL IMAGERY EXERCISES

The following script can be used as a warm-up exercise to promote relaxation breathing with imagery.

"With your eyes closed, draw and exhale several very deep breaths. Notice the rising and falling of your abdomen. Each time you breathe in, imagine that you are taking in energy from the universe. This is exactly what you are doing. As you exhale, notice that your body is becoming more and more relaxed, more and more peaceful.

Now imagine that you are seated on a large rock, overlooking a quiet pool of water in some pleasant forest or wooded area. Imagine that nothing disturbs the tranquility of this scene except the occasional jumping of a small fish to the side of the pond. Imagine that, in slow motion, you have picked up a small round stone near where you are sitting, and in very s-l-o-w motion, you are lobbing this stone into the air and watching it descend s-l-o-w-l-y into the very center of the glassy pond. Watch the stone as it travels up and then down through the air. Watch it slowly enter the water, and watch the ripples begin to form. Watch the ripples spread slowly outward towards the edges of the pond. Watch the surface of the water until it is completely still once again.

Stay with this scene until you are aware of feeling very relaxed and refreshed. When you are ready, notice the sounds around you in the room, gently open your eyes, and go about your day's activities."

Source: Richard McKnight, Ph. D., *Staying Relaxed in a Tense World*, Learning Project Press, 103 Avon Road, Narberth, Pa 19072.

Here is a sample script used to help lead a group of employees through the process of preparing to receive a performance appraisal.

"I'd like you to close your eyes for a few moments as you explore how to prepare to receive your next performance appraisal. Close your eyes, slow your rate of breathing down, and listen as I walk you through the evaluation process. (pause) First, I would like for you to imagine yourself working at your job. Consider aspects of your job that you truly enjoy. (pause) Think about the satisfaction that you receive as you complete that task. (pause) Now, imagine how you would describe the accomplishment of that task to your closest friend. Go ahead, brag about yourself. Explain just how well you like doing that task and why. Consider why you do that task better than anyone else.

As you continue to keep your eyes closed, I would like for you to turn your thoughts in another direction. This time, I would like for you to consider an aspect of your current responsibilities that you really do not enjoy. Think carefully about a task related to a responsibility that you do not enjoy. (pause) What is it about this task that you do not like? (pause) Consider all of the different components of this task. Are there any that you believe that you could improve upon? Imagine yourself improving your performance of this task. Consider how you would feel if you handled this task to the best of your ability.

Now you are ready to walk into your manager's office. Instead of being nervous, you feel confident in your abilities. Think back on the images you have just seen. Consider that in an appraisal both positive and negative evaluations of work performance will be discussed. Think back to how you evaluated your own performance as you discuss your appraisal with your manager."

Source: Carol Auerbach, M.Ed. Reprinted with permission.

The following exercise is called Visions and Values. It is used for team building in a hospital setting.

"Spend a little time getting as comfortable as you can . . . find a comfortable spot . . . clear your mind . . . relax . . . take a deep breath . . . as you breathe out, silently say, 'relax and let go.' . . . feel yourself relax even further . . . as you think about each part of your body, allow that part to relax, feel all the tension flowing away, feel calm, comfortable, peaceful . . . each time you breathe out you will become more relaxed and feel the relaxation spreading slowly through your body.

"I want you to imagine yourself on a typical day, on your way to work. Picture yourself enroute, in your car, on the bus, train or however you normally travel to the hospital. As you are traveling, you are thinking about work and who you are . . . what your job is . . . the way you do it . . . how you'd like to be to feel more successful . . . what you would do differently . . . what you would change.

"As you get to work you suddenly realize it's not the same place it was yesterday . . . something has changed . . . something is different . . . suddenly it's YOUR IDEAL PLACE TO WORK.

"You enter the hospital, the same entrance you usually use . . . what do you see, what do you hear? You walk through the halls into your department . . . who is there, who do you see . . . what are people doing . . . what are people saying . . . what are you saying . . . what is different? You sit at your desk thinking about the day ahead . . . you have a busy schedule . . . you will be traveling all around the hospital today.

"The first thing you have is a Department Head meeting . . . most of your colleagues are there . . . what do you see . . . what do you hear . . . what are people saying . . . what is different?

"After the meeting, you walk through the halls of the hospital back to your department . . . you see your employees . . . what are they doing . . . what do you say . . . what is the interaction like?

"You need to follow-up on a problem with another department head . . . you go to that department . . . it's very busy . . . you and your colleague talk about the problem . . . what is that interaction like . . . how are you acting . . . what are you saying . . . how does it feel?

"At lunchtime, you are in the cafeteria . . . what's it like . . . what do you hear . . . what do you see . . . how is it different?

"You have a busy afternoon . . . you spend time at your desk doing paperwork . . . how do you feel . . . what's it like . . . what's different than before?

"It's time to wind up the day . . . you are getting ready to leave . . . you think back on the day . . . think about the people you saw and talked with . . . think about the sounds . . . think about the work you did . . . what's different . . . what's better about now?"

Have group members slowly bring themselves back mentally into the room.

Stand and form a circle. Instructions: "One person will start by answering a question. The person to their left will go next. The questions will keep going around the group still I stop the flow. You may pass. Do not try to be original. If someone else gives the answer you would have, please repeat it."

PERSONAL

1. A word to describe yourself at work.

2. Something you'd like to express more of at work.

3. How you would like to be at work.

4. What do you want others to think or say about you?

5. What is a hidden quality you have that others don't see?

6. You had an option for passing . . . I want you to think about how often you passed . . . how typical is this for you? Think but don't answer out loud.

ORGANIZATIONAL

1. Who is *(name of hospital)*? (We are!)

2. What positive qualities would you like to see more fully expressed by the people at _____?

3. What is one word to describe your vision of the full potential of _____ _____?

4. What value would you personally like to guide and direct at _____ _____?

(Source: Albert Einstein Healthcare Foundation, Philadelphia, Penn. 19141. © 1988. Reprinted with permission.)

WRITING TASKS

Yet another experiental medium to consider is writing. Like mental imagery, writing is usually an individual activity. It allows each participant to reflect slowly on his own understanding of and response to training input.

Writing activities range from short responses to long essays. The most common short form is the **worksheet,** such as those found at the end of each chapter in this book. A worksheet provides rather specific instructions concerning what the participant is to write. It can be used at any time during a design. For example, a trainer in a course on customer relations might ask participants to fill out a worksheet that asks for brief descriptions of recent encounters with customers. A worksheet might also be assigned at the end of such a course, perhaps asking participants to set goals for applying course techniques back on the job. **Longer writing** generally works best in the middle of a training design; assigned at the beginning or the end, it can make a program drag. One example of longer writing comes from a course on dealing with problem employees. Participants were asked to recall an especially disturbing incident that happened to them in the past. They were then asked to write an action account of the incident in the present tense (as if it were happening in the 'here and now'). This writing assignment was used to help participants distinguish behaviors from the feelings that accompany them.

Writing tasks are, of course, useful when any written skill (e.g., business correspondence) is being taught. They can also be used, as above, to describe events. Furthermore, trainers can ask participants to record plans, develop verbal scripts, and review material in written form.

GUIDELINES

When you are about to introduce a writing task, keep these five tips in mind.

HELP PARTICIPANTS TO GET IN THE MOOD TO EXPRESS THEMSELVES IN WRITING. Do something beforehand to inspire or challenge them. Make them feel that the writing has a good purpose and is not just busy work.

MAKE SURE YOUR INSTRUCTIONS ARE CRYSTAL CLEAR. If appropriate, you may even want to provide a model for participants to emulate.

ARRANGE A GOOD WORK ENVIRONMENT FOR WRITING. Provide a clear, firm surface on which to write. Provide workbooks in which all pages lie flat or ask participants to remove worksheets from loose-leaf binders. Establish privacy and quiet.

ALLOW ENOUGH TIME FOR WRITING. Participants should not feel rushed. They may need time to get started. On the other hand, don't let the exercise go on too long. Involvement will slacken.

ALLOW ENOUGH TIME FOR FEEDBACK. When participants have finished, they often want to share what they have written. One alternative is to invite a limited number of volunteers to read their finished work. A second alternative is to have seat partners share their writing with each other.

EXAMPLES OF WRITING TASKS

1. In a training program on interviewing skills, participants were taught five steps to follow in planning an interview: (1) study the job description; (2) gather information on the organization/career advancement; (3) study the candidate's resume; (4) list skills to evaluate during the interview; and (5) write a list of open-ended questions to ask in the interview. At this point, participants were asked to outline questions for use in an interview they might actually conduct. Figure 6–4 reproduces the written instructions.

Figure 6–4. Interviewing Skills: Planning the Interview

Instructions:

Outline questions for the job description you developed earlier in class. Please list at least two technical questions and six categories of performance questions. Remember that you will be asking follow-up questions to discover situation/ action/result. Here is an example of a preplanned question outline.

You are interviewing a candidate for the fitness trainer for our class. Using the job description already prepared for you, the preplanned questions include:

TECHNICAL

1. Are you certified to teach aerobics?
2. Do you have knowledge of first aid?

PERFORMANCE

1. In the past, when you have sensed that a class was losing interest in maintaining the workout schedule, what have you done? (Team building)
2. When conflicts have arisen among class members concerning _____, what have you done? (Problem solving)
3. Describe a typical class. (Planning)
4. Suppose that several class members have back problems. What would you do to accommodate them? (Adaptability)
5. Tell me about the largest group you've had and describe how you maintained control over the group. (Controlling)
6. How would you design/market a new aerobics class for a fitness center? (Organizing)

YOUR PREPLANNED QUESTIONS

TECHNICAL

1.

2.

Figure 6–4. continued

PERFORMANCE

1.

2.

3.

4.

5.

6.

---

2. The writing task in figure 6–5 was given as part of a workshop entitled "Helping Women Pursue Their Dreams."

Figure 6–5. Your Ideal Day

Below, write a description of your ideal day exactly as you would like it. Tell about this fantasy day in the present tense and in detail, describing each thing you would like to do, with whom (or alone), where, and when.

Figure 6–5. continued

Now divide the events in your ideal day into the three categories below.

Essential   *Optional*   *Frills*

Pair up with someone else, share your lists, and discuss these questions:

1. What elements, if any, of your ideal day do you already have?

2. Which elements are conspicuously absent from your present life?

3. What obstacles stand in the way of your having your ideal day tomorrow?

3. A vision is an inspiring picture of a desired future state. Figure 6–6 presents a writing task for enabling managers to learn what a vision is and how to create one.

Figure 6–6. Creating a Vision Statement

1. Have participants make two columns on a piece of paper. Have them entitle the first column *"What doesn't work."* They are to write here any major or minor glitches in the department that impede its effectiveness. Give them plenty of time to write this list. Encourage them to state these problems negatively. Give them lots of possibilities, e.g., "Our people are burning out from all the work."

Figure 6–6. continued

2. The second column should be entitled, *"Instead, I choose . . ."* In this column, they should transform the negative statements in the first column into very positive, desirable statements. For example, if in the first column was written, "We have way too much turnover," the corresponding entry in the second column would read, "Our staff turnover is only 5% per year." *Encourage participants not to concern themselves with what they think is possible* and to be sure to state these as positives.

3. Now participants should be instructed to write a detailed description of how their unit would be functioning eighteen months from now *if anything were possible*. This description should address all of the following:

   - the unique contribution the unit is making to the company
   - how the unit is perceived by other units in the company
   - the effective ways people in the unit are relating to one another
   - how much fun people are having because they are a part of the unit

   Participants should now be encouraged to write this *as if it were true now*. This will include phrases such as, "We are creating new approaches to customer service all the time." This should be so simple and clear that an eighth grader would be able to understand it.

4. Next, have participants write five to eight declarative statements about *what people in the department will be doing* to fulfill this vision. Examples are, "Everyone in the department takes personal responsibility for quality," and "We hold to the commitments we make." These may well come right out of what was written in step 3. They should be the most important ingredients of the scenario described in step 3.

5. The participants should be instructed to regard what was written in step 4 as a list of "means," not the "end." Now, it's time to write a brief sentence or two describing the end state. This is what most people think of as the vision statement.

   Some sample vision statements are:

   - (for a customer service unit) "We make customers glad they bought our product."
   - (for a hospital dialysis unit) "Because of us, patients feel more dignity and hope."
   - (for a manufacturing plant) "Our customers know when they operate one of our units they are operating the finest equipment money can buy."

Source: Richard McKnight and Associates. 1988. *Training for Leadership* (103 Avon Rd, Narberth, PA 19072).

PROJECTS

The project method of learning involves assigning lengthy tasks to participants. Such tasks should challenge them to obtain additional information not given by you and to apply what they have learned. If you design projects that participants find meaningful, you will find that this method has significant learning value. Naturally, time is the biggest constraint to including projects in a training program.

We will describe and illustrate four kinds of projects commonly used in training programs.

IN-BASKET ASSIGNMENTS

In-basket assignments are a form of the project method in which letters, memos, phone messages, and so forth, are given to the participant playing an assigned role. She is then given time to write actual responses to the items in her in basket. Figure 6–7 provides instructions for such an assignment. This assignment could be used in its present form as part of a time management program for managers.

Figure 6–7. In-Basket

For the purpose of this exercise, you are to assume the role of Pat Ladder, Manager, Operations Department, the J. R. Jones Company. As manager of the Operations Department, you report to the Division Head, Kelly MacDonald. The following people report to you:

- Jamie White, Secretary
- Mike Crossman, Facilities Maintenance Supervisor
- Linda Stevens, Property and Supplies Supervisor
- Stan Powell, Security Supervisor
- Jay Snyder, Transportation Supervisor

All are capable people and have been in their respective jobs one year or more. The situation this exercise deals with is as follows:

Today is Monday, December 14. You have been away for several days, so you have come into your office at 8:00 a.m. (early) to "catch up" and get ready for the day. The normal working day begins at 8:30 a.m. Promptly at 8:30 a.m. you must leave to attend a training meeting. Therefore, you only have about thirty minutes to organize your work, and you want to get as much done as possible. You do not expect to return to your office from the meeting until 10:00 a.m. As you reach your desk at 8:00 a.m., you find items in your "in-basket."

Figure 6–7. continued

As you go through the material, take whatever action is needed assuming you are Pat Ladder. Use your own experience as a basis for your decisions.

Make notes to yourself or to others by writing directly on the message, letter, or memo or by attaching notes (use note paper provided by the facilitator). Draft or write letters and memos where appropriate. Note any phone calls you plan to make, including information about when you plan to make the call and whom you plan to call. Note follow-up dates where further action is necessary. Write on the items themselves where you want them sent such as "Follow Up 12/15" or "File."

After the exercise, you will have an opportunity to compare your actions with others in the group. Remember:

- Put yourself in the position of Pat Ladder.
- Today is December 11.
- You have come in before regular working hours. There is no one else available to help or call.
- You want to get as much out of the way as possible in the thirty minutes you have to spend organizing.
- Record (make mention of) every action you make or intend to make.
- Be prepared to discuss how you handled the exercise with the group.

RESEARCH PROJECTS

If preparation time and the necessary data are available, asking participants to conduct some research and present their findings is a valuable form of learning. This research can be done in small teams or individually. Teams or individuals can have the same or different assignments. Data can be obtained either from people or from written materials.

- An interesting example of a research project comes from a course for insurance claims adjusters. The trainer wanted to avoid long periods of dry lectures intended to give participants a crash course in tort law and medical terminology, two things adjusters dealing with accident claims need to know. Instead, she divided participants into small research study groups. Every evening during this week-long course, participants were given assignments (and reference material) that they did individually. For one hour each afternoon, the groups met to study the information they had obtained and to draw up test questions for the other study groups. Twice during the week, test questions were swapped among the groups, and the answers discussed. In post-tests, knowledge of tort law and medical terminology was shown to have increased 60% over that gained from lectures in previous courses.

TEACHING PROJECTS

It is said that one really has learned something if one can teach it. Another project assignment is to ask participants to teach new information or skills to each other. The teaching can be performed by either individuals or teams in front of the full group or in small groups.

- In a four-week course on family therapy, for example, participants are formed into teaching teams. Each team is assigned one model of family therapy. In the last week of the course, the team is expected to teach others about the assumptions, key concepts, and intervention methods of its assigned model. Teams are urged to use active training methods. A natural competitiveness usually develops among the teams, which has the effect of producing teaching designs that are creative and of high quality.

- Similarly, a team-building trainer assigns teams to demonstrate one of the following attributes: flexibility, interdependence, trust, and openness. Some groups display skills, some conduct meetings, and some use visual aids such as flip charts or banners in their teaching exercises. Once a demonstration is complete, the rest of the participants critique it, highlighting the positive aspects.

TASK FORCE PROJECTS

The purpose of these kinds of projects is to give participants confidence in their ability to do the same tasks back on the job. Typically, groups are asked to generate a plan or other specific outcome that can be used by other participants in their actual work situations.

- In a course on planning and organizing skills, participants were given a planning task based on a real case situation in their company. Task force groups were formed, relevant materials were given out, and a request was made for each group to complete its work on a specific form (which was then duplicated and shared among the groups). A debriefing of the work of the task forces followed. The case study (minus the exhibits) and the planning chart that was to be completed are presented in figure 6–8.

Figure 6–8. Task Force Assignment

You are the Director of Distribution Services and Planning and you have been given approval by the President of XYZ to pilot a new teleselling program. You have been waiting some time for this moment and the decision represents a victory for your department. Now the hard work of planning and organizing the project must begin.

BACKGROUND

The teleselling approach is a new one for XYZ. In teleselling (or telemarketing as it is more commonly called) a small, highly trained team uses advanced telephone technology to sell to a broad group of customers. To be successful, the teleselling team needs strong training in product knowledge as well as telephone selling and communications techniques.

Typically, the XYZ sales force has operated on a face-to-face basis. The teleselling team would not supplant the regular sales force. Instead they would be an adjunct to the sales force and help them reach smaller accounts more efficiently.

Upper management feels that teleselling would be especially useful in reaching Class 19 accounts between $500 to $2500 with a special emphasis on products other than hypertensives. In 1985 there were 15,000 Class 19 accounts with a total sales of just over $6 million for the year. Teleselling is viewed as a way to boost these sales.

Most of these accounts are too small for regular visits and detailing by the sales force. On the other hand, they represent an excellent source of business if there were a way of reaching them efficiently. That is why upper management at XYZ finds teleselling so attractive.

But there are problems, too. For one thing, the wholesalers would feel that XYZ was impinging on their turf. The wholesalers are a key link between XYZ and its customers, both large and small, and relationships with wholesalers would have to be handled carefully.

There are also turf issues within XYZ. The sale force feels that teleselling should be under their control. On the other hand, regional sales offices are located at most of the distribution centers which also handle inventory and transportation control. Ultimately, upper management decided to put the administration of the teleselling program in the hands of distribution but the sales force would set the criteria for whom to call and what to sell and provide the training. Thus, to be successful, the program would require excellent relations between sales and distribution personnel.

Figure 6–8. continued

CURRENT STATUS

It is now August 1 and the President has passed on to you final approval to pilot the teleselling program in the St. Louis region. Ultimately, he would like to see four teleselling locations set up, including the pilot. He wants the pilot up and running by the beginning of November. The company has set the following objectives for the program:

- Provide consistent coverage of mid to low volume Class 19's and allow more detailing time to field sales
- Increase market penetration
- Increase coverage of ethical and consumer products
- Improve XYZ's image with customers
- Increase sales at less contact cost

The President has given you a list of target products (Exhibit 1) and suggested that you work closely with the sales and marketing groups on strategies for promoting these products through special offers and other approaches. You have on your desk the draft of an introductory letter to be sent to accounts in the St. Louis region by the Branch Operations Manager (Exhibit 2).

You have also been working up proposed staffing and budgets for the program (Exhibit 3). Current plans call for two part-time telesell workers at the St. Louis pilot site working for four hours per day per person. Each worker should be able to make thirty calls a day. You know that a key issue will be training and continued motivation for those involved in the program. From what you have been reading about telemarketing, burnout among workers in such a program can be very high. The total budget for the St. Louis pilot program will be $152,000.

Under current plans, distribution will handle the operations of the teleselling program but will work closely with sales representatives. The Division Manager will send a list of all accounts below $2500 to the sales representative. The sales rep will in turn determine which of these accounts should be called under the teleselling program and this information will be given to the branch operation manager.

You have very little time to put the program together and you are now mulling over how to plan and organize the work for the pilot. You are reviewing a memo prepared by a member of your staff on some of the key issues that will arise in the program (Exhibit 4). You know that the first and perhaps the most important step is to organize the work well and to plan for any contingencies that might arise.

Figure 6–8. continued

PLANNING CHART

Prioritized Action Steps   Time Reference

_____   _____

_____   _____

_____   _____

_____   _____

_____   _____

_____   _____

_____   _____

_____   _____

_____   _____

_____   _____

_____   _____

_____   _____

_____   _____

_____   _____

Source: Training Management Corporation, 245 Nassau Street, Princeton, N.J. 08540.

Worksheet

USING EXPERIENTIAL LEARNING APPROACHES

Now that you have been introduced to these experiential learning approaches, consider which ones you would want to utilize to achieve the objectives in your next training program.

_____ Role playing
_____ Games and simulations
_____ Observation
_____ Mental imagery
_____ Writing tasks
_____ Projects

Strategy Outline:

_____
_____
_____
_____
_____
_____
_____
_____
_____
_____
_____
_____
_____
_____
_____
_____
_____

DESIGNING ACTIVE TRAINING ACTIVITIES

7

With objectives set and a variety of training methods at your disposal, you are in a position to develop all of the specific training activities you will need in an active training program.

THE THREE MAJOR INGREDIENTS OF ANY DESIGN

Earlier, we compared opening exercises to appetizers at the beginning of a full meal. Continuing this delectable analogy, let's consider all the separate activities in an active training program as items on a menu or, if you prefer, dishes in a meal. Each item or dish has, of course, certain ingredients. With regard to individual training activities, there are three: a **purpose,** a **method,** and a **format.** How the purpose, method, and format combine together is the basic recipe for the design. Your decisions about what is to be accomplished (purpose), how it is to be accomplished (method), and in what setting (format) will determine the design you wish to create. Let's examine two activities as cases in point.

The first case example is an activity called Prejudice. In this activity, the following major decisions have been made:

1. The **purpose** is to share feelings and ideas about prejudices in a non-threatening manner.
2. The **method** employed is a simulation game.
3. The **format** is mostly small group with full group interaction at the end.

Figure 7–1 presents the details of this design.

Figure 7–1. Prejudice: An Awareness-Expansion Activity

On *each* of *ten* index cards, write the name of *one* group that is commonly the object of prejudice (e.g., women, blacks, homosexuals, Republicans, etc.). Group three chairs in a triangle with one chair facing the other for each subgroup.

1. The facilitator distributes two blank index cards and a pencil to each participant. He reads the list of ten groups from the prepared cards and directs the participants to write one additional object of prejudice on each of their two blank cards, with a different item on each card.
2. The facilitator collects the index cards, adds them to the ten prepared cards, and shuffles the stack.
3. The facilitator divides the participants into triads. One member from each group takes two cards off the top of the stack, looks at both, and selects one. The other card is returned to the stack. Each of these members then returns to his place, facing the other two members of the triad.
4. The member with the card in each triad announces the subject of his card to his group. The other group members verbally assault and make disparaging or stereotyped remarks about the object of prejudice, while the member holding the card refutes their statements and defends the item or group being attacked. (Three to five minutes)
5. Each member takes a turn being the person who selects a card and defends the object of prejudice.
6. The facilitator leads the total group in a discussion of the following points:
   1. What types of prejudicial statements were made by the participants?
   2. Did any participants admit to having any prejudices? What were they?
   3. Were any prejudices held in common by a number of members?
   4. How did the selected members defend the objects of prejudice?
   5. How did the members feel when they were seated alone defending their subject against the other group members?

Figure 7–1. continued

6. How did members feel if they perceived themselves as fitting a stereotyped subject?
7. How did members feel when they were making stereotypical remarks?
8. What did this experience tell group members about their own prejudicial perceptions and behavior?

The facilitator then leads a discussion of the fallacies of the usual prejudices found in society today, the results of such attitudes, and ways to deal with or refute them.

Source: J. William Pfeiffer and John E. Jones. 1979. *A Handbook of Structured Experiences for Human Relations Training,* vol. 7 San Diego, Calif.: University Associates, pp. 15–18. Reprinted with permission.

The second case example is an activity called Absentee. In this activity, the following major decisions have been made:

1. The **purpose** is to study the dynamics of decision making.
2. The **method** employed is role playing.
3. The **format** is intergroup (two groups interacting with each other).

Figure 7–2 outlines the terms of the game.

Figure 7–2. Absentee: A Management Role Play

1. In a brief introduction, the facilitator gives an overview of the activity. He does not state the goals of the activity.
2. The facilitator forms two groups of five to seven members each. He announces that each group is to sit in a circle away from the other group. One group is designated "top management" and the other "middle management."
3. The facilitator distributes the Absentee Information Sheet below to all participants and tells them to spend ten minutes studying it and making notes on how they would resolve the problem.

ABSENTEE INFORMATION SHEET

BACKGROUND

Bob Ford has been a test supervisor in the quality-control section for five months. He was promoted on the basis of excellent performance in the research and development (R&D) section. Although his new subordinates do not question

Figure 7–2. continued

Ford's engineering ability, they are still grumbling about the fact that their fellow worker, Bill Novak, was passed over in favor of an "outsider."

THE CRITICAL INCIDENTS

a. Ford's supervisor had asked to have a "good man" sent over to R&D to help out with a special problem for four days. Looking over the job and surveying his staff, Ford decided that Novak was best qualified.

Friday afternoon, Ford called Novak into his office and said, "Bill, the superintendent has a special project going in the R&D section and needs some help. Since our schedule is flexible, I'm sending you over there for a short time starting Monday."

Novak answered, "Why pick me? I like the work I'm doing here. Do you have any complaints about my work?"

Ford shook his head. "No, but I don't have time to argue with you. Be over there Monday morning."

Novak stormed out of Ford's office without saying a word.

b. Late Monday morning, the superintendent called Ford. "I thought you were sending Novak over here to help me out. I'm on a tight schedule with a subcontractor, Bob, and I need Novak now!"

Ford replied, "I told him to report to you this morning. He hasn't shown up here, and he should have called in by 9 o'clock if he wasn't coming in today. I assumed he was over there working with you. I'll send one of the other men over in a few minutes."

As Ford picked up the phone to call Novak's home, his secretary walked in and announced that Novak's wife had just called. "She says Novak is sick and will probably be out for a few days."

c. Wednesday morning, Ford was holding a staff meeting; he had to leave to answer a telephone call. Returning to the conference room, he was just in time to hear one of his men, whose back was turned to him, say, "Novak really made a pile on that poker game last night, didn't he?"

For the rest of the meeting, the men avoided Ford's glances. On Friday, Novak handed in a doctor's certificate for four days' sick leave.

Ford knows that the crew is waiting to see what he will do.

4. The facilitator then tells the groups that they have twenty-five minutes to discuss the problem and to reach consensus on a solution. After the groups have been working for ten minutes, the facilitator interrupts and randomly appoints one member of each group to be its leader for the remainder of the time.

5. At the end of twenty-five minutes, the facilitator stops the discussion. He directs the middle-management leader to assume the role of spokesperson for his group.

Figure 7–2. continued

6. The spokesperson goes to the top-management group and presents the recommendations of his team. The remaining middle managers silently observe this meeting.

7. The middle-management group is instructed to reconvene in its original meeting place to give its leader feedback and to speculate on the pending decisions of top management. Concurrently, the top-management team makes its final decisions. (Five minutes)

8. The top-management team summons the middle-management spokesperson to receive its decision. (The other middle-management members continue their meeting.)

9. The middle-management spokesperson returns to his group to announce the decision of top management. The top-management members observe the reactions of the middle-management group and discuss their observations. (Ten minutes)

10. Participants pair off with a member of the other group to discuss their learnings. (Ten minutes)

11. The facilitator leads a discussion of the outcomes of the experience. He keeps the discussion from stressing the "correct" solution and focuses instead on the process.

Source: J. William Pfeiffer and John E. Jones. 1975. *A Handbook of Structured Experiences for Human Relations Training*, vol. 5 San Diego, Calif.: University Associates, pp. 49–52. Reprinted with permission.

For many topics, it is possible to make a variety of choices concerning the purpose, method, and format of the designs intended to cover them. Let's take, for example, the topic of leadership behavior and, in particular, the concepts of authoritarian, democratic, and laissez-faire leadership styles. Your purposes as a trainer may range from deepening participants' understanding of the consequences of each style (cognitive learning) to allowing participants to experience their differing levels of comfort with each style (affective learning) to providing them with practice in utilizing each style in appropriate situations (behavioral learning). Just as the same menu item can be prepared with different recipes, so, too, can each one of these purposes be achieved by a variety of methods and group settings. For example, participants could experience their comfort levels with each style through role playing, mental imagery, or a writing task. Any of the basic formats (full group, individual, pairs, small group, intergroup) could serve as well. In training, as in cooking, art, or music, a desired end can be accomplished by varied means.

BASIC QUESTIONS ABOUT ANY DESIGN

When shaping a design, there are several considerations to take into account.

1. Does the design achieve the activity's purpose? This, of course, is the most important consideration. To take an obvious example, a demonstration may show participants a skill or procedure in action without giving them actual practice. Even when the choice of method is appropriate, a particular design may not achieve its purpose. For example, a role play, if poorly designed, may provide little skill practice for participants.

2. What knowledge or skill level does the design require of participants? Your assessment of participants is often critical in creating a specific design. For example, a complicated task force exercise on project planning might be premature for novice project managers. Or another design might not be sufficiently challenging for a particular situation.

3. How much time will it take? At any particular point in a program, you may feel that time is limited or, conversely, that a longer design is perfect for the occasion. In general, it is a good rule to keep afternoon activities shorter than morning ones. Further, it rarely pays to skimp on time when you are seeking to accomplish an especially important objective. You would not want, for instance, to allot only ten minutes to a discussion of a company's controversial system for disciplining employees.

4. Is the design slow or fast paced? Regardless of the overall time needed for a design, some activities are slow moving and others have a quicker pace. Fast-paced activities work best to get the total group involved. Leisurely paced activities are more appropriate in a small group format.

5. Is it suited to the size of the group? Some designs simply don't work well with large groups. For instance, dyadic role-playing practice is very hard to monitor when the training group consists of more than thirty people. On the other hand, some designs require a critical mass. For example, it can be uncomfortable to participate in a mental imagery exercise in a very small group (six or less); the anonymity of a somewhat larger group helps participants to relax.

6. What skills are required to conduct the design? It's important to assess how much expertise or facilitation skill a design demands. For example, a read-and-discuss approach to cognitive material requires less in the way of Socratic skills than does a guided teaching mode.

It is not always possible to answer these questions in advance. Experience is the best teacher when it comes to designing; often, the most you can hope for is to anticipate what might occur if a particular design is used. Taking small risks is absolutely essential to your development as a trainer—the only way to find out if a design will work for you is to give it a try. A good approach is to change the design of *one* part of your module/course every time you teach, in order to expand your repertoire.

THE REMAINING DETAILS

When the purpose, method, and format for a single design have been chosen, several details remain.

1. **Time allocation:** How many minutes will the design take?
2. **Buy-in:** What will you say or do to get participants involved?
3. **Key points and/or instructions:** What are the major ideas in the presentation, and what exactly do you want participants to do?
4. **Materials:** What do you or the participants need in the way of materials to implement the design?
5. **Setting:** How should you set up the physical environment for the design to succeed?
6. **Ending:** What remarks do you want to make and/or what discussion do you want the participants to have before proceeding to the next activity?

Once these decisions have been made, a design is complete. Let us illustrate this process.

- Assume that you are conducting a course on assertive behavior for a group of sixteen managers. You are using a large training room with four windows. Participants are seated around U-shaped tables, which occupy only half the room. It's right after lunch. During the morning, you discussed and demonstrated the differences between nonassertive, aggressive, and assertive styles of coping with conflict. Your goal for the early afternoon is to teach how body language is a large part of style. *You decide that the purpose of your first design is to introduce the topic of body language in a dramatic way and to help participants become aware of how they now use body language during a power struggle.*

  The next decisions concern method and format. Looking over several possibilities, *you decide to use a game that involves every participant.* This decision allows for a fast-paced, active activity, desirable after lunch.

With sixteen people to accommodate and with the need for practice time later in the afternoon in mind, *you decide to use pairs as the most efficient format for the game.*

With these tentative decisions in mind, you now need to find or, if necessary, invent a game that will achieve your purpose. Luckily, a colleague has told you about a nonverbal "persuasion" game that might suit your purposes. The only problem is that this game usually takes forty-five minutes and appears to you to be too threatening for your clientele. You decide to redesign the game, paying attention to such details as time allotment, buy-in, activity instructions, materials, physical setting, and ending. Your final design might resemble the one in figure 7–3.

THREE TIPS FOR CREATIVE DESIGNS

Many trainers wish they were more creative. However, creative designers are not a special breed; they *work* at being creative and use several tricks to help them do their best. Here are some of their tips.

ONE DESIGN CAN ACCOMPLISH TWO THINGS AT ONCE

Economy is the trademark of a good design, and, with a little care, most can serve double duty. For example, you could brief participant observers about nonverbal aspects of communication to watch for while their peers are giving sales presentations. By watching how you change your own facial, vocal, and postural communication during the briefing, the observers could gain observation practice before trying it out for real. Or suppose that you wanted to help a participant through a role play requiring him to coach a confused employee. As you did this, you yourself could provide a demonstration of effective coaching behavior.

THE SAME DESIGN CAN OFTEN BE USED FOR DIFFERENT PURPOSES

Many creative trainers have a few exercises in their repertoires that they use over and over again with different topics because these exercises are easily adaptable.

- For an energizer late in the afternoon, a trainer of a team-building course had participants make paper airplanes and attempt to hit a target. Noticing that some participants helped each other out with their

Figure 7–3. Nonverbal Persuasion

After greeting the participants who have just returned from lunch, say the following:

"I thought it would be a good idea to wake us up after lunch with a lively activity. It will help us introduce the topic of body language and its effect on our style."

There are no materials needed for the activity, but the instructions are very important and the physical setting plays a role. With those factors in mind, do the following:

1. Ask participants to pair off with their seat partners and to establish whose birthday falls earlier in the calendar year.
2. Give the person with the earlier birthday in each pair an index card with the following instructions: "Leave your seat and go somewhere else in the room (e.g., look out a window, stand in the corner of the room, play with some object). Soon, your partner will come to fetch you and want to bring you back to your seat. Resist him or her, saying or doing whatever you like. Don't go back to your seat until you feel persuaded to do so."
3. After these participants leave their seats, ask their partners to go and fetch them. Explain to them that they can approach the task in any way they like except for one condition: *they may not talk (or write) during the entire time they are trying to get their partners back to their seats.* (Allow the "resisters" to overhear your instructions to the "persuaders.")
4. When all participants have eventually returned to their seats, ask the resisters to give feedback (privately) to their persuaders. Urge them to identify which kinds of nonverbal communication were effective and which ineffective. (Effective nonverbal communication tends to include some of the following: good eye contact, decisiveness, firm but gentle physical movements, persistence, and calmness.)
5. Ask resisters to brag about their partners' effective nonverbal behaviors to the rest of the group.
6. Invite partners to reverse roles and redo the exercise.
7. End the activity by stating that research indicates that nonverbal aspects of communication (vocal, facial, and postural) influence the impact of our messages more (some even say by 93%) than does the verbal content. Write on a flipchart: "It's not what you say, but how you say it." Invite participants to react to the statement, then go on to the next design.

airplane designs while others did not, he initiated a dramatic discussion about teamwork. At a problem-solving course, he used the same exercise to point out how many people changed their designs when their first attempts didn't work while others repeated the same essential solution (design) with each attempt.

PUBLISHED DESIGNS CAN OFTEN BE MODIFIED TO SUIT YOUR OWN NEEDS

Whenever you examine a published design, think how you might change its purpose, its direction, its length, and so on to achieve the design you are seeking.

- A well-known activity based on a drawing of a young girl/old woman originally published in *Puck* in 1915 uses the ambiguous picture to examine stereotyping and group pressure on perception. Typically, participants are asked to relate their feelings and opinions about the woman they see in the drawing, not realizing that it can be viewed in two different ways. Instead of using this drawing for its traditional purpose, however, a trainer used it as the basis for an interesting coaching or teaching exercise, employing the following instructions:

  1. Obtain two volunteers. One is to serve as a teacher. She should be a person who has previously seen the drawing. (There are always some participants who have.) The other is to portray a student who needs assistance in seeing both women.

  2. The teacher should try to show the student how to see both women. (If the student is successful in a matter of seconds, replace him with someone else.)

  3. After the student has seen both women, observers should tell the teacher in terms as descriptive as possible what she did to cope with the student.

  4. Then discuss what behaviors were helpful or harmful in loosening up the student's perceptions of the drawing. Compare these behaviors to common teaching or coaching situations.

- In a popular exercise called "Towers: An Intergroup Competition" (Pfeiffer and Jones, 1974, 3:17–21), teams compete to build the best construction-paper tower. The towers are judged by height, aesthetic appeal, and sturdiness. In a group dynamics course, a trainer was looking for a group-building activity to help in the development of new teams that would eventually work cooperatively with each other. He decided to change "towers" to "houses" and asked each team to construct a model of the dream house in which all members would like to live. Instead of using construction paper, teams were given index cards. With these noncompetitive instructions, three completely different and highly creative designs emerged, and each team was able to display proudly a model of its dream home. Through a simple change in design, the activity went from a competitive to a noncompetitive experience.

Worksheet
DESIGNING A TRAINING ACTIVITY

Try your hand at designing a training activity. Choose a purpose of your own and develop a creative design with the suggestions you have been given.

Purpose:

Method:

Format:

    ____ Individual

    ____ Pairs

    ____ Small group

    ____ Full group

    ____ Intergroup

Outline:
(include time allotment, buy-in, key points/instructions, materials, physical setting, and ending)

_____

_____

_____

_____

_____

_____

_____

_____

_____

_____

_____

_____

_____

SEQUENCING ACTIVE TRAINING ACTIVITIES

8

What you do as a trainer is not all that counts. Equally important is *when* you do it.

No matter how well you design a particular activity or presentation, its impact and value may diminish greatly if it is misplaced in the overall sequence of events. For example, participants may be tired just when you need them to be alert. Or the group may not be able to grasp abstract ideas before experiencing concrete examples.

Sequencing is partly an art; some trainers just know where to place different pieces in their overall designs. Most trainers, however, learn to master sequencing through experience and trial and error. Nonetheless, some basic guidelines remove the mystery from effective sequencing.

BASIC SEQUENCING GUIDELINES

1. **Build interest and introduce new content before you delve more deeply.** Set the stage for learning by using an activity that hooks participants' interest or gives the big picture.

2. **Have demanding activities follow easy activities.** Get participants settled in and warmed up before you put them through hard work.

3. **Maintain a good mix of activities.** Vary training methods, the length of activities, the intensity of activities, the physical setting, and the format. Variety is the spice of good training.

4. **Teach easier concepts before teaching more difficult ones.** Generally, we learn more easily when one idea is an outgrowth of another.

5. **Provide sub-skills before practicing complex skills.** Often, difficult skills cannot be learned until some basic ones have been mastered.

6. **Close training sequences with a discussion of "so what."** Have the participants consider the implications of the course content for themselves.

How would you apply these guidelines to specific situations? Figures 8–1 and 8–2 present two opportunities for you to try your hand at sequencing. There are no correct answers. Use your own judgment.

Figure 8–1. Sequencing Activity 1

You have been asked to design a brief introductory training module on using a PC. Assume that you have enough PCs for half of the class. The activities you have chosen include:

A. Showing how to boot up the machine and insert a diskette.

B. Setting up a race in which pairs compete with each other to prepare the printer for producing a letter.

C. Obtaining participant feelings about learning how to use a PC.

D. Explaining the components of the PC and the differences between hardware and software.

E. Demonstrating how a word-processed letter is composed.

F. Giving quartets an exercise in getting to know the main computer commands (e.g., *Save, Directory, Edit*) by exploring the computer manual.

In what order would you sequence these activities? Why?

1. ____

2. ____

3. ____

4. ____

5. ____

6. ____

One way to sequence the module in figure 8–1 is:

1. C. Obtain participants feelings about learning how to use a PC. (A good on-the-spot assessment opener)

2. D. Explain the components of the PC and the differences between hardware and software. (An overview of the topic)

3. A. Show how to boot up the machine and insert a diskette. (A simple first learning step)

4. F. Give quartets an exercise in getting to know the main computer commands by exploring the computer manual. (A way to engage participants actively after they have listened to and watched the trainer)

5. E. Demonstrate how a word-processed letter is composed. (A demonstration of what participants can do with the knowledge they have gained)

6. B. Set up a race in which pairs compete with each other to prepare the printer for producing a letter. (A fun way to end and see the results of the letter composed in the previous step)

Of course, many other sequences might also work. For example, you could begin with the demonstration so that participants would see immediately the outcome of what they will learn. You could also end with obtaining participants' feelings about learning how to use a PC (after having tried it out a little).

Figure 8–2. Sequencing Activity 2

You have been asked to design a training module for supervisors on giving feedback. The design is to be based on a handout containing the text below.

What Makes Feedback Useful?
Constructive feedback is a way of helping another person look at his own behavior without putting him on the defensive. It is communication to a person (or group) that gives that person information about how he affects others. If we wish to avoid creating defensiveness with our feedback, we must appear not to be attacking the *person* but rather to be commenting on his *behavior*.

Here are some criteria for useful feedback:

1. **It is descriptive rather than evaluative.** Describing one's own reactions leaves the individual free to use or not use the feedback or to use it as he sees fit. Avoiding evaluative language reduces the need for the individual to react defensively.
2. **It is specific rather than general.** Telling someone that he is "dominating," for example, would probably not be as useful as saying, "just now when we were deciding the issue, you did not listen to what others said. I felt forced to accept your arguments or face attack from you."
3. **It takes into account the needs of both the receiver and the giver of feedback.** Feedback can be destructive when it serves only our own needs and fails to consider the needs of the person on the receiving end.
4. **It is directed toward behavior that the receiver can do something about.** Reminding a person of some shortcoming over which he has no control only causes frustration.
5. **It is solicited, rather than imposed.** Feedback is most useful when the receiver himself has formulated the questions that those observing him answer.
6. **It is well timed.** In general, feedback is best offered as soon as possible after the given behavior (depending, of course, on the person's readiness to hear it, support available from others, etc.).
7. **It is clear.** Feedback is worthless if the receiver misinterprets it. One way of checking is to have the receiver try to rephrase what he has heard to see if it corresponds to what the sender had in mind.

The training activities you have chosen to support the handout include:

A. Asking participants to assess themselves as givers of feedback.
B. Setting up role plays so that each participant can practice giving feedback to a difficult employee and obtain feedback from others on her performance.
C. Dividing participants into small groups and asking them to discuss and clarify the handout.

Figure 8–2. continued

D. Setting up skill-building exercises to practice each skill suggested by the handout.

E. Asking participants to discuss what they value when receiving feedback.

F. Having participants identify employees to whom they would be willing to give feedback according to the guidelines in the handout.

In what order would you sequence these activities? Why?

1. ____

2. ____

3. ____

4. ____

5. ____

6. ____

One way to sequence the module in figure 8–2 is:

1. E. Ask participants to discuss what they value when receiving feedback. (A good lead-in to the handout)
2. C. Divide participants into small groups and ask them to discuss and clarify the handout. (A read-and-discuss method for teaching about feedback)
3. A. Ask participants to assess themselves as givers of feedback. (A useful way of reviewing the handout and motivating participants to improve their skills)
4. D. Set up skill-building exercises to practice each skill suggested by the handout. (An activity that allows the group to learn the subskills of giving feedback)
5. B. Set up role plays so that each participant can practice giving feedback to a difficult employee and obtain feedback from others on her performance. (An opportunity for participants to pull together the skills learned in the previous step)
6. F. Have participants identify employees to whom they would be willing to give feedback according to the guidelines in the handout. (A consideration of on-the-job application of the skills taught in the module)

Another way to end the design would be to ask participants to assess themselves as givers of feedback (after having had had a chance to practice the skill).

CASE APPLICATIONS OF SEQUENCING GUIDELINES

Active training programs contain sequences of activities or modules that adhere to the six guidelines presented at the beginning of this chapter. Figure 8–3 presents an example of a two-hour training sequence for teaching force field analysis, a well-known problem-solving tool based on the concepts of Kurt Lewin. As you read the design, note (1) the use of several methods described in previous chapters (initial case problem, key terms, demonstration, etc.) and (2) the way in which sequencing guidelines are respected (interest building, easy activities first, a good mix, etc.).

Figure 8–3. Teaching Force Field Analysis

I. Introduction

Participants are invited to write down a personal and/or work related problem they are currently experiencing. They are told that a suitable problem is one in which they have been pursuing or thinking about pursuing a goal (e.g., stopping smoking; obtaining more business) but have thus far not succeeded.

Next, they are introduced to the term "force field analysis" and told that it is a tool for obtaining *unattained goals* such as those they have just listed. By contrast, it is *not* a tool to make a decision (e.g., should I quit my job?).

A request is then made for a few participants to share with the group one of the problems they have selected. The trainer either verifies that the problem chosen will "work well" with force field analysis or helps to modify the problem statement so that it does.

II. Lecturette

The trainer discusses with the groups some common patterns people use when they have trouble obtaining desired goals. One way these patterns can be described is to utilize the following list:

Procrastination—not dealing with the problem and perhaps even denying it.

Fretting—continually stewing about the problem but taking no clear directions with it.

Scheming—generating many solutions to the problem but not committing oneself to implementing any of them.

Repeating—utilizing basically the same solution over and over again even though it fails to produce change.

III. Dyadic Discussion

Participants are invited to pair off and share with each other those patterns which they use most frequently. It is suggested that the participants especially consider the patterns used with the problems each has identified in I (above).

IV. Lecturette

The trainer emphasizes that force field analysis is an effective way to counteract procrastination, fretting, scheming or repeating. It is a useful tool because it provides a focused framework for solving problems and builds in social support for implementation.

Figure 8–3. continued

The trainer proceeds to identify four principles in force field analysis: (1) getting clear about what is happening right now with the problem; (2) defining more precisely the goal one is seeking; (3) identifying some of the obstacles which prevent goal attainment; and (4) selecting a concrete place to begin solving the problem.

V. Demonstration

Participants are given form A below. This form streamlines the process of force field analysis by eliminating the identification of helping forces. It also uses simple language.

FORM A

I. The Situation as It Is Now:

II. The Situation as I Want It to Be:

III. What Will Keep the Situation from Changing?

IV. My Top Priority Obstacle:

V. Possible Action Steps: Resources Needed:

Figure 8–3. continued

Next, the participants listen to a pre-recorded case demonstration in which an interviewer asks probing questions to help a "client" identify responses to each of the five steps on the form. Form B shows the results of an interview with a client who distributes watches.

FORM B

I. The Situation as Is Now: *Over 25% of our accounts complained that they did not receive their Xmas order in sufficient time.*

II. The Situation as I Want It to Be: *In the future, our accounts should receive their Xmas order by November 10th.*

III. What will keep the situation from changing?

   Delivery delays

   My own disorganization

   Our drivers don't want to work overtime

   Orders from our accounts are late

IV. My Top Priority Obstacle: *Orders from accounts are late.*

V. Possible Action Steps: Resources Needed:

   Survey accounts re: their obstacles   *Ask Ass't. to develop survey*

   Establish discount for early orders   *Get fiscal projections*

   Establish deadline for order date   *Meet with shipping*

VI. **Dyadic Activity**

Participants are asked to pair off with their partner from III. Each is instructed to interview the other as per the case demonstration. The problem selected for each interview is one previously identified by the participant.

VII. **Ending**

Participants are invited to share their reactions to and questions about the previous activity. The trainer may discover that some participants were plagued by a problem which was not sufficiently concrete. Some resistance to the limits placed by the process (e.g.—selecting only *one* obstacle) may be anticipated and deflected with assurances that problem resolution begins with specific first steps which are actually implemented. The trainer should also encourage participants to announce publicly those action steps they intend to undertake and suggest that one's partner be used as support during the process.

Source: Mel Silberman, "Force Field Analysis: A Suggested Training Design," in *Lewin's Legacy*, ed. Eugene Stivers and Susan Wheelan (New York: Springer-Verlag, 1986). Reprinted with permission.

Another example sequence is given in figure 8–4. Taken from a parenting course, the topic is obtaining support from other adults. Again, take notice of the techniques and guidelines as they are employed.

Figure 8–4. Obtaining Support from Other Adults

This session is devoted to how a parent obtains support from (and gives support to) other adults who care for their child; such as spouse, relative, teacher, child caregiver, etc. The key assumption is that parenting does not occur in a vacuum. There are always other significant adults who can support or undermine an individual parent's efforts.

 I. **The Lone Ranger** (Game)

   A. Ask participants to stand up and form a line. If they see themselves as a person who usually faces personal problems alone, they should go to the head of the line. By contrast, if they typically seek the help of others in solving their personal problems, they should find a place to the rear of the line. Participants who do not identify with either choice should find a place somewhere in the middle. Don't allow participants to "bunch up" in the middle. Urge them to create a "single file" line. Use humor to help participants feel relaxed during the activity.

   B. When the lineup is completed, ask participants to form a semi-circle so that they can see each other while keeping their place.

   C. Interview the two participants at each end of the semi-circle as to the factors influencing their self-placement. Ask them if they feel good about their position in the line.

   D. Indicate that a parent needs to combine both ends of the spectrum: he must stand on his own two feet and also be willing to involve others in the problems posed by his children. Compare this notion to the Lone Ranger, a rugged individual crime fighter who nonetheless had someone to depend upon—Tonto.

 II. **The Need for Support, Feedback, and Planning** (Lecturette)

   A. Ask the group to sit down.

   B. Write: *support, feedback,* and *planning* on a chalkboard or newsprint.

   C. Point out that adults in charge of the same children need to give and receive these three things in order to maximize their effectiveness as a team. *Support* is available if you can count on someone else to help out, listen to your frustrations, and appreciate your efforts. *Feedback* is a constructive evaluation of your strengths and weaknesses as a parent. *Planning* is a joint commitment to discuss rules, expectations, and discipline strategies for specific problem behavior.

III. **Your Own Resistance to Team Collaboration** (Discussion)

   A. Indicate that every parent has some resistance to including others in the parenting of their children. Share your own resistance in order to

Figure 8–4. continued

give participants an example of what you mean. Perhaps you consider yourself more interested, better informed, and more capable of helping children than someone else. This attitude, although understandable and maybe even true, nonetheless blocks a team approach to parenting.

B. Request participants to form pairs and share with each other some of their resistance to including others in the parenting of their children.

IV. **How Adults Disqualify Themselves** (Guided Teaching)

A. Illustrate the five major ways adults "disqualify" each other:
- allowing others to parent your children
- keeping a rigid role division
- acting impulsively
- not standing on your own two feet
- directly interfering with the other adult

B. Ask participants to provide examples from their own lives.

V. **Guidelines for Team Parenting** (Read and Discuss)

A. Divide participants into small groups and ask them to read and discuss the handout—"Guidelines for Team Parenting." Be sure to indicate that these are general guidelines—not hard and fast rules.

B. Ask participants to share their questions and comments about the five guidelines. Remind participants that the major activities done in this course are useful to do with their partners.

VI. **Making Requests** (Mental Imagery and Role Playing)

A. Share with participants that they are more likely to practice team parenting if they feel comfortable and skillful making specific requests of other adults.

B. Ask participants to select someone (spouse, relative, teacher, child caretaker, etc.) of whom they wish to make a request. The request should be something they want from that person which will improve their relationship with him or her or his/her relationship with their child. Invite them to relax (perhaps close their eyes) and then ask them to imagine making the request of the person they selected. Ask further, "When would you do it?" (wait 15 seconds) "Where would you be?" . . . "What exactly would you say?" . . . "How do you think the person you selected would respond?" . . . "How would you respond back?" . . . "Can you make your request more specific?"

C. Ask a volunteer to describe the dialogue he or she just imagined. Role play the scene with you as the other person. If the person experiences difficulty, provide coaching.

D. Ask participants to pair off and role play making their request to their partner.

Figure 8–4. continued

VII. Quaker Meeting (Ending Activity)

    A. As a closing event, ask participants to share their completions to any of the following sentence stems:

       1. Something I'm going to do as a result of tonight's session is

       2. I'm still not sure that

       3. Tonight, I learned

    B. Explain that participants can share any of these thoughts as the spirit moves them (as in a Quaker meeting). There is no need to raise hands or agree/disagree with what others have said.

Source: The Confident Parenting Program, 26 Linden Lane, Princeton, NJ 08540.

THE FINER SIDE OF SEQUENCING

Now that we have looked at some basic rules of thumb, we can explore more subtle sequencing issues. A trainer has a number of sequencing choices at his disposal. In this respect, he can be compared to a musical composer. Although a composer follows certain "rules" in writing music, he still has a seemingly endless variety of directions to take. Sometimes, like Beethoven, he may even pull off breaking the basic rules and obtain a stunning result. Likewise, the content you are teaching may seem to dictate a certain logical sequence, but content is not the only determining factor.

Imagine, for example, that you are teaching somebody how to use a manually operated 35-mm camera. If the student knows little about such a camera, what would you do first? We posed this question to several groups of trainers, and the most common response is "start from the beginning"—show how to load film into the camera and then explain the camera's parts (shutter, lens, etc.) and their function. It seems logical, doesn't it? Yet starting at the end could be just as effective. You could show a series of photographs, some unfocused, some too light, some too dark, and so on, then invite your student to speculate about why these results occurred and lead her, in a Socratic fashion, to the unfortunate actions taken by the photographer. Along the way, you could explain the parts of the camera and how they interact to get different results.

In this example, the learner, rather than the content, influences the sequence. By beginning with the end result, you immediately involve the student, stirring up curiosity and grabbing her attention from the start. Nor is this method the only alternative to the more traditional approach. There are many other possibilities. The critical thing is to avoid what Ora Spaid (1986, P. 156) calls "the deadly predictable sameness that shortens attention spans." *The hallmark of active training programs is the variety of sequences employed to keep participants not only awake but also learning.*

Let's consider four ways to alter a training sequence.

1. Your design can go from **the general to the specific** *or* from **the specific to the general.**

You are teaching participants how to establish customer credit. You could define what makes up a good payment record and then give a case example illustrating the positive payment history of one customer. Or you could reverse the sequence by providing the case example followed by the definition.

2. When teaching a procedure, you could start with **the first step** of a procedure *or* **the last step.**

You are teaching participants how to compile a profit-and-loss statement. You could start by explaining the basic elements and proceed with a step-by-step demonstration of how to compile the statement. Or, you could present a completed financial statement and work backwards, showing how the bottom line represents a profit or loss.

3. You could place **an experiential activity** before a content presentation *or* follow a **content presentation** with an experiential exercise.

You have decided to discuss four manipulative communication roles that people play (blaming, distracting, placating, and intellectualizing).

To reinforce the presentation, you have designed a role play in which the different members of groups of four each exhibit one of these roles. Placing the role play before the presentation would allow you to hook participant interest immediately and provide examples to refer to in the presentation. However, placing the role play after the presentation would also work well, helping to clarify (experientially) what has already been presented (didactically).

4. You could teach from **theory to practice** *or* from **practice to theory.**

You begin a counseling module by explaining how direct confrontation increases resistance in defensive employees. You follow your theoretical input with a chance to practice indirect ways to correct performance and lower resistance. Alternatively, you might begin by practicing indirect approaches and then discussing why employee resistance is lower when this strategy is used.

In addition to reversing sequences, you can also place design components in a variety of *positions.* Take, for example, practicing a complex skill. The practice session usually comes **at the end** of a long sequence of explanation and demonstration. If often makes sense, however, to have participants practice a skill **at the beginning** without benefit of prior instruction just to see how well they do. You can then go back and examine the skill, piece by piece. Frequent practice sessions can also occur **during** the explanation and demonstration phase. The trainer can show the skill as a whole, and the participants can practice it; the trainer then focuses on a specific aspect of the skill, and the participants practice the entire skill once again. Each time, the skill is broken down by the trainer further and further, but the participants always attempt to practice it as a whole.

The success of an effective training sequence often lies in the *flow* from one piece of the design to the next. The worst kind of training sequence is a steady progression of topics with little regard for building participant interest, highlighting the links between pieces, recycling earlier material, or concluding satisfactorily. Here are some tips to improve the flow of a design.

1. Use what Ruth Colvin Clark (1989) calls the "Zoom Principle." When introducing participants to new information, given them a broad picture before going into the details. The learner needs what she calls an "advanced organizer" before he can sort new information out. After presenting the big picture, the trainer "zooms in" on some detail, returning

to it periodically to show him how each detail relates to the whole. Clark provides the following example:

- When teaching the customer service representative job to new-hires, you could describe the process flow of work among functional units in the customer service department. Then, you might proceed with an explanation of the representative job, returning at critical moments to the flow chart to show the interfaces between their job and other department functions. The new customer service representative could also be presented with an overview of the major types of customer calls he will be taking and how they relate to each other. Then, as detailed information is given about each call type, the big picture can be presented again, giving more detailed information on how the call types relate to each other.

2. A training sequence should look like a spiral rather than a straight line. Reintroduce later on skills and ideas taught earlier in a sequence. If the skill or idea in question is complex, introduce it first on a simple level and then teach it at greater levels of complexity as the course unfolds. Training in conflict management provides a good example.

- A core skill in conflict management is the ability to listen attentively to one's opponent. Typically, active listening skills are stressed early in the program. As she introduces mediation and negotiation techniques, the trainer can easily point out how active listening is the basis of these more sophisticated tools. Moreover, being in the difficult spot of mediating or negotiating intense conflicts of interest dramatically tests the ability to listen attentively.

3. Avoid the urge to plunge right into an important part of your design. Add a brief activity or short presentation to set up the main event and build motivation. Before an important task, warm up a group with a lighter exercise similar to but not as serious as the one to follow. Sometimes, a shift in the design that widens or redirects the focus is necessary for the next experience to be more effective.

- In team-building or leadership development programs, a crucial moment occurs when each participant is about to receive serious peer feedback about his behavior in the program thus far. The anxiety level of the group rises precipitously. Before giving the final instructions, a trainer decided to present the Johari Window (see figure 4–8). He ended his remarks with an analogy: "Feedback is like a gift. Take it as such. Like any gift, you may not like it. But, if it's from a reputable source, you can always return it 'to the store' without the giver knowing." Inserting this piece into the design helped reduce the tension, and participants were more receptive to their first experience receiving peer feedback.

4. From time to time, build a training sequence around a critical incident, a problem to be solved, or a task to be accomplished rather than around a set of concepts or skills to be learned. Often, trainers employ didactic teaching methods when the participants can learn instead from their own inquiries. Inquiry modes of learning are always more active than trainer-dependent ones.

- Novice bank tellers are required to learn how to identify counterfeit bills. The usual training sequence is an orderly presentation, with handouts, of the flaws to watch for, such as the whiteness of the portrait, broken sawtooth points around the rim of the seal, uneven spacing of the serial numbers, and blurry lines in the scroll work surrounding the numerals. A more active approach would be to ask the trainees to attempt to distinguish between counterfeit and noncounterfeit bills without benefit of prior instruction, sharing their evidence as they do so. The trainer could then point out other telltale signs of forgery. Yet another approach would be to request the trainees to examine some genuine bills and develop hypotheses about how they are printed to discourage counterfeiting.

5. Closing a training sequence can be climactic or reflective. Sometimes a sequence should end with a bang to emphasize the accomplishment. A dramatic finish can consist of a scintillating final lecture, an intergroup competition, a role play that serves as a dress rehearsal for later application, a challenging case study, and so on. At other times, however, it may be more appropriate to wind down by processing reactions to the material, making connections to skills previously learned, or generating final questions about topics that are still unclear.

- In designing the closing of a training module on how to assess the roles played by members of an alcoholic family, the trainer had two ideas. One was to end with a live interview of a family in treatment, so that, watching and listening, participants could test in their minds how they would assess the family roles in an actual situation. The trainer would easily be able to arrange such an experience, and it certainly would be memorable. His other idea was to end with a panel discussion in which participants would take turns answering questions posed by the moderator (i.e., the trainer). There was insufficient time for two ending events, so the trainer selected the second because it would serve well to help participants review what they had learned.

Opportunities for testing this knowledge, he reasoned, could come later in the training program.

EXPERIENTIAL LEARNING SEQUENCES

The sequencing of strongly experiential training requires special consideration. In such training, learning flows not from didactic presentations but from what participants discover for themselves as a result of powerful experiences that the trainer has designed for them. William Pfeiffer and Arlette Ballew call it "an *inductive* process proceeding from observation rather than from *a priori* 'truth' (as in the *deductive* process)" (1988, p. 3). They go on to describe a five-step experiential learning sequence:

1. **Experiencing:** Participants engage in one or more structured experiences.
2. **Publishing:** Participants share their personal reactions and observations concerning the experience(s).
3. **Processing:** Participants discuss patterns and dynamics that occurred in the experience(s).
4. **Generalizing:** Participants infer principles about the real world based on what they learned from the experience(s).
5. **Applying:** Participants plan more effective behavior back on the job.

Any experiential training sequence can incorporate some of these steps. When time permits, all five should be taken for maximum learning to occur.

The best way to explain each step is with an example. As mentioned in chapter 6, many games resemble the classic competition/cooperation exercise, the Prisoner's Dilemma. One example is appropriately called The Game of Life. Figure 8–5 presents the instructions.

Figure 8–5. The Game of Life

This game should be played by six groups of any size, although adjustments can be made to accommodate fewer groups. Each group should have approximately the same number of players. The objective is for each group "to win as much as it can."

Procedure

There are six rounds to the game. For each round, each group chooses either Y or X (without knowing what the other groups have chosen) and writes its choice on a slip of paper. All slips are handed to the trainer who tallies them and announces the results. Each group's payoff depends on the combination of choices made by the groups. For six groups, there are seven possible combinations:

Combinations	*Payoffs*
All choose *X*	All lose $2
Five choose *X*; one chooses *Y*	*X*s win $2; *Y* loses $10
Four choose *X*; two choose *Y*	*X*s win $4; *Y* loses $8
Three choose *X*; three choose *Y*	*X*s win $6; *Y*s lose $6
Two choose *X*; four choose *Y*	*X*s win $8; *Y*s lose $4
One chooses *X*; five choose *Y*	*X* wins $10; *Y*s lose $2
All choose *Y*	All win $2

Other payoff schedules can easily be generated for fewer than six groups.

After the third and fifth rounds, allowance is made for a ten-minute negotiation session among single representatives from any group that wishes to participate. The negotiations, if held, should be loud enough for everyone in the room to hear. Before these opportunities for negotiation, the trainer announces that the payoff (wins and losses) will be tripled, for the fourth round, and tenfold, for the sixth (last) round.

After **experiencing** The Game of Life, participants will have many reactions, especially anger at teams that did not cooperate (rarely, do the six groups choose to cooperate by all choosing *Y*) and disdain for any groups that used deceit. Some participants will protest that "it's only a game," while others will take it very seriously. **Publishing** these reactions and observations is a critical first step in realizing the potential of this experiential activity.

In the **processing** stage, participants begin to have many insights. They note that the world is not simply divided into good guys and bad guys. They understand that behaviors could have occurred during the negotiations that would have inspired trust and cooperation. They also observe how groups that were losing heavily often behaved like victims and failed to see that they had the power to turn their fortunes around.

After achieving these insights, participants can be helped to do some **generalizing.** Among the principles and learnings that might emerge are that:

- all parties in an organization are responsible for creating its ultimate climate.
- the actions of one unit invariably affect the actions of the others.
- groups with power are reluctant to negotiate.
- negotiation is most effective when each side acknowledges its needs in a straightforward fashion and acknowledges its differences with others in a nonblaming manner.

At this point, participants are usually motivated to start **applying** the experience to their own organization(s). When all participants belong to the same organization, discussion can address the intergroup competition within their own ranks and ways to alleviate it. When participants come from different organizations, individual participants can share case situations for the advice and counsel of peers.

As you can see, this experiential learning cycle allows you to base an entire training sequence on one experience. Two ingredients are key to an effective sequence: a structured **experience** that is rich in potential and a set of **questions** to follow it up, including (1) What happened? (2) How did you feel about it? (3) What did you observe about your behavior and the behavior of others during this experience? (4) What can we learn from this experience? and (5) How can you apply these learnings to your life or work?

Worksheet

SEQUENCING TRAINING ACTIVITIES

Consider all of the sequencing ideas in this chapter and select one or more to use in designing or redesigning your own training module. Outline your thoughts below.

Objectives:

_____ Obtaining a different mix of activities
_____ Improving the flow
_____ Reversing commonly used sequences
_____ Altering placement of activities
_____ Improving beginnings and endings
_____ Providing experiential learning cycles

Outline:

_____

_____

_____

_____

_____

_____

_____

_____

_____

_____

_____

_____

_____

_____

_____

_____

_____

PROVIDING FOR BACK-ON-THE-JOB

APPLICATION

9

What truly separates effective training programs from ineffective ones is the explicit attention given to back-on-the-job (or back-home) application. The "Now what?" phase is often the most neglected part of a training design. In this phase, participants determine how they personally want to change what they do, think, or feel as a result of the training designs you have taken them through. The "Now what?" phase is also the most difficult part of training, both in the design and implementation. Happily, there are many ways to design your program so that the training sticks and back-on-the-job application occurs. Our suggestions will cover three time periods: **before the training event begins, while it is in progress,** and **as it concludes.**

PRIOR TO THE TRAINING PROGRAM

Perhaps the single best insurance policy you might obtain to assure that participants will transfer what they have learned from classroom to job is to pretrain their supervisors. When supervisors receive such training, they are able to serve not merely as managers but also as mentors. They are available as coaches, role models, and encouragers.

Of course, such an insurance policy is expensive and hard to come by. Yet, while it is rare to pretrain supervisors, frequently you will have the chance to brief them about the training their employees are receiving. In such briefings, it is important for you to discuss the following:

1. The objectives of the training program
2. The course outline
3. The kinds of training activities utilized in the program
4. Course materials
5. Suggestions for facilitating further practice and application of skills

Another way to make supervisors your allies is to enlist their cooperation with regard to any precourse preparation you may ask of their employees. Giving the participants time off from their regular responsibilities to read advance materials or complete precourse assignments is a real contribution. It is even better when supervisors sit down with their employees and help them define a personal case problem or two to bring to the training program. This problem then becomes the basis for real-life problem solving in your instruction. Here is such a case.

• For a course in managing difficult employee behavior, the trainer requested participants to write up brief descriptions of two incidents in which subordinates acted irresponsibly. These incidents were to be discussed in small groups during the program and were also to serve as a basis for role-playing exercises. The trainer asked participants to select incidents in consultation with their own supervisors. After the training program, they would then be able to share with their bosses what they had learned.

Prior to the training program, it is also possible to ask participants and their supervisors to select a project to undertake as a result of what participants will have learned. Coming to the training program with a project in mind that has already been discussed with upper management means that back-on-job application is built into the program design.

DURING THE TRAINING PROGRAM

As you teach new skills, there are certain things you can do to promote retention and on-the-job application. Our first tip is to *allow enough practice time for skill mastery*. Some trainers have a tendency to move quickly from skill to skill without enough rehearsal. For example, they may give participants the opportunity to role-play how to conduct a hiring interview and provide (or have peers provide) feedback on the performance but neglect to provide a chance for participants to redo the role play based on the feedback received. Some degree of overlearning is required for participants to feel confident about exercising a new skill. Skill mastery is like the process of breaking in new shoes. At first, it feels unnatural but, with enough wear, it begins to feel comfortable. Confidence grows even more when participants master exercises of increasing levels of difficulty. Eventually, they feel that they truly own the skill. Here is a case in point.

- In a training program on conflict mediation, participants practice mediation skills in a variety of situations. Experience has shown that, when role-playing practice is limited to certain types of clients, trainees often have difficulty applying the skills in real life, where clients vary considerably. Because of this, a conflict mediation trainer designed a series of role plays that included a broad range of clients. Participants underwent two days of videotaped practice before seeing (under supervision) real clients. Frequently, role plays were redone after video feedback. Participants were pleased by the ample opportunity to practice and felt confident that they were ready for the real thing.

Participants are more apt to use skills back on the job if they have been able to practice them realistically. The more similar the training situation is to the back-on-the-job situation, the more likely it is to last. Even recreating the physical environment of the job can be helpful. For example, bank teller training is greatly enhanced if the classroom is fitted with realistic teller stations.

As participants learn new skills, they should be encouraged to express their attitudes about the skills being taught and their feelings about their performance. Paradoxically, participants are less likely to resist changes if they have the chance to express their reservations and trepidations about them. Some trainers hard sell the value of the skills, ideas, and procedures that they are advocating. It is far better to encourage participants to draw their own conclusions—ultimately, it is they who will decide whether to use what you have taught them. Here is a case example in which this process was encouraged.

- Using a fishbowl design, a trainer invited participants to examine their feelings about his company's performance appraisal system. One-third of the group was asked to participate in the first fishbowl discussion. The trainer suggested that they begin by describing their positive and negative reactions to the system. After ten minutes, the second third was brought into the fishbowl to react to the discussion of the first group. Then, the final third replaced its predecessors and wrapped up the discussion. By providing ample time to air viewpoints, the trainer gave a clear message about his respect for the participants' views.

Our final tip can be implemented if you are able to arrange for time back on the job between training sessions. *Give assignments to be completed in the participants' own work settings.* When you resume the training, you can ask participants to share how well the real-life practice went and to pose any questions they may still have about the skills they have been learning.

- In a course on overcoming shyness, the trainer requested that participants complete a between-sessions practice sheet. The sheet required participants to identify one situation that occurred between sessions in which they attempted to be less shy than usual. Also required was information about who else was present, what the participants said and/or did, what they wished they had done instead (if anything), how they felt during the situation, and how they felt after the situation.

AT THE END OF THE TRAINING PROGRAM

Before ending the training program, you can employ several strategies to encourage application back on the job.

SELF-ASSESSMENT

Ask participants to evaluate what they have learned about themselves, including their knowledge, behavior, and attitudes. Taking stock of oneself is a great motivator of change. A wide variety of techniques can help participants with their self-assessment. Make use of questionnaires, post-tests, or final role-play performances. Even gamelike activities, such as the one below, can be appropriate.

- At the end of a one-week management development program, participants evaluated the extent to which they saw themselves along three style spectrums: (1) *directive* versus *delegating;* (2) *well planned* versus *spontaneous;* and (3) *challenging* versus *nonthreatening.* For each spectrum, they were asked to stand up and place themselves in a line according to how they viewed themselves. For example, if they saw themselves as more directive than other participants, they went to the head of the line. By contrast, if they saw themselves as more delegating than others, they went to the rear of the line. Participants who did not identify clearly with either choice were to place themselves somewhere in the middle. Each physical continuum was discussed, with participants disclosing their reasons for placing themselves where they did and commenting on their self-peers' placement. Finally, they were asked if they wanted to change their "place in the line" and to indicate what they would need to do back on the job to achieve this.

JOB OR BACK-HOME AIDS

Job or back-home aids include checklists, worksheets, and a variety of other forms that are used as course materials. These aids provide a structure for participants to apply what they have learned in the course. Job or back-home aids are most effective when they are explained and tried out first in the course itself.

- Participants in a management training program were given the checklist in figure 9–1 to use in preparing their upcoming interviews with problem employees.

Figure 9–1. Corrective Interviews Checklist

1. Begin on a positive note.
2. State your purpose.
3. Identify the changes desired.
4. Obtain and listen to the employee's point of view.
5. Get agreement.
6. Involve the employee in generating solutions.
7. Have the employee summarize corrective actions.
8. Express support and encouragement.

REENTRY ADVICE

Any training program might end with a closing session on reentry advice. Such a session should present some realistic first steps for applying the training back home or on the job. First steps might include setting up a meeting with one's supervisor to discuss the training program and how to use it, consciously identifying tasks that would use skills learned in the program, or networking with others who have taken the course or similar courses to compare experiences and applications.

- As a program on improving technical training skills was ending, the training consultant advised the employees of a large retail organization to begin observing each others' work. He urged the group to adopt this practice as the best way to build support and continued reinforcement for what they had learned in the training program.

OBSTACLE ASSESSMENT

Future planning must include a realistic assessment of the obstacles to applying training. Just as any dieter will have a hard time resisting a midnight snack, so a participant subjected to the pressures of his job may slip back into his old ways of doing things. The most common obstacle is a lack of support from peers, supervisors, or others on the job. Another common obstacle is a lack of time to apply new skills consciously, assess how they've been used, and get feedback from others. In addition to offering reentry advice, a training program should build in some time for participants to discuss some of the obstacles they expect to meet and ways to overcome them.

- A stress management trainer was so concerned about the obstacles to carrying out the techniques she had taught participants that she decided on an unusual strategy. Instead of giving her usual pep talk at the end of the course, she asked participants to predict the circumstances of their first moment of faltering. Using a mental imagery approach, she encouraged participants to visualize the scene in great detail. She then asked them to develop positive images of coping with the situation that they would be able to keep in their mind's eye when the predicted negative scenario began to unfold in the actual work setting.

PEER CONSULTATION

One of the best designs we know to bring together the learnings from a training program and to encourage their back-on-the-job application involves peer consultation. Participants are arranged in small groups for the purpose of discussing a specific back-home issue of each of the members. After each issue is clarified, the client (the participant with the issue) receives advice from the consultants (the other group members). This process gives participants the opportunity to summarize and apply the knowledge and skills they have gained and to try out their new expertise.

- At the end of a workshop on managing cultural diversity, participants were formed into quartets. Each participant took turns being a client with a specific problem (based on her own work situation) concerning racism or sexism. The job of the other group members was to recall and select concepts and action ideas examined earlier in the workshop that might apply to the problem posed by the client. By taking part in this process of peer consultation, participants were able to prove their expertise to one another and to pull together the content of the workshop.

PEER TEACHING

An excellent way to master new ideas and skills is to try to teach them to someone else. Teaching others is also bound to increase one's own commitment to actually using what is being taught. Consequently, there is considerable benefit in encouraging participants to present what you have taught them to others. This can be done within the program by assigning participants to different projects and having them present their findings to others in the training group. Participants may also be able to present the material to peers back on the job who have not yet received the training.

- One-half of a sales staff was given training in how to build rapport with different types of clients. Each participant was then paired up with a salesperson who had not received the training. Pairs were expected to meet with each other three times to share the ideas and skills gained from the training. The trained salespeople did such a good job that it was unnecessary to conduct a program for the other half of the staff.

SELF-MONITORING

A well-known technique in behavior modification is to request the client to monitor his own behaviors. For example, in a weight-loss program, a client might be asked to note in writing everything he eats on the assumption that increased awareness will bring about greater self-control. Likewise, you could suggest to participants that they closely monitor their own behavior back on the job as a way to make training benefits last. Keeping a personal diary is one way to perform self-monitoring. The use of ready-made checklists is another approach. Whatever tools are chosen should ideally be tried out before the training program ends so that the participants can gain comfort and understanding of the procedure.

- At the end of a business writing seminar, the trainer asked participants to design their own checklist for monitoring their future business memos. The training group received guidelines on checklist construction and a sample checklist as a working model. The trainer then divided the group into teams, each of which developed a series of checklist questions covering such areas as organization (e.g., "Have I used subheadings?"), conciseness (e.g., "Do I make my point in the fewest words possible?"), sentence and paragraph length (e.g., "Do I use too many choppy sentences?" or "Are my paragraphs short?"), redundancy (e.g., "Do I repeat ideas instead of elaborating them?"), phrasing (e.g., "Have I used antiquated phrases like 'pursuant to your request'?"), passive language (e.g., "How tentative is my language?"), tone (e.g. "Is my style conversational or stuffy?"), spelling (e.g., "Is the memo free of spelling errors?"), and grammar (e.g., "Do my subjects and predicates agree?"). Each participant then devised a checklist suited to her needs based on the input of the group.

CONTRACTING

A popular device for promoting the application of training is a simple written expression of the intent to change one's behavior in some respect or to undertake a particular action appropriate to the goals of the training program. The contract can be made with oneself or with others (a co-participant, the trainer, one's boss, or a colleague). The format of the contract can be formal ("The undersigned hereby commits himself to . . .") or informal (a letter to oneself). Often, trainers will offer to collect the contracts and mail them back to participants for review in one month. Pairing participants, who commit themselves to exchanging contracts and supporting each other, is an excellent way to conduct this process. A follow-up phone call or get-together helps to cement the contract.

- The peer contract in figure 9–2 was used in a time management seminar.

Figure 9–2. Peer Contract

As a result of our training on time management, I want to incorporate the following ideas into my work:

1.

2.

3.

4.

Signed _____

I will follow up with the above person in one month.

Signed _____

Date _____

ACTION PLANS

A more detailed tool for future application is the action plan. In this approach, the participant defines appropriate outcomes and steps to achieve them as a result of the training program. Obstacles are anticipated as well. In a work setting, an action plan is often utilized as a mechanism by which the participant and her supervisor agree on a project that has benefits for the organization. An action plan can also be viewed as a self-motivational tool for the employee without specific monitoring by the supervisor.

Figure 9–3 presents a basic format for generating an action plan.

Figure 9–3. Developing an Action Plan

1. List three actions you would like to undertake as a result of this program.

   a.

   b.

   c.

2. Choose the action that you would like to plan to do first and enter it below.

3. List the potential roadblocks to implementing this action.

4. Discuss with your seat partner how you might overcome these roadblocks.
5. Describe in detail the action you will undertake and the steps you will take to ensure that it will happen.

Action plans have the virtue of pushing the writer to be clear about what he is going to do. In the form in figure 9–4, the writer is asked to specify how and when he will assert himself in the near future.

Figure 9–4. An Assertive Action Plan

I want to be more assertive with *(person's name and title)* in this situation:

The skills I will use:

Roadblocks that could get in the way:

Sample script/conversation:

I will make my first attempt by *(date)*

Figure 9–5 reproduces an elaborate example of action planning used in a management development program. It involves a serious commitment on the part of the participant and others in the organization to apply what has been learned in the training program and simultaneously to benefit the organization.

Figure 9–5. Action Plan Design and Development Guidelines

Directions for Use

One of the greatest shortcomings of management development programs is the absence of any tools to measure their effectiveness. To be sure, the participants can complete an evaluation sheet that asks what the participants like most, least, and so on. However, such questions are not able to fully gauge the impact of training.

The only true measure of impact is the degree to which the participants return and use the skills learned in the program. In order for this to happen, two conditions must be met:

- The participant must work on a plan of action that spells out the specific steps for implementing change.
- This plan is shared with the Mentor and Manager and supported by them.

This ACTION PLAN is designed to assist participants in meeting these two conditions, thereby enabling both them and XYZ to realize a return on the investment made through participation in the program.

. . .

Subject

Many topics are covered in this module. Select a project (one of those covered or one of your own) that you plan to focus on. As you complete your ACTION PLAN, try to be as specific as possible in stating your subject. For example, if you were writing an ACTION PLAN for Communications, "Written Communication" would be too broad. A more specific subject would be, "Developing a Highlight Report Format for the Department."

Within the subject you have selected, state your purpose or reason for doing so. This will be a brief description of your intent or goal. Using the example above, "Developing a Highlight Report Format," the goal might look like this: "Highlight Reports contain numerous details. They need to be organized so that the details appear in a logical sequence. After obtaining permission from my Manager, I plan to format one of my Manager's Highlight Reports using an eye opener, transition one, supporting details, transition two, and action conclusion."

Goals are stated in broad terms: objectives are quite specific and should include measures by which your progress toward them can be measured. Objectives are the things you must achieve (deadlines, performance indices, etc.) in order to meet your goal. Building on the same example, the objective might look like this: "To spend one day formatting a Highlight Report that can be used as a model for subsequent Highlight Reports."

Figure 9–5. continued

To achieve your goal, you must schedule activities to move toward your goal. This section is your blueprint and timetable for reaching the goal. Following our example above, the activities list might look like this:

ACTIVITIES	TIME
1. Meet with Mentor to explain my ACTION PLAN.	1. One morning next week—two hours.
2. Meet with my Manager to explain my ACTION PLAN and obtain three latest Highlight Reports written by Manager.	2. One morning next week—two hours (after meeting with Mentor).
3. Read over my Manager's Highlight Reports.	3. Two hours following week.
4. Develop a format for organizing a Highlight Report.	4. Two hours same week as 3.
5. After obtaining necessary facts, data, etc., write an actual Highlight Report for my Manager.	5. Four hours—before Highlight Report is due.

As you carry out your schedule of activities, problems or barriers inevitably occur. Sometimes these can be anticipated in advance. Others may not. This section of the plan asks you to list and number all problems, present and potential, that you foresee as barriers to completing your activities.

Next, state how you plan to deal with each, numbering each solution to agree with the problem it addresses. Following our example, this section might look like this:

PROBLEMS	SOLUTIONS
1. Manager may not be able to get me all the facts, data needed to complete actual Highlight Report.	1. Work directly with Manager in writing Highlight Report.

Resources

Some ACTION PLANS are easy to carry out, requiring no resources other than your own time. Others may need help to be implemented (your Manager, other professionals, other Managers, etc.) This section asks you to detail other sources you are depending on.

Figure 9–5. continued

Costs/Benefits

Some activities you plan may involve a cost to the organization. If you don't know actual costs, estimate them. For example, the cost of completing our sample ACTION PLAN involves "Word Processing Services from Support Staff." Then list the payoffs you expect to realize from carrying out the ACTION PLAN. Some may be intangible (improved morale, systematic approach, increase in performance, better customer service, etc.). If possible, estimate the dollar value of your benefits, both tangible and intangible. For example, one benefit of the plan is "developing a format usable in writing Highlight Reports."

Commitment

Finally, the last section asks you, your Mentor, and your Manager to make a commitment to carry out the plan. As described in the directions, you will review the plan with your Mentor and agree upon any changes. Then you will want to review the plan with your Manager.

Then you, your Mentor, and your Manager should sign the plan confirming your intent to carry out the plan. You should set one or more dates for reviewing progress.

Source: Training Management Corporation, 245 Nassau Street, Princeton, NJ 08540.

Worksheet

FOSTERING BACK-ON-THE-JOB APPLICATION

Now is your chance to think about strategies for back-on-the-job or back-home application of your training program. Use this worksheet to guide your planning.

Strategies prior to the Program:

_____

_____

_____

_____

Strategies during the Program:

_____

_____

_____

_____

Strategies at the end of the Program:

_____ Self-assessment

_____ Job or back-home aids

_____ Reentry advice

_____ Obstacle assessment

_____ Peer consultation

_____ Peer teaching

_____ Self-monitoring

_____ Contracting

_____ Action plans

Notes:

_____

_____

_____

_____

PLANNING ACTIVE TRAINING PROGRAMS

10

At this point in the design of your active training program, you've established your objectives and designed and sequenced activities to support them. You've also taken into consideration back-on-the-job or back-home application of the skills your program is intended to teach. You have now reached the point where you can organize all of your design ideas on a given topic into a complete program. This final step in designing involves the creation of the outer shell of the program, sometimes referred to as the *macrodesign*.

THE MACRODESIGN OF AN ACTIVE TRAINING PROGRAM

Back in the introduction to part 1, we proposed that an active training program was characterized by:

- a moderate level of content
- a balance between affective, behavioral, and cognitive learning

- a variety of learning approaches
- opportunities for group participation
- utilization of participants' expertise
- a recycling of earlier learned concepts and skills
- real-life problem solving
- allowance for reentry planning

With the above characteristics in mind, we would like to present a macrodesign for a total program. If your time is limited, it may be difficult to employ all five aspects of this plan. In this case, you might eliminate the middle and advanced activities.

OPENING EXERCISES

Design activities that build interest in the entire course and introduce some of the major ideas of the first part of the program. Also use this time for group building and learning about the participants. An initial case study that invites participants to start thinking about the subject matter may be a good starting point. This is also the time to solicit participants' initial questions about the topic being studied. If the course is skill oriented, ask participants to try out the skills without the benefit of prior instruction just to see how well they do.

BUILDING BLOCKS

Design activities that teach the basic knowledge and/or skills as well as explore the attitudes and feelings about the topic. Actively involve participants by interspersing lecture presentations with opportunities for group participation. Utilize alternative methods to lecturing and experiential learning approaches for variety.

MIDDLE ACTIVITIES

Design activities that help participants review the building blocks and introduce ideas to be covered at the next stage of the program. Role-playing, simulation, observation exercises, case studies, assigned projects, and other comparable methods can be featured.

ADVANCED KNOWLEDGE/SKILLS

Design activities that teach the course material at a more advanced level. Emphasize real-world problem solving. Be careful to recycle information and skills presented earlier. Be especially mindful of utilizing the participants' expertise. Draw out their feelings about what they are learning.

APPLICATION ACTIVITIES

Design activities that help participants test their knowledge and skill and encourage them to apply these to new problems and on-the-job (or back-home) situations. Allow time for goal setting, action planning, and consideration of on-the-job or back-home application issues.

A CASE EXAMPLE OF AN ACTIVE TRAINING PROGRAM

To illustrate this five-part macrodesign, we have chosen to present in figure 10–1 an actual training program on coaching and counseling skills that was designed by the authors as part of an ongoing development program for a group of new managers in a large pharmaceutical company. The details of each activity have been eliminated so that you can easily follow the general outline of the macrodesign. As you read this outline, keep in mind that the program design was developed as an intensive two-day seminar. If the program had been longer in duration or allowed for time back on the job during it, the specific designs of each section could have been quite different. A program you are designing may differ because of the nature of your training topic, your assessment of participants, and your overall training objectives. Still, you should find this macrodesign adaptable to your situation.

Figure 10–1. Coaching and Counseling Program

This two-day program is designed to increase a manager's skills as a coach and as a counselor. As a coach, the manager identifies a need among employees for instruction and direction, usually directly related to their current work assignments—for example, an employee may be having difficulty learning a new computer system. In a coaching relationship, employees are open to advice and show little defensiveness. As a counselor, the manager identifies a problem that is interfering with the work performance of his employees—for example, an employee may be suffering from burnout and lack interest in her work. A manager needs to switch from a coaching to a counseling mode when employees are *not* as open to his input. In a counseling relationship, the manager builds trust by approaching the employee in an especially supportive, nonthreatening manner.

This program gives equal weight to affective, behavioral, and cognitive aspects of the topic. It builds on training that participants have already received about

Figure 10–1. continued

the Myers-Briggs Type Indicator, a tool in which the effects of one's own personality type on one's performance as a manager can be been examined.

I. **Opening Exercises**
    A. *Introduction and Objectives*
        1. Key Terms
           a. **Coaching**
           b. **Counseling**
        2. Objectives
           a. To value the role that coaching and counseling play in a manager's work
           b. To learn and practice coaching skills
           c. To learn and practice counseling skills

(The trainer begins with remarks about the terms "coaching" and "counseling" and shares her objectives with the training group.)

    B. *The Role of Coaching and Counseling*
        1. *Discussion:* Experiences being coached and counseled by others and opinions about effective and ineffective approaches
        2. *Activity:* Identifying specific examples in which coaching and counseling have (or might) take place in participants' work as managers
        3. *Discussion:* Participant views on the benefits of coaching and counseling
        4. *Videotape:* "Coaching and Counseling" (an overview of the two skills)

(This section is a sequence of activities designed to achieve group building, on-the-spot assessment, and immediate learning involvement. Although participants already know each other, they become reacquainted by discussing their prior experiences and current views. At the same time, the trainer can assess participants' attitudes about the training topic. The video is used not only to clarify further the distinction between coaching and counseling but also to stimulate interest in further skill development.)

II. **Building Blocks**
    A. *Coaching Employees*
        1. *Activity:* Paper-tearing exercise
        2. *Activity:* Observing a role play demonstration in which someone is learning something new

Figure 10–1. continued

3. *Activity:* Dyadic practice in teaching a new skill or procedure
4. *Discussion:* Myers-Briggs and coaching: implications

(The first major training sequence begins with an exercise demonstrating common foibles in coaching another person. Participants are then asked to observe effective coaching procedures and apply what they have observed in teaching a skill or procedure (from their real-life work situation) to another participant. The sequence concludes with an interesting exchange between participants with contrasting MBTI profiles concerning the needs each has in a coaching situation.)

B. *Counseling Employees*

1. *Discussion:* Feelings about counseling others
2. *Lecturette:* Guidelines for giving performance feedback
3. *Activity:* Practicing feedback skills
4. *Discussion:* Myers-Briggs and counseling: implications
5. *Activity:* Learning to listen actively, reflect back what people are saying, and ask probing questions
6. *Demonstration:* A counseling interview
7. *Activity:* Practicing counseling interviews

(The second training sequence begins with an affective consideration of the problems inherent in counseling employees. It then presents basic counseling skills (feedback, listening, questioning, reflecting) and provides opportunities for practice. In the middle of the sequence is a second discussion of the Myers-Briggs Type Indicator, this time examining how contrasting styles affect the success of the counseling process.)

III. Middle Activities

A. *Case Review Problem*

1. *Activity:* Determining whether a case situation requires coaching or counseling and outlining the actions needed
2. *Discussion:* Questions that remain concerning when and how coaching and counseling skills should be applied

(Before launching into advanced topics, the trainer asks participants to reflect on what they have learned by clarifying their understanding of the respective roles of coaching and counseling.)

IV. Advanced Skills

A. *More Issues in Coaching and Counseling*

1. *Demonstration:* Dealing with anger and resistance
2. *Activity:* Practicing dealing with anger and resistance

Figure 10–1. continued

3. *Demonstration:* Motivating higher performance

4. *Activity:* Practicing motivating higher performance

5. *Discussion:* Feelings of confidence and trepidation about coaching and counseling

6. *Activity:* Behavior rehearsals: performing, critiquing, and redoing role plays of a variety of coaching and counseling situations

(The purpose of this section of the program is not only to consider new issues (anger/ resistance and motivating higher performance) but also to process emerging feelings and polish difficult skills. The last two activities recognize that coaching and counseling are a confluent mixture of affective and behavioral elements. Participants are asked to rehearse their newfound skills in a variety of situations to maximize the transfer of training back on the job.)

V. Ending Activities

A. *Peer Consultation*

1. *Activity:* Using fellow participants as consultants on back-on-the-job problems with difficult employees

B. *Action Planning*

1. *Discussion:* Steps to ensure retention of skills

2. *Activity:* Developing a self-contract for improving coaching and counseling skills

(By asking participants to act as consultants for each other, the peer consultation activity becomes a review of the knowledge participants have gained. Action planning is incorporated into the design to motivate back-on-the-job application.)

Worksheet

PLANNING AN ENTIRE ACTIVE TRAINING PROGRAM

Use the space provided in this worksheet to outline a total active training program of your own. Check the result against the characteristics of an active training program.

Opening Exercises

_____

_____

_____

_____

_____

_____

Building Blocks

_____

_____

_____

_____

_____

_____

Middle Activities

_____

_____

_____

_____

_____

_____

Advanced Skills

_____

_____

_____

_____

_____

_____

Ending Activities

_____

_____

_____

_____

_____

_____

Qualities of my program:

_____ Moderate level of content

_____ Balance between affective, behavioral, and cognitive learning

_____ Variety of learning approaches

_____ Opportunities for group participation

_____ Utilization of participants' expertise

_____ Recycling of earlier learned concepts and skills

_____ Real-life problem solving

_____ Allowance for reentry planning

CONDUCTING AN ACTIVE TRAINING PROGRAM

II

You can build active learning into the design of your program, but it is in the delivery of that program that your efforts are truly tested. As we have already stressed, designing is not complete at the time of delivery. Instead, the delivery phase of a training program is a period of continual adjusting, refining, and redesigning.

Ensuring the successful delivery of a training program is a process that actually begins before the participants arrive. Preparation is one of the most important ingredients for success. Since much will happen during the actual program, you need to make sure that materials and equipment are ready and that the physical layout of the training room is suitable. As the trainer of this event, you need to be mentally prepared as well. Greeting participants, establishing early rapport, presenting your training agenda, and inviting feedback are also important beginning steps.

Once that you have *connected* with your participants, you then have the opportunity to *lead* them through the program. Your credibility as a leader depends on your ability to set group norms, eliminate training time-wasters, get the group's attention, win over wary participants, and manage difficult behaviors. This can be a forbidding task for many trainers. Fortunately, there are many techniques to help you gain control and establish yourself as an effective leader of the training group.

The challenge of delivering an active training program is most apparent during the middle section of the program, when the majority of your content is covered. Here, you have two different roles as a trainer: one as a *stimulator* when you give presentations and lead discussions and the other as a *facilitator* as you guide participants through structured activities. At this point, your success will depend upon how well you present information, lead discussions, direct participants through structured exercises, and make effective transitions from one event in the program to the other.

Concluding a training program can be as difficult as beginning one. Key skills involve how you review the program, handle remaining questions, guide reentry planning, and evaluate training results.

The five chapters that constitute part 2 focus directly on your actions in the training room as you conduct active training programs. Chapter 11 tells how to prepare yourself mentally and arrange the physical layout of the classroom and illustrates four ways to establish immediate rapport with participants and introduce the program. Chapter 12 suggests ways to foster constructive group norms, control timing and pacing, avoid confrontations, assert positive authority, and utilize humor to handle difficult situations that occur in training programs. Chapter 13 describes ways to overcome anxiety, make eye contact, maintain natural and positive body language and voice quality, handle props, and make smooth transitions. It also outlines a ten-point menu of training behaviors that facilitate discussion. Chapter 14 explains how to motivate participants to buy into a training activity, how to give clear instructions, how to manage group behavior, and how to assist participants in processing what they have learned and examining its implications. Finally, chapter 15 identifies techniques for reviewing program content, eliciting final questions and concerns, promoting self-assessment, focusing on back-on-the-job application, and expressing final sentiments. Specifically, it describes how to obtain ongoing feedback and determine the focus, tools, and timing of evaluation.

Each of these chapters is filled with examples of how the ideas it contains have been translated into many different types of training programs covering a wide variety of content areas. Every chapter also ends with a worksheet where you can practice applying the suggestions to your training situation.

At times, it will be helpful to refer back to design ideas in part 1 as you apply the advice we give. We will alert you to instances where material from part 1 should be considered side by side with material from part 2.

BEGINNING AN ACTIVE TRAINING PROGRAM

11

You have assessed your group participants in advance, designed course objectives and activities, and are now ready to conduct your active training program. If you have designed some effective opening exercises, you're likely to have a strong beginning. For added insurance, however, it is wise to think about these questions: How are you going to arrange the physical setup of your facility? How are you going to establish rapport with participants as they walk in the door? What are you going to say to introduce your program?

No training program can be totally successful based upon the written design alone. Programs that look gorgeous on paper are worthless if the trainer does not have the delivery skills to carry out the design requirements. In this chapter, we will give you tips for conducting the beginning portion of a previously designed training program.

PREPARING YOURSELF MENTALLY

All trainers are a little nervous when starting a program. However, the anticipation of preparing to train rather then the training itself is usually the worst part. If you have planned your activities and are well organized, the butterflies will probably settle down. If, on the other hand, you have left preparation details until the last minute and have not thought out your design carefully, you will have a far greater chance of losing the confidence you will need to sell the group on your ideas.

The preparation of materials and activities for a training program may begin days or weeks before the participants walk into the classroom. Typical preparations include determining the date and time for the course, reproducing manuals and course materials, arranging for room space and audiovisual equipment, and confirming course attendance. People who are not directly involved with training usually don't consider all of the little things that go into making a program successful—that is, until something like a miscommunicated date and time or a training room without enough chairs interferes with the conduct of the session. Attention to all of the details establishes an atmosphere of order, organization, and professionalism.

In addition to preparation, you will find that making the effort to connect with participants before you begin will reduce your tension and build your confidence. This way you avoid the self-absorption that breeds anxiety. Remember that it is the participants who are responsible for acquiring skills or information from the training experience. They are present not to be impressed by you but to take something away with them when they leave the training session. Here is a case of someone who needed this advice.

- One trainer in a large service organization was famous for theatrics during his one-day training programs. Employees were always anxious to sign up for his classes because they were known to be fun. The trainer's style seemed to be effective until he was asked to deliver a five-day program for midlevel managers. After three days, the theatrics had worn thin, and attendance began to drop. By the fifth day, the trainer had lost half of his group, and the participants who remained weren't able to demonstrate anything except that they had been entertained by the experience.

Another consideration is your own comfort with the course content. Creating a training program from scratch and delivering it for the first time can be tremendously exciting as you participate in the learning process step by step with the participants. The drawback to presenting new material is the hesitancy and uncertainty with which you may deliver the course.

If you are not well versed in the subject matter, you might be especially concerned about handling questions from the participants. Remind yourself that one way to field questions to which you don't know the complete answers is to draw upon group expertise: throw the question out to the group as a whole to determine if they can discover the answer collectively. Another approach is to write down any questions to which you cannot respond immediately and promise to find out the answers. Make sure to get back to the participants as soon as you have the correct answers to their questions. Here is an example of how one trainer fielded a participant's question.

- "How will our documents be archived once that the new system is in place?"

  "I'm not sure that I can answer that question right now. I'll have to check with our systems administrator to find out how archiving will be handled in the future. If I don't have the information by the end of today's class, I'll make sure to send the archiving procedures to you by the end of the week."

A different kind of mental preparation is needed if the course content is something that's second nature to you. Boredom is a problem for anyone who teaches a subject repeatedly. If you are in the position of training course material that you could recite in your sleep, try to remember that, although the information is not new to you, it is new for your group members.

- A sales trainer was asked how she could possibly look forward to conducting a session on customer relations the next day in light of the fact that she had conducted the same session every other day in the past three weeks. Her answer was simple: "I just tell myself to focus on the participants and not myself. I find it interesting to watch the way that they respond to what I'm saying, and try to find as many opportunities as possible for them to contribute to the discussion. In that way I can learn from their experiences, and add their contributions to the subject matter the next time that I teach the course."

Other ways to prevent trainer burnout are as follows:

1. Be flexible with your lesson plans and designs. Use repeat sessions of the same program to experiment with new ways to deliver the same material or to try out new activities.

2. Vary the location and the environment. If you always teach in the same room, see if a different one is available instead. If conditions permit, try bringing your program to the participants' work area rather than having them come to your training facility.

3. Watch others train the same program. If an outside vendor offers a program similar to yours, attend the class to get new ideas on how to handle the same subject matter. If there are other trainers within your organization whom you can observe, do so in order to pick up new delivery techniques and styles.

As a professional trainer, you may be asked to conduct a program many times more than you would prefer. However, the preceding tips may help you to extend your endurance and postpone burnout a bit longer than you would ordinarily expect.

One final recommendation as you mentally prepare for the training program ahead: remember that what works well for one audience may not work at all with another group. Course content may not vary from one session to the next, but the mix of people most likely will. Success in an active training program depends upon your ability to modify the content and design of a course according to the overall goals of that particular group of participants. All course time should be centered around the particular knowledge, skills, or attitudes that are supposed to be learned. Walk through your program keeping in mind the participants you are currently training. Try to be as flexible as possible as you think through your program, always considering a backup exercise if a planned activity does not fit the characteristics of your current training group.

ARRANGING THE PHYSICAL ENVIRONMENT

The physical setup of a training facility makes the first impression that participants will receive as they begin their session. Large corporate training centers may have hotel-type accommodations and extensive recreation areas, but your program may very well be scheduled to take place in an unused classroom in a church basement or elementary school. Regardless of your surroundings, you can directly affect the physical layout of the training classroom in a number of ways.

By considering the physical arrangement of the room as a continually flexible backdrop to your active training program, you can make it provide continued action and support for your activities. Don't be afraid to move the furniture within your classroom; even request the participants' help. By asking them to work with you to rearrange the room, you offer them the chance to take control of their surroundings. Training conducted in less than optimal environments is sometimes more successful than that undertaken within the best possible facilities because everybody has to pitch in to make things work. Here is an example in point.

- A trainer walked into a classroom with twelve rectangular tables arranged in three rows (see figure 11–1). Since there was little time to rearrange the tables, he decided to leave things as they were for his opening remarks. When he needed participants to be seated as subgroups, he asked them to help him do some interior decorating, rearranging the tables as in figure 11–2.

  Later on, when he wanted a fishbowl design (one group surrounding another group), he used the arrangement in figure 11–3.

Figure 11–1. Table Arrangement 1

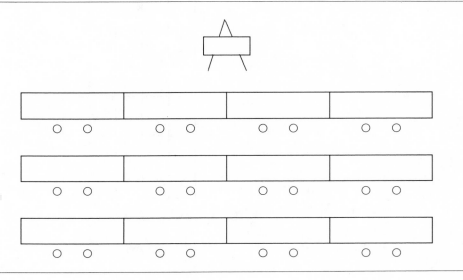

Figure 11–2. Table Arrangement 2

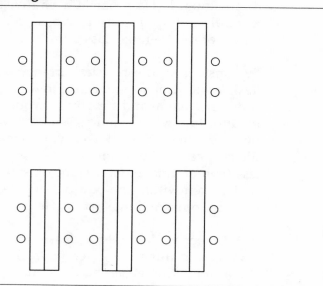

Figure 11–3. Table Arrangement 3

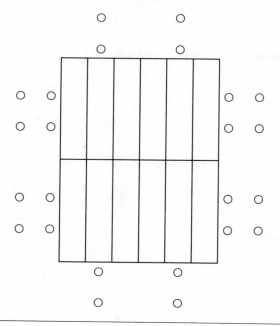

There are times, of course, when nothing can be changed physically to create new arrangements. Even then, however, all is not lost, as evidenced by this case example.

• A trainer had designed a fishbowl activity as part of a course on conflict management. He walked into a small room furnished with one large square conference table and space enough only for chairs around it. His solution was to treat each side of the table as a potential fishbowl group. Participants along successive sides of the table became the center of the discussion, with all those seated elsewhere acting as observers (see figure 11–4).

Figure 11–4. Musical Fishbowls

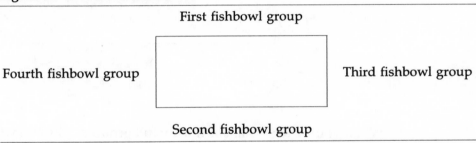

First fishbowl group

Fourth fishbowl group   Third fishbowl group

Second fishbowl group

Even fixed seating in an auditorium does not have to inhibit interaction. Participants can still have dyadic conversations with seat partners and can also be divided into groups of four, with two of the participants sitting directly in front of/behind the other two.

Probably the most common seating arrangement in the training world is a horseshoe (see figure 11–5).

The virtue of a U-shaped layout is that participants can see each other while a traditional teacher-in-the-front presentation is going on. Whenever the trainer wants to break into full group discussion, participants can interact face to face without having to move. The arrangement is also convenient for handing out materials as the need arises: the trainer simply moves into the U and gives a stack of handouts to participants at each side of the horseshoe. If the room is large enough, participants can pull away from the tables and form small groups. For a more intimate full group discussion, some participants can move their chairs into the mouth of the U to create a circle.

Figure 11–5. Seating Arrangement 1

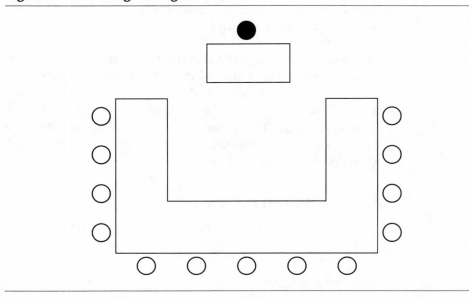

When your design calls for mostly full group discussion with few trainer-led presentations or subgroup activity, furniture can be arranged in a circle or square (see figure 11–6). Circles and squares afford the best view for each participant, although sometimes the room dimensions dictate an oval or rectangular arrangement.

Figure 11–6. Seating Arrangement 2

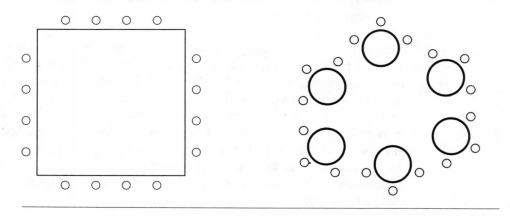

If you plan to have participants work in subgroups, try to locate groups as far from each other as possible so that they do not disturb one another. In these circumstances, if you must address the full group at any time, keep your remarks brief because you will be too far away to connect with your entire audience for a long period of time. Use breakout spaces, if available, for maximum privacy for the subgroups, but do so only when the task is sufficiently lengthy to warrant the physical isolation between groups. For short tasks, sending groups to breakout areas may be too time-consuming.

In the event that your design involves little need to write, take notes, or read from training manuals, you can do away with tables entirely. With only chairs to maneuver, any layout can be set up easily and quickly. Circles for small or large groups are easiest to achieve without any tables as obstacles.

GREETING PARTICIPANTS AND ESTABLISHING RAPPORT

The first moments of getting acquainted with your group members can be awkward for both you and the participants. Consider the following example:

- Michael Taylor was responsible for putting together a one-day program on team building for two small manufacturing companies that had recently merged. The program was scheduled to run from 9:00 A.M. to 4:00 P.M. at the in-house training facility of one of the two companies. Participants had been informed by a preclass confirmation memo that coffee and doughnuts would be available at 8:30.

  By 8:35, the first few participants had walked into the training room and had begun helping themselves to the refreshments. This was the first opportunity for employees from the two companies to meet each other, and, even within the same company, some of the faces were unknown to fellow workers. As more people entered the training room, small groups of participants began to form, with little interaction between groups. A few participants made no effort to socialize; after getting coffee, they began to read a newspaper at their seats. Several other participants wandered around the room, looking unsure of where to put themselves.

  The trainer, Michael Taylor, did not help himself to coffee and doughnuts. He was in his office around the corner from the training room doing some last-minute preparations for the day's class. When he looked at his watch and discovered that it was 8:50, he realized that he still had a chance to make a couple of quick phone calls before the official start of the class. When Michael finally entered the classroom at 9:00, he greeted the participants with a brief hello and launched into the program.

By 9:45, Michael experienced the first feelings that perhaps all was not going as well as he had hoped. Although he could not identify exactly what was wrong, he noticed that very few participants responded when he asked general questions. He had seen several people yawn openly as he talked, and many participants appeared to be restless. Two participants near the back of the room had begun a private conversation, and it looked like others were more interested in this conversation than in the information that Michael was delivering.

Michael decided to give the class a morning break a little earlier than he had planned to give himself a chance to figure out why the group wasn't relating to his material. He kept asking himself, "What went wrong?"

Consider Michael's experience a warning of what can happen if you do not take the time to greet participants one by one and connect with your group as a whole. A simple way to ease those tense moments is to make sure that you are available and ready to greet participants at least fifteen minutes prior to the start of the program. Walk around the room casually as people enter, make eye contact, and try to shake hands with the participants as they get comfortable with the training environment. *Learn as many names as you can. Introduce participants who don't know each other.* This getting-to-know-you process may relax your nerves as well, for you will begin to see the group members as individuals with whom you can share your interests. If you have not had a chance to do a thorough assessment of your group previous to the class, informal conversations with the participants at this time can help you gather valuable information before you begin the program.

Informal conversations are also valuable for establishing rapport with your participants. This can be very difficult with a new group, yet is essential if you are to gain your participants' acceptance and respect. Consider using the following approaches as you attempt to connect with your audience, whether in informal conversations or in the first moments of your training program. Not all may work for you, but utilizing even one of these approaches will create a bond between you and the participants.

1. "I've got something for you." Let participants know about your expertise and your ability to transmit it to them. Don't be boastful but do let them know that you are confident about your knowledge and skills.

- Management training is difficult to deliver unless you can convince participants of your expertise and experience. In a management training class designed for newly promoted supervisors, one trainer began the session, "I'm pleased to be your trainer for this class. Luckily, I have both the management and the training experience to help you. For those of you who aren't familiar with my background already, I'd like you to know that I've worked at the bank for the last twelve years, eight of which were spent working at all levels in the branch system. In addition, I've worked for four years in training, three of which were prior to my most recent experience as a branch manager. I hope my experiences at the bank will enable me to relate to your questions."

2. "I've been through this, too." If you have been through the same training and work assignments as the participants, let them know that you can identify with them.

- A trainer used this approach to connect with her group when she was asked to deliver a training program for clerical employees in a production environment. The employees were responsible for processing high volumes of mail and were employed only at peak times of the year. Before beginning the training session on quality awareness, the trainer let the participants know that she had also worked an off shift at one time in her career. She began the session by encouraging participants to compare stories about the difficulties of coping with an irregular work schedule. The group was pleased to discover that the trainer understood some of the pressures of their work. Without this mutual exchange of stories, it is doubtful that the employees would have paid as much attention to the new information presented in the training program.

3. "I admire you." Express your admiration for qualities that you respect in your participants. Praising their efforts, their intelligence, and their goodwill can help you to build a positive rapport.

- A trainer asked customer service representatives in a program on telephone skills to describe what it was like to be on the firing line with angry customers. The initial response was hesitant. Once the first story had been told, however, more and more participants joined what quickly became a very animated discussion. The trainer wrapped up the conversation by saying, "It's very interesting for me to hear about some of the frustrations you face on the job. I really respect you for having the patience and control to be able to deal with so many customers every day. I'm not sure I could do as well."

4. "You interest me." Get to know the participants and express interest in their backgrounds, life experiences, and concerns. The more you let participants know that you care about who they are, the more they will care about what you have to offer to them.

- A group of Indonesian managers came to the United States for a two-month training program. One of the trainers began the first day of his section of the program by asking the participants if they already missed home. Most nodded affirmatively. A participant added that that day was a special national holiday back home. The trainer asked the group if they would sing their national anthem for him to hear. Immediately, all twenty-eight participants rose and sang in unison. The trainer tried to learn the melody by humming along. To the delight of the participants, he successfully got through the opening notes. A tradition was then started, and, during breaks in the program, the participants taught the trainer several Indonesian songs. Showing this degree of interest in the participants' native music enabled the trainer to form a strong bond with the group.

GETTING THE BEST FROM THE FIRST THIRTY MINUTES OF TRAINING

Any progress that you might have made toward establishing rapport with your group can go to waste immediately if you are not careful during the most important period of your training program: the first thirty minutes. The first half hour is a kind of "grace period," according to Napier and Gershenfeld (1983, p.104), "during which any overt hostility or antagonism will be submerged under a veneer of politeness, watchfulness, and reserve." It is during this initial segment of time, however, that participants decide how they perceive you, what role they expect to play during the training program, and what they intend to accomplish during the course. As a trainer, it is your responsibility to make sure that each of these concerns is resolved positively during the first thirty minutes of your program. Be aware that participants may be asking themselves any of the following questions about their involvement with you and the training:

1. When are we actually going to start learning? How long will this thing last? (Impatience)

2. What am I doing here? I already know this stuff. Does the trainer really know what she's doing? (Competence)

3. I don't think that I'm going to like this trainer. I wonder what the trainer thinks of me? (Compatibility)

4. Is he really interested in solving *my* problems? I wonder if what I say in class will get back to my manager? (Trust)

5. Who will handle my regular work while I'm here? Is somebody going to be able to get in touch with me if there's a problem at home? (Out-of-Class Concerns)

Knowing that the first thirty minutes of your training set the tone for the entire program, try following these tips for making a positive first impression on your group:

1. Impatience: Begin the class promptly at the time previously announced for the start of the course. Work to focus the group on the course objectives, trying to hook participants' interest on to the course content as opposed to what time they will be released for breaks and lunch.

2. Competence: Don't assume that everyone in a course needs exactly the same content delivered to the same degree. Assess the range of differences in participant knowledge, skills, and attitudes either as part of a formal needs assessment or during informal conversations previous to the class. Opening exercises also can be used to explore participant skills more fully. Let the participants know that you are confident in your abilities, yet don't pretend that you have all the answers or the final word, and never pretend that you know more than you really do.

3. Compatibility: Neutralize the traditional teacher-pupil relationship as quickly as possible during the opening moments of the training program. Let participants know that your purpose is not to preach *at* them but to interact *with* them. Establish a community-like atmosphere in which contributions from the group are welcomed and supported by you and by the other members of the class.

4. Trust: Emphasize that you respect class confidentiality. Show the participants that you want to hear what they have to say and that you will be responsive to their needs.

5. Out-of-Class Concerns: Allow the participants the opportunity to speculate about how the training program will affect their work. Begin to establish the transition from the classroom back into the real world during the first, not the last, hour of the program. And, of course, inform participants of the schedule so that they can arrange communication with the outside world if necessary.

REVIEWING THE AGENDA

No discussion of the beginning moments of a training program would be complete without a reference to reviewing the agenda or program objectives. After your introductory remarks, clue the audience into what they can expect out of the training program and what detail is expected of them. There are several ways to do this.

1. Include your training objectives in the participants' manuals. Briefly clarify what you mean by each objective. Giving participants a copy of the objectives up-front allows them to be clear about what learning is expected of them. Figure 11–7 presents an example.

Figure 11–7. Objectives

After completing this time management course, you will be able to

- complete a time-study analysis.
- specify time-savers and time-wasters that affect your personal productivity.
- establish priorities to maximize your work in future.
- develop a time plan to use both at work and at home.

2. List what you hope to accomplish on a flip chart. You can make the flip chart ahead of time, or you can fill it in as you make your remarks. One way to do this is to list the issues to be covered in the program. Figure 11–8 reproduces an example from a training program on selling skills:

Figure 11–8. Agenda

- How to feel more comfortable asking for business
- How to improve group selling skills
- How to draw out and understand client needs better
- How not to subvert the salesperson if you are the manager

3. Orally describe the overall program objectives to your group. This approach is suitable if you have a very short or informal program that you would like to keep casual in tone.

A trainer began a management training program for new supervisors by saying, "The transition from coworker to supervisor can be difficult. Many first-time supervisors ask questions such as:

- How do I manage relationships with former coworkers?
- Do I need to keep my distance?
- How do I define my role as supervisor to them?

Today's workshop is designed to help you adjust to your new position."

In addition to informing participants about your goals, you should be sure to tell them how the program will be run and what you need from them in order for the program to be successful. Include the following information:

1. A content outline
2. A description of the kinds of training activities you have designed
3. The schedule
4. Requests you will make of participants during the program
5. Housekeeping information (eating arrangements, location of rest rooms, coffee breaks, telephone messages)

INVITING FEEDBACK TO THE AGENDA

One of the basic decisions that you will face at this point is the degree to which you will solicit participants' feelings about the impending program. Some trainers are reluctant to risk the possibility of opening a Pandora's box. They enthusiastically present their agenda and then proceed directly to the opening exercises, bypassing participant feedback. There is little problem with this if time is limited and you have every reason to believe that the program is as eagerly desired as it has been advertised. In most instances, however, there is much to gain from inviting feedback. How else can you check whether your agenda fulfills participants' expectations?

The simplest approach is to ask directly: "Does this match what you hope to gain from this program? Is there anything you would like to add to the agenda?" By asking these questions, you are not implying that the agenda is up for grabs. You are merely expressing your willingness to consider any wishes that participants may have. Most participants will understand when their wishes cannot be accommodated.

Another common approach is to ask participants, once they have learned about your plans, what hopes and concerns they have. This formula allows them to express a wide variety of wishes, from wanting the program to have more real-life application to allowing for smoking breaks. Some trainers prefer to separate the discussion into two parts. First, they elicit from the group *what* they want to learn. Then, they encourage the participants to discuss *how* the program will proceed and *how* they will work together as a group.

In the event that you have gathered assessment data about the participants prior to the program, it makes a great deal of sense to summarize that information at this point. Let the participants know that you have done your homework and are aware of their needs. This recognition is particularly important if participants have some resistance to the program. Instead of ignoring their resistance, you are better off bringing it out into the open. Showing interest in their misgivings is a sign that you are supportive and not afraid to listen to negative comments. Even if you do not agree with participants' views, you can still empathize with their feelings and acknowledge their valid points without compromising your own beliefs concerning the value of the program you have planned.

By the time you complete your agenda review, your training program should be well under way. You can now continue with opening exercises outlined in chapter 3. Remember that a well-planned beginning can save you hours of later frustration and prepares the stage for the rest of your active training program.

Worksheet
BEGINNING YOUR ACTIVE TRAINING PROGRAM

Use this worksheet to think about the beginning of your next program.

Physical Layout

Shape of tables:

_____

_____

_____

Arrangement:

_____

_____

_____

Establishing Rapport

"I've got something for you"—describe:

_____

_____

_____

"I've been through this, too"—describe:

_____

_____

_____

"I admire you"—describe:

_____

_____

_____

"You interest me"—describe:

_____

_____

_____

Reviewing Agenda

_____ Printed list of objectives

_____ Flip chart presentation

_____ Informal remarks

_____ Inviting participant feedback

Notes:

_____

_____

_____

_____

_____

GAINING LEADERSHIP OF THE

TRAINING GROUP

12

In the early stages of a training program, your leadership needs to be established. Even though all learning does not depend upon you, the active training program that you have designed requires your direction and guidance. Setting appropriate group norms, controlling the timing and the pacing of the program, getting the group's attention, winning receptiveness to your message, and dealing with problem participants are all aspects of gaining leadership within a training group.

SETTING GROUP NORMS

One of the first steps in gaining leadership is to set appropriate group norms. Consider what behavior you want to foster within the training and then focus on guiding the group in this direction. Establishing firm ground rules lets everyone understand how the training program will operate and where it will go. These ground rules should not just be set and forgotten; you should model and reinforce them continuously throughout the session. Group norms that are firmly established from the outset of the training program help to guide the remainder of the course.

The following group norms have been found to be helpful within an active training environment.

1. Encourage participants to express themselves honestly. Let them know that the open expression of ideas, concerns, and attitudes is appreciated and will enhance the overall learning process.

Sample script: "Please feel free to add your own opinions to our discussions; your ideas and experiences will contribute greatly to the value of this class for all of us."

2. Ask that confidentiality be respected. Let participants know that you want what everyone says during a session to remain confidential. Conversations about people outside the training group should not be disclosed to others once the session is over.

Sample script: "I realize that many of you know the same people within your organization. Let's have a rule of trust between us that whatever we say and do as individuals during the training session will remain in this room."

3. Urge risk taking. A training session is a unique opportunity for participants to step away from their usual roles and responsibilities and consider information from another point of view. Encourage participants to use the training environment to their advantage by taking risks that they normally would not consider.

Sample script: "Sometimes people shy away from role plays because they feel uncomfortable acting in front of the group. It is my hope that you will find role plays to be quite useful for examining your own behavior in a variety of situations and that you will feel comfortable participating in the activities planned for today."

4. Expect participation from everyone. Remind participants that if they hold back initially from participating, it becomes increasingly more difficult to join in as time goes on. Tell them that you have planned opening exercises designed to encourage participation.

Sample script: "Do you remember how when you were a student in high school or college the same people always spoke up in class? I don't want that to happen here, so I have put together some introductory activities designed for all of you to participate in right from the beginning.''

5. Promote the value of performance feedback. Let participants know that they are expected to give helpful feedback to each other and that all comments, both given and received, should be considered constructive criticism.

Sample script: "As part of this interviewing skills training course, I will ask each one of you to participate in an exercise that will be videotaped and then critiqued by the class. I hope that you will view this as an opportunity to sharpen and enhance your existing skills and not see it as a personal attack on your own interviewing style.''

6. Require participants to sit in different spots. This way more people meet, the social climate of the group evens out, and cliques cannot form.

Sample script: "We will be together for three days. I'd like you to switch seats twice a day so that you will get a chance to work with everyone in the group.''

7. Reassure participants that their questions are welcomed. Let them know that you expect them to ask questions whenever they are confused and to speak up when they don't understand.

Sample script: "The best questions are those that, at first, you might think are dumb. These questions truly seek an answer and are asked at a risk. These same questions might also be on the minds of many others.''

8. Insist on punctuality. Let participants know that you will be able to start and end on time as long as they return promptly from breaks and lunch.

Sample script: "We have a jam-packed program, and I need your cooperation to make it run smoothly. One thing that would help me a lot is if you are punctual when it's time to resume after a break. Even one person missing can be a problem because often we will be involved in team activities and therefore can't start until all members are present.''

As an alternative to stating norms yourself, you can invite group members to express their own norms. Break the group up into pairs and have participants identify behaviors they want and don't want to occur. When pairs report their lists, there will probably be considerable overlap. Wishes expressed by more than one pair can be listed on a flip chart (ask a participant to jot them down). Attaching the list to a wall will serve as a reminder to all throughout the program.

- In a public workshop with a diverse group, some participants expressed the wish that people get to know others different from themselves. This encouraged participants to seek out during breaks, lunch, and evenings people with whom they might not have been comfortable initially. This level of social integration would probably not have occurred if the wish to have different kinds of people get to know each other had been expressed solely by the trainer.

Norm setting does not, of course, have to rely on direct verbal statements. Your opening exercises can set in motion positive group behavior without any direct suggestions from you. Setting positive group norms through opening exercises can go a long way toward preventing negative situations from arising within your training program.

CONTROLLING TIMING AND PACING

One way to lose a grip on your leadership is to lose control of time. Few feelings are worse than the panic a trainer experiences on discovering that she has one hour left to cover half a day's worth of material. Running out of material also can be embarrassing and give participants the feeling that they have been cheated of time that they have already allocated and purchased. And, while you may decide during the design phase of development how you would like to pace your program, it is not until you actually begin delivering that program that you will be able to ascertain the appropriate timing and realize its benefits. Both the participants and you will feel a sense of completion and organization when a program remains on target and moves at a steady pace through the planned agenda. On the other hand, a program that moves too slowly or too rapidly will leave participants either bored or breathless.

A leisurely pace is suitable for small group activities to allow sufficient time for each person to be heard and directly involved in the activity. A much faster pace is necessary to keep the attention of all of the participants when you are working with the group as a whole. Regardless of the format, stay alert to signs of restlessness and conclude any activity before the participants' interest is lost. Keeping things moving will help to give the entire program a sense of organization and accomplishment.

Also make sure that no time is wasted during your training programs. This may mean giving short breaks, letting participants know that work will begin as soon as breaks are over, and taking care not to waste time when you move from one part of your program to the next. A list of potential training time-wasters and their more efficient alternatives is given below:

Time-waster	*Alternative*
Starting late after breaks or lunch	Start exactly at the time that you had indicated. If all of the participants are not yet in the room, begin the session with a discussion or filler activity for which complete attendance is not necessary.
Starting an activity when participants are confused about what they are supposed to do	Give clear and precise instructions. If the directions are complicated, putting them in writing beforehand will avoid the need for lengthy oral instructions.
Writing lecture points on flip charts while participants watch; recording all output from subgroups	Prepare flip charts ahead of time or ask a participant to record information as you moderate a discussion of responses; use only key terms; decide if recording is really necessary.
Passing out participant materials individually	Prepare stapled packets of handouts ahead of time; distribute packets to strategic areas so that several people can assist with their distribution.
Demonstrating every part of a new skill	Show only the parts of a skill that are new to the participants or are key for their understanding of the whole skill.
Having every subgroup report back to the whole group one by one	Ask participants to write key findings on flip-chart paper and post these lists on the walls of the training room so that each group's work can be viewed and discussed at the same time. Or, going from group to group, have each team report only one item

Time-waster	*Alternative*
	at a time so that everyone can listen for possible duplication. The groups should not repeat what has already been said.
Letting discussions drag on and on	Express the need to move on but be sure to call on those who were cut off during a subsequent discussion. Or begin a discussion by stating your time limit and suggesting how many contributions time will permit.
Waiting for volunteers to emerge from the group	Recruit volunteers during breaks in the program; call on individual participants when there are no immediate volunteers.
Pulling ideas or questions from a tired or lethargic group	Provide a list of ideas or questions and ask participants to select those they agree with; often your list will trigger thoughts and queries from participants.

You can affirm the value of your training program by monitoring how you allocate time within the session. A program that provides both adequate time for participants to learn and a quick pace to assure participant attention helps to establish your control. You can then keep that control by eliminating busywork and time-wasters.

GETTING THE GROUP'S ATTENTION

In a school setting, a teacher calls the class to order in ways that often won't do for a trainer who wants to emphasize an adult-to-adult relationship. There are several friendly, unobtrusive ways to accomplish this. For example, as participants are chatting, you can simply raise your voice slightly and say nonapologetically, "May I begin?" To vary your cues over a longer program, try any one of these attention-getting devices:

1. Ask a silly, joke-type question such as, "Excuse me. I have a question for you. If George Washington were stopped by a police officer, would he show a quarter or a dollar for identification?"

2. Clear your throat and gently grab the participants' attention by saying humorously something like "Testing, 1, 2, 3. Testing," "Now hear this, hear this," or "Earth to group, earth to group."

3. Flick a light switch ever so slightly. This isn't offensive if done tastefully.

INCREASING RECEPTIVITY TO YOUR LEADERSHIP

The way a trainer talks to adult participants makes a big difference in how receptive they will be to his leadership (Repplier 1986). As you converse with your group, particularly in the early stages of the program, try to use some of the following approaches to win participants over.

1. **Make "liking" statements:**

   "I'd like to get the chance to know all of you."

   "I hope that, through the comments I give you, you will feel as though you're getting some personal attention."

2. **Convey respect and appreciation:**

   "Don't worry about waiting for a break to get your coffee."

   "Thanks for having me here."

3. **Share what you have in common with participants:**

   "I guess we all wear a number of different hats."

   "A lot of us don't plan."

4. **Use informal language as a way of reducing your status:**

   "You've got to get out there and fight sometimes."

   "In today's career development jargon, we talk about 'the right fit.' "

5. **Phrase your advice and directives indirectly:**

   "I guess I'd like to start by asking you . . ."

   "Let me tell you how I propose to do this."

6. **State what's positive about participants' contrary viewpoints:**

   "It's exciting for me to get to try out these ideas with you."

   "It's always more interesting to get different points of view."

7. **Encourage disagreement:**

   "Nothing is carved in stone; I just want you to know that."

   "This is the aspect that people are most resistant to."

8. **Convey a desire for collaboration:**

"You're going to have a lot of input in this program."

"I'd like to spend most of today finding out how you would handle these matters."

HANDLING PROBLEM SITUATIONS

Any experienced trainer can tell you anecdotes about difficult moments with entire training groups or with individual participants. The unfortunate truth is that a trainer is an easy target for hostile participants' frustrations. Even more difficult can be the uninterested participants who would much prefer to be at home or at work rather than in your training program. Dealing with those feelings of hostility and uninterest can be the most difficult aspect of delivering a training program.

Why might an **entire group** become hostile toward you? Quite simply, because participants are likely to turn on you any dissatisfaction or frustration that they are feeling at the time of the program. The hostility actually may have nothing to do with you personally but instead may stem from irritation at having to attend your program or anxiety about learning new skills. Additionally, the participants may make an "us" versus "you" distinction in which they perceive you as the natural opposition.

As we mentioned in chapter 11, acknowledging class resistance is the first step to overcoming it and breaking through the "us"/"you" barriers. A well-known strategy is to acknowledge that often participants do not come to a training program as voluntary, eager *learners*. Instead, they may have been sent by their managers and feel like *prisoners*. Or they may just have wanted a break from the daily grind of their jobs and be attending essentially as *vacationers*.

You may want to tell the prisoners with gentle humor, "I'll try to keep your sentence as short as possible." To the vacationers, you might say, "We'll be having some fun and will be taking frequent breaks." In a more serious tone, you might try asking participants to identify their roles and place themselves in a group with fellow learners, prisoners, and vacationers. Begin to ventilate resistance by asking these questions: (1) Why are you in this group? (2) Why do you feel the way you do? (3) What can you get from others in the room? (4) What can you give?

The more you encourage group members to explain their positions, the better chance you have of reducing their hostility. This may mean leaving the course content for a while, but more productive learning in the long run will make up for the time spent dealing with the situation. An efficient approach is to use the conflict as a learning tool by incorporating it into the discussions and exercises planned for the course.

If you sense resistance when introducing a new skill or some new information midway through a program, you should again take the time to focus on the resistance and identify it before the situation gets out of control. Don't be afraid to stop the program, ask what's happening, and propose a discussion of the problem.

Negative behaviors of **specific individuals** create another difficult situation. Below is a list of some common behaviors you might face within the training environment.

1. **Monopolizing:** taking up a great deal of time
2. **One-upping:** trying to appear more skilled and knowledgeable than the others in the group, including the trainer
3. **Complaining:** continually finding fault with the procedures of the trainer
4. **Intellectualizing:** excessive rationalizing and justifying of one's ideas and beliefs
5. **Withdrawing:** not participating (and sometimes distracting the group by doing so)
6. **Arguing:** taking vocal exception to any comments with which one disagrees
7. **Questioning:** stopping the flow of presentations by frequently asking questions
8. **Clowning:** joking at inappropriate times

The key to handling such behaviors is to not take them personally. Napier and Gershenfeld (1983) suggest several reasons why problem behaviors that have nothing to do with you occur. The participant may have been ordered to attend the training to shape up. Or he may be hiding fears about failing to do well in the program. Or she may be a long-time employee who doesn't believe anything will change. Or he may feel that he is too old to learn new approaches. Or, after years of hostility toward her boss, she may be displacing her anger on you. Or he may like the attention he attracts with his behavior.

Coping effectively with participant problems is an extremely important training skill. When a participant exhibits problem behaviors, the whole group likely will become involved and therefore be distracted from the actual training program. Negative behaviors also tend to rattle the trainer and distract from the delivery of the course content.

Your responsibility is to the entire class, not just to one participant. You should not allow the disrupter to monopolize your attention to the point where the program begins to suffer. If you do need to say something to a participant exhibiting a problem behavior, it is far better to do so privately. Introduce your request with a statement such as "I think that it would be helpful if . . ." or "I'd like to ask you to . . ."

One way to control potential troublemakers is periodically to remind the whole group to adhere to the norms or ground rules established at the beginning of the program. In addition, make some new requests from time to time to prevent problems from occurring. Common requests used by experienced trainers include:

- "Please hold your questions for a few moments."
- "I think that it would be helpful for us to agree that people should speak only for themselves."
- "Let's just have one comment per person for now so that everyone has a chance to speak."
- "Try to build on each other's ideas."
- "When you go into your groups, I'd like to ask you to listen to the opinions of each member before getting into further discussions."
- "Let's have a rule that a different spokesperson be nominated every time that a subgroup is asked to report its findings."
- "Please, no cheap shots."

As conflicts between you and one or more participants arise in a class, you may begin to feel annoyed with the participant(s). Be wary of becoming unsettled by a conflict: *managing your feelings and remaining in control is important to your overall leadership of the class.* Do everything you can to defuse and depersonalize the situation. Try to acknowledge the challenge openly and to respond in warm but businesslike tone of voice. This will tell the rest of the group that you are confident and in charge. Some tips on maintaining control in the face of participant conflict are:

- **Don't get caught in one-to-one power struggles.** Acknowledge the value of a participant's views even when they are contrary to your own (e.g., "You've got a good point"). Empathize with his feelings. Show interest by asking the participant to go into more detail about his concerns. Summarize the participant's position. Agree to disagree. Offer to discuss the matter further at the coffee break.

- **Use good-natured humor.** One way to deflect conflict is to humor the combatant. Be careful not to be sarcastic or patronizing. Gently protest the harassment (e.g., "Enough, enough for one day!"). Humorously, put yourself down instead of the participant (e.g., "I guess I'm being stubborn, but . . .").

- **Connect on a personal level.** Whether the problem participant is hostile or withdrawn, make a point of getting to know him during breaks or lunch. It's unlikely that a person will continue to give you a hard time or remain distant if you've taken an interest in her.

- **Broaden the participation of others.** The more you use small groups and other devices to involve everyone, the harder it will be for just a few individuals to dominate the group. Also, ask for the opinions and comments of others (e.g., "I'd like to hear from those of you who haven't spoken so far").

- **Protect participants as needed.** If a participant or a subgroup is being attacked by a barrage of criticism, find something positive or provide a plausible explanation for what occurred. (e.g., "I agree that John was heavy-handed in that role play but I did really like his honesty.")

Here is a list of several problem situations that can occur in training programs. How would you handle them?

1. A participant monopolizes discussions.
2. A participant goes off on a lengthy tangent unrelated to the current discussion.
3. A participant continually holds private conversations with another participant.
4. A participant disrupts the session with jokes.
5. A participant strongly expresses disagreement with what the trainer says.
6. A participant has a distracting habit (e.g., pencil tapping, pen clicking, paper shuffling, etc.).
7. A participant does other work during the training session.

8. A participant does not adhere to time schedules, arriving late or coming and going at will during class.

9. A participant does not participate at all during discussion.

10. A participant does not do the in-class assignments or the homework.

Here are potential solutions to these situations:

1. **Monopolizing**
   - Summarize the participant's viewpoint (active listening), then move on.
   - Ask others for their input.
   - Ask the participant to hold off until a break.

2. **Tangents**
   - Ask the participant to hold off till later in the seminar.
   - Summarize the participant's viewpoint and move on.
   - Address directly the fact that a tangent has been raised—"That seems to be a different issue,"—and restate the purpose of the discussion, asking others for input.

3. **Private conversations**
   - Use nonverbal methods to regain the participants' attention (make eye contact, move closer).
   - Ask one of them a question (making sure to say the participant's name *first*).
   - Ask them to refrain from talking (privately, if possible).

4. **Jokes**
   - Privately ask the participant to minimize jokes.
   - Resume the session after the humorous interjections (be as serious as possible).

5. **Disagreeing**
   - Summarize the participant's viewpoint; ask others for their opinions.
   - Agree to disagree.
   - Agree *in part*, then state how you differ and way.

6. **Distractions**
   - Use nonverbal means to get the participant's attention (e.g., eye contact).
   - Ignore if the behavior is not detracting from the session.
   - Privately ask the participant to stop.

7. **Doing own work**
   - Use nonverbal methods to get the participant's attention.
   - If a group activity is under way, ask all to participate.
   - Ignore the behavior if it is not affecting others.
   - Privately ask the person to participate actively in the program.

8. **Time schedules**
   - Ignore the behavior.
   - Adhere to time schedules; don't let everyone suffer for one person's lateness.
   - Remind participants of time frames.
   - Privately request promptness (as a courtesy to the rest of the group, not just to you).

9. **Nonparticipation**
   - Use nonverbal means to draw the person into the discussion.
   - Ask direct but nonthreatening questions.
   - Connect with the participant during breaks.
   - Ask the participant to be the leader in a small group activity.
   - Leave such participants alone (just because they're not participating doesn't mean they aren't learning).

10. **No assignments**
    - Reemphasize the purpose of assignments (either to the class as a whole or one on one).
    - Ignore the behavior.
    - Recapitulate major learnings from assignments so that delinquent participants don't lose out.

One final thought as you consider handling problem situations: remember that it may not be necessary for you to intervene every time that a participant exhibits a problem behavior during your training program. Very often, other participants will make it known that they find such behavior inappropriate and unnecessary. A good guideline is to intervene only if the problem behavior is repetitive or affects the entire training program. Also, realize that participants who have been difficult often want to find a way out themselves. Give them some space to discover a graceful, face-saving way to change their behavior.

To gain leadership of your training group effectively, it is important to keep in mind that prevention and intervention are the keys to establishing and maintaining control. Setting positive group norms and modeling those behaviors throughout the session help participants know what guidelines to follow. Controlling the timing and pacing of your program prevents boredom and keeps participants focused on the course content. The way that you handle problem situations will give further credibility to your leadership, allowing you to concentrate on giving presentations and leading discussions.

Worksheet

GAINING LEADERSHIP OF A TRAINING GROUP

Use this worksheet to figure out how you will establish your leadership in your next training program.

Group norms to be encouraged:

_____

_____

_____

_____

_____

Time-wasters to be avoided:

_____

_____

_____

_____

_____

Comments to win participants over:

_____

_____

_____

_____

_____

Ideas for preventing problem behaviors:

_____

_____

_____

_____

_____

GIVING PRESENTATIONS AND LEADING

DISCUSSIONS

13

Although a lecture may be an efficient way to transmit information, its value for the participant is minimal if your delivery is dry, boring, or too lengthy. In chapter 4, we suggested several ways to design presentations to build interest, maximize understanding and retention, involve participants, and reinforce the content. The tips and illustrations of successful delivery techniques provided here are intended to complement those ideas. In addition, this chapter will cover how to make smooth transitions between phases of your program and facilitate lively discussions.

KNOWING YOUR GROUP

To many people both in and out of the training profession, the ability to deliver an effective presentation is the mark of a good trainer. Sometimes, sessions that are called training programs are really just forums for presentations by speakers with expertise in a particular area. Whether your presentation is the only component of your session or you have designed a lecturette midway through a full training program, a successful presentation can stimulate new thoughts and ideas in others.

To create an effective presentation, first consider the nature of the participants. What are their concerns, their backgrounds, and their reasons for attending? Tailoring your remarks specifically to your audience is the first step toward a successful presentation. If you originally designed a lecturette on writing techniques for college undergraduates, for example, edit your examples to make sure that they are appropriate in an adult working environment before presenting the same information to a corporate audience. The more aware you are of the composition of your audience, the better your chances of suiting your remarks to its needs. Following these other tips also will help you connect with your presentation audience immediately:

1. Aim your initial remarks at the immediate concerns of your listeners. Participants will be more attentive if they think that you are going to address the questions that matter most to them. Until these questions are answered to the participants' satisfaction, they will have difficulty relating to the information that you are trying to get across. Typical concerns might be

- "Why are you telling me this?"
- "How does this affect me?"
- "Why should I be here instead of elsewhere?"

If you do not address these concerns at the outset, you risk losing your listeners before you even begin and having to spend the rest of the time fighting to gain their attention and interest.

2. Understand why you are communicating this information. Have you been invited to speak as an expert consultant, a helpful intermediary, or as a decision maker who is telling the group what is about to happen? If you have been asked to present information about a new benefits program that will require employees to make major concessions, are you prepared to handle the hostile and angry responses that are likely to come from your audience? If you are lecturing as an expert consultant, do you have the credentials to back up your statements? Anticipate your group's perceptions of your role and plan your reactions accordingly.

3. Use language familiar to your listeners to establish bridges between your experiences and theirs. Avoid jargon or unfamiliar terms that might confuse people or prevent your overall message from getting through. Provide examples that relate to your audience.

Below is a transcript of the beginning of a class given by a corporate trainer responsible for teaching employees how to use a new word processing system. Pay attention to how the trainer attempts to answer the listeners' concerns immediately, explains her role, and uses language accessible to the participants.

Welcome to word processing transition training. Today's class is intended to help you, as experienced word processors, to make an easy transition between what you are using currently and the new version of word processing that our company will be using in the future.

Although a full conversion between the two systems will not take place until all word processors in your area have been trained, you will find that as of tomorrow morning the new system will be available to you on your terminals at work. It is important that you try out the new software on your own as soon as possible so that you can gain the full advantage from your hours spent in training today. I have been tracking previous attendees very closely and have found that the people who are having the best results use the new system immediately. I'd like to give you a follow-up call approximately three days from now to find out if you have accessed the new system and if you have experienced any problems when using it. Before I go any further, are any questions already forming in your mind?

"Will we still be able to access the old version of word processing?"

Yes, for a limited time period you will have access to both the new [and] the old software. I will be explaining more about conversion time frames at the end of our class today.

Let's start by finding out why our company has decided to change to a new version of word processing. The vendor that developed our system received numerous requests from word processing operators for enhancements that the old system simply didn't have. The programmers decided to put all of the enhancements together into one new word processing package, which is what you are going to be trying out today. I think that after you practice on the new version you'll agree that the enhancements are really terrific and make our word processing system much easier to use.

"What if I decide that I don't like the new version?"

The truth is that our company has definitely decided that everyone will be converted to the new system by mid-October. Any time that you move away from something that you're comfortable with you are bound to feel a bit awkward at first. However, I think that once you experiment with the new version and then try to return to the old system you will say to yourself: "I can't believe that I lasted with the regular word processing program for so long."

Instead of just talking about the system, let's go ahead and have you try out some of the new features for yourself. Please sign on by entering your user ID and password. . . .

In this extract, the speaker addressed the participants' potential concerns by identifying the reason why she was giving the presentation as well as the short- and long-term impacts of the new system on the word processing operators. A concern that the trainer overlooked (giving up a familiar word processing system) was brought up by a listener very early in the presentation. The purpose for the session was clearly identified (to help word processors learn how to use the new system), and the trainer used jargon that the audience would understand ("software," "users," "operator enhancements"). The trainer knew her audience and presented the information in a way that they could understand.

Here is another excerpt, this time from a lecture presented as part of a program entitled "Strategic Selling Skills." The immediate topic is sales presentations. As with the previous example, notice how the trainer focuses his initial remarks on the concerns of his listeners, understands his role in communicating this information, and uses a common language to bridge his experiences with those of the participants.

Right now we're going to be focusing on the sales presentation framework. Taking a look at our list of course objectives from yesterday, you'll remember that several people had mentioned improving their sales presentation delivery skills as one of their personal goals for our training program.

I know from my previous experience that making a sales presentation can be a very nerve-racking experience, especially if making these types of presentations is new to you. However, I think that you will find that you may already possess much of the knowledge that you should have in order to be successful when you give a sales presentation. What you will see by comparing the information covered yesterday to what will be covered today is that there are a lot of similarities between a sales call, a sales telephone call and a sales presentation. Let's look at the framework of the sales call as a review right now. [The following list appeared on a flip chart labeled "Framework of a Sale."]

- Opening
- Client's Primary Needs
- Probing Questions
- Listening
- Positioning Product Knowledge
- Resolving Objections
- Close
- Action Step

The framework for a sales presentation will follow the framework of a sales call very closely because all of the elements are very much the same. The skills that are required for handling a successful sales call will also be required for successfully handling a sales presentation, with some extra attention given to specialized delivery techniques such as voice inflection and positive language. We will have a chance to practice these delivery techniques later in today's program.

Let's begin, however, by discussing the opening or the introduction within the framework of a sales presentation. When you start giving your presentation to a group of individuals, and in this I mean within a sales situation, one of the most important things to do is to immediately thank everybody in the room for the opportunity to speak to them. You are taking time away from their work, so you want to thank them for coming to your presentation and giving you the opportunity to present your organization and your company's solution to them.

Another thing that you want to do up front is to clarify just how much time that you have to speak. Many of us will prepare for an hour presentation only to have someone come in and say, "I'm sorry, I have to leave in forty-five minutes," or somebody might come in and say, "You're going to have to cut your presentation to twenty minutes because we have a big problem and we have to run out on you." Some advice that I'm going to give you is to always have a short program and a long program, because you never know what the situation is going to call for. Above all, you want to make sure that you save enough time to get through your major points, close effectively and allow time for questions and answers.

So, initially, prepare yourself for your presentation by planning for both a long and a short program, and don't forget to thank your listeners up front for the opportunity to present to them.

ORGANIZING YOUR PRESENTATION

Although the actual design of your presentation may vary widely from one course to the next, several organizational principles apply to all lectures and presentations regardless of content or structure. Some ideas to keep in mind as you organize your presentation follow.

1. Make sure your opening is effective. A good opening will help the rest of your presentation to go much more smoothly. If you have a great opening story or joke that makes sense within the context of the rest of your presentation, use it. However, don't think that your opening has to be entirely your responsibility. Poll the group or ask the participants a few initial questions designed to elicit their opinions before you launch into your presentation. Asking the group to participate immediately will be as effective as the most humorous or captivating opening story.

2. Cover a few points of information thoroughly rather than many points incompletely. Set limits on how much you plan to cover and stick to those limits during your presentation. All listeners have finite attention spans, no matter how interesting or scintillating the speaker is. Trying to cram in as much information as possible can overwhelm your key points as well as confuse the listener.

3. Avoid tangents and getting off track. While it is not necessary always to stick to a logical sequence, prevent yourself from going off the deep end when delivering your presentation, especially in response to participant questions. Stay on target, in focus, and pace your presentation so as to keep everyone's interest in your subject matter alive.

4. Be as specific as possible in your lecture points. The clearer your message, the greater the likelihood that your audience will understand what it is that you are trying to convey. Give examples or make analogies that truly illuminate your points.

5. Estimate the time each part of your presentation will take. By doing so, you can adjust your remarks as needed. Sometimes, you will need to shorten certain parts of a prepared presentation to fit into the time constraints of a particular training group. Before delivering the presentation, decide which segments can be shortened or lengthened if necessary.

WATCHING YOUR BODY LANGUAGE

Underlying all presentations is your body language and the expressiveness of your voice. The maxim "it's not what you say but how you say it" holds true. In fact, research shows that *what* you say accounts for only 7% of the impact of your presentation. Ninety-three percent of how people respond to you stems from *how* you are communicating nonverbally. The keys to effective nonverbal behavior are how you present yourself *vocally*, *facially*, and *posturally*. Remember that the participants will primarily be focused on you as the lecturer or presenter. The effective communication of your message can be sabotaged by delivery techniques that are annoying or irritating to your listeners. Following these suggestions will enhance your personal presentation skills:

1. Establish your comfort level with the group through natural, positive body language. Maintain good posture and a firm stance as you address the group. Avoid putting your hands near your mouth or your face, as those gestures signal insecurity. Watch out for such bad habits as fidgeting, playing with your hair, or tapping a pencil, as they distract the participants from your message.

2. Individualize your audience by making eye contact with your participants. Resist the temptation to stare at your notes or read from a written page. You are speaking to an audience, not a piece of paper. Pick out two or three friendly faces and look at them frequently for support. Alternate looking at those specific people with a general panning of the group, allowing your eyes to rove from one corner of the room to another.

3. Be aware of the pace and volume of your voice as you speak. Try to speak slightly more slowly than you would in normal conversation so that all participants can catch what you are saying. Speak at a volume that is loud enough for all to hear yet not so loud that you find yourself shouting. Varying both the rate and the tone of your voice can help to keep the audience's attention, much as a master storyteller modulates her voice to complement the plot and characters of the story.

4. Alter speech habits that are annoying to your listeners. Fillers like "ah," "um," and "er" are irritating when used repetitively by a speaker. Especially guard against the continual use of "you know," which is a popular conversational phrase but out of place in a lecture or presentation. Excessive coughing or throat clearing takes a listener's attention away from the information being presented and instead focuses it on the presenter himself.

As you try to make any desired changes in your nonverbal behavior, be careful, however, not to overdo it. Eye contact that becomes a stare, a forced smile, or an overly enthusiastic voice will diminish your credibility.

Listening to a tape recording of yourself giving a sample presentation may help you pick up annoying speech mannerisms of which you may be unaware. Viewing a videotape (ask a friend or colleague to help) is even better, since you can both hear and see your delivery style.

Changing your presentation style may be difficult at first. Your habits have probably developed over a long period of time and may be hard to break. However, constant awareness of your body language and voice patterns while you speak in front of a group will help to ensure that your message is not only delivered but also heard and understood by your participants.

If you wish, utilize the feedback form reproduced in figure 13–1 to assess how you are doing.

Figure 13–1. Feedback on Nonverbal Behaviors

VOICE

Volume	(loud)	5	4	3	2	1	(soft)
Tone	(animated)	5	4	3	2	1	(monotonous)
Fluency	(smooth)	5	4	3	2	1	(halting)
Speed	(fast)	5	4	3	2	1	(slow)

FACIAL EXPRESSIONS

Eyes	(engaged)	5	4	3	2	1	(removed)
Mouth	(friendly)	5	4	3	2	1	(stern)
Forehead	(relaxed)	5	4	3	2	1	(furrowed)

POSTURE

Posture	(erect)	5	4	3	2	1	(slouched)
Movement	(controlled)	5	4	3	2	1	(fidgety)
Hand gestures	(natural)	5	4	3	2	1	(robotic)

HANDLING PROPS

One of the things that do the most harm to a presentation is the mishandling of props. If you decide to use notes for a lecture, number the pages or notecards so that you don't get lost midspeech. Try to look at your notes rarely and don't give in to the temptation to read your written information verbatim. *Your best approach is to use already prepared flip charts for your notes.* When your key points are posted, not only does the audience receive visual backup of your material, but you can keep track of what to say next. A useful trick is lightly to pencil notes concerning your presentation on the flip chart itself—you'll be able to see them but your audience won't.

A **flip chart** is the most effective prop to use in presentations to groups of fewer than thirty participants because it does not require lights to be dimmed. A flip chart is also versatile, correctable, and portable. Be sure to print big and use few words. Draw pictures if you have the talent and write in different robust colors. A number of other flip chart hints may come in handy.

1. Leave a blank page between each already prepared flip-chart sheet in case you want to write spontaneously during a presentation. Or use a second flip chart for this purpose.

2. Number, paper clip, or otherwise flag important pages so that you can locate and flip to them quickly.

3. Hide lines on the flip chart if participants' reading ahead will lessen the impact of your presentation. You can accomplish this with strips of paper or by folding up lower portions of the sheet.

4. Build curiosity and provide an opening summary of your presentation by posting all the flip charts you plan to use along a wall or blackboard.

5. Tear off and post around the room sheets from the flip chart that you want the group to be able to refer to throughout the program. Have strips of tape ready so that you can paper the walls quickly.

Although they are not as personal as flip charts, **overheads** can add impact to your presentations to large audiences, especially when the transparencies are clear, concise, and easy to read. If you do supplement your presentation with overheads, however, be aware of the "6-6" rule: there should be no more than six lines on each overhead, and each line should contain no more than six words per line. Limit yourself to one idea per transparency, and use graphics whenever possible. In order to stay connected with your audience, turn the lamp off whenever the projector is not in use.

A **handout** spares your listeners the burden of notetaking and provides a helpful reminder of the points that you covered in your lecture. Make sure, however, that your handout is concise and designed for easy reading. And think carefully about when you should distribute your handouts. Many trainers do so before their presentations and then wonder why they have trouble getting the group's attention when they begin speaking. If you want the group's full attention, let them know that handouts covering the major points of your discussion will be available after you speak. The participants will then be free to concentrate fully on what you have to say rather than on what you have written on the handouts. If you feel that participants will follow your presentation more easily if they have a handout in front of them, be explicit about asking participants for eye contact when you need it.

Following the suggestions outlined above should assist you with any presentation that you are asked to make, regardless of the size of the group or the subject matter. Well-designed visual aids can help you communicate your message quickly and effectively to the participants of your training program.

MAKING SMOOTH TRANSITIONS

In the previous section, we excerpted a segment from a lecture on strategic selling skills. In this section, on linkages and transitions, we will be taking a look at another passage from that same lecture. This time pay attention to how the trainer leads the group from one topic to the next.

I hope that you didn't forget the framework of a sales presentation over lunch because it's important that you keep that framework in the back of your mind as we move on to our next topic. By taking a look at our agenda, you'll notice that we're now going to be discussing *differentiation.* Mark, I believe that it was you who had asked me this morning about how to differentiate proposals, wasn't it? Now is the time that I finally get to explore your question in detail.

As you'll see on this overhead, I have listed three specific ways to differentiate your proposal from the competition's. The first method listed, team strategy, focuses on introducing the team of individuals that is with you when you make your sales presentation and the expertise of those individuals. It is important that you make sure to introduce whoever is accompanying you from your company and give the group a brief idea as to how and when they are going to be contributing to your presentation that day. . . .

Making smooth linkages and transitions between one topic and the next in your lecture or presentation involves briefly reminding the participants of what you have already covered then indicating what is to follow. The best transitions appear to be seamless and flowing, easily connecting what you have already covered to what you will be discussing next and letting the group know that you are ready to move on. There are several techniques for either tying together sections of your presentation or linking together various parts of your training program. These techniques and examples of how they can be used are described below.

1. References to periods of time. Mentioning specific periods of time—"yesterday," "this morning," "today," "this afternoon"—helps participants to organize the sections of your training program in their minds and gives them a clear indication of where you are headed.

"This morning, we took a look at what *not* to do in an interview; this afternoon we will be focusing on what positive approaches you can take to make the most of an interview."

2. Mini–subject review. Taking a few moments to review what has been covered allows participants to reflect on what they've already learned and to prepare themselves for the next part of your presentation.

"Let's quickly review what we've covered so far before we move on to our next topic of discussion."

3. Agenda check. Hanging your planned agenda on the wall not only helps to keep the group on track but also serves as an easy reference when you are making subject matter transitions.

"Taking a look at our agenda for today, you'll see that we have already covered writing and speaking communication skills and are now ready to address the topic of listening."

4. Change of visual aid. Introducing a new visual aid or changing to a different type of presentation tool can indicate a transition to a new lecture topic.

"Turning to our flip chart, you'll see that I have listed the five assertive communication techniques that we will be discussing today."

5. Change of group format. Reorganizing the group into a new configuration is probably the clearest way of marking a transition from one segment of your program to another.

"I think that it makes more sense for us to be together in one group for our next discussion topic. If everyone would just move their chairs from the small groups we were in for our last activity and form a large circle, we can begin."

Logical linkages between sections of your presentation or program ensure that both you and your group are ready to address a new topic. With just a bit of practice, elegant linkages will become a natural part of your delivery style.

FACILITATING A LIVELY DISCUSSION

For many presenters, encouraging discussion after a lecture consists of introducing a question-and-answer period with the classic line, "Are there any questions?" All too often what follows is an uncomfortable silence as participants wonder who will dare to speak up first. After a few awkward moments, the trainer sighs and says, "Well, if there are no questions, I thank all of you for listening."

But what if participants do have questions that they are simply too shy to ask? How do you coax lively discussion out of a group intimidated by the quiet aftermath of a presentation or lecture?

Starting a discussion is no different from beginning a lecture. You first have to build interest! Note how the opening remarks below are designed to generate a discussion about the benefits and problems of work teams.

Now that we have looked at the nature of work teams, I'd like to use the next ten minutes to get your thoughts about their advantages and disadvantages. Everyone these days is touting work teams as if they had discovered the Holy Grail. But maybe there hasn't been a critical enough look at when it makes sense to do things in teams and when it's better to get work done individually. I also know people who feel that work teams place an unfair burden on the people who take up the slack of the team members who don't pull their own weight. It's as if there is no individual accountability in work teams. You have a lot of experience working here at ABC Corporation. What do you think about the pros and cons of getting work done around here using teams?

Most experts agree that open-ended questions trigger better discussions than closed questions. Avoid questions that can be answered simply yes or no, such as "Did you like this training video?": "What are some things that you liked and didn't like about this video?" invites a longer response.

Remember that once a discussion topic is introduced, you can use many interesting formats to further participation. Back in chapter 3, we discussed the following methods:

- open sharing
- anonymous cards
- questionnaires
- subgroup discussion
- seat partners
- whips
- panels

- fishbowl
- games
- calling on the next speaker

Many of these options allow you to sit back and let the participants take charge. You might, for example, ask participants to form small groups to discuss the question, "What do you think about the pros and cons of getting work done around here using teams?" and then summarize their conclusions on newsprint. Other options require your leadership. In such cases, your role is to facilitate the flow of comments from participants. Although it is not necessary to interject after each person speaks, periodically assisting participants with their contributions can be helpful. Here is a ten-point facilitation menu from which to select as you lead group discussions.

1. Paraphrase what someone has said so that the participant knows she has been understood and the other participants can hear a concise summary of what has just been said at greater length.

"So, what you're saying is that you have to be very careful during an interview about asking an applicant where he lives because it might suggest that you are looking for some type of racial or ethnic affiliation. You also told us that it's okay to ask for an interviewee's address on a company application form."

2. Check your understanding against the words of a participant or ask a participant to clarify what s/he is saying.

"Are you saying that this plan is not realistic? I'm not sure that I understand exactly what you meant. Could you please run it by us again?"

3. Compliment participants on interesting or insightful comments.

"That's a good point. I'm glad that you brought that to our attention."

4. Elaborate on a participant's contribution to the discussion with examples or suggest a new way to view the problem.

"Your comments make an interesting point from the subordinate's perspective. We could also consider how a manager would view the same situation...."

5. Energize a discussion by quickening the pace, using humor, or, if necessary, prodding the group for more contributions.

"Oh, my, we have lots of humble people in this group! Here's a challenge for you. For the next two minutes, let's see how many ways you can think of to increase cooperation within your department."

6. Disagree (gently) with a participant's comments to stimulate further discussion.

"I can see where you're coming from, but I'm not sure that what you are describing is always the case. Has anyone else had an experience that is different from Jim's?"

7. Mediate differences of opinion between participants and relieve any tensions that may be brewing.

"I think that Susan and Mary are not really disagreeing with each other but are just bringing out two different sides of this issue."

8. Pull together ideas, showing their relationship to each other.

"As you can see from Dan and Jean's comments, personal goal setting is very much a part of time management. You need to be able to establish goals for yourself on a daily basis in order to manage your time more effectively."

9. Change the group process by altering the method of participation or prompting the group to evaluate issues that have been raised during the previous discussion.

"Let's break into smaller groups and see if you can come up with some typical customer objections to the products that were covered in the presentation this morning."

10. Summarize (and record, if desired) the major views of the group.

"I have noted four major reasons that you have suggested that may account for managers' unwillingness to delegate work: (1) lack of confidence; (2) fear of failure; (3) comfort in doing the task themselves; and (4) fear of being replaced.

All of the actions described above can be used alone or in conjunction with the others to help stimulate discussions within your training group. You may find that, as participants become more and more relaxed about contributing their ideas and opinions, you may shift from being a leader to being an occasional facilitator and perhaps just another person with an opinion. As your role in the conversation diminishes, the participants make the learning process their own.

Worksheet

GIVING PRESENTATIONS AND LEADING DISCUSSIONS

Answer the questions below.

1. What do I know about my audience?

_____

_____

_____

_____

_____

2. What is the core organization of my presentation?

_____

_____

_____

_____

_____

3. What nonverbal behaviors do I want to increase? Avoid?

_____

_____

_____

_____

_____

4. What props will I use?

_____

_____

_____

_____

5. How will I make transitions?

_____

_____

_____

_____

_____

6. How will I introduce a discussion?

_____

_____

_____

_____

7. What facilitation methods do I want to pursue?

_____

_____

_____

_____

FACILITATING STRUCTURED ACTIVITIES

14

In part 1, we examined alternatives to lecturing as well as several experiential learning approaches. Because these kinds of activities play a central role in active training programs, you will need to develop an array of facilitation skills to make them effective learning experiences. Listening to a lecture, watching a demonstration, or even participating in a discussion demand less effort and risk than does taking part in a role play, an exercise, or a project. Consequently, one of your basic responsibilities as a facilitator of experiential learning is *motivating participation*. Since it is difficult to get participants to do exactly what you want them to do, especially if any of your activities are complicated, you also need to become an expert at *directing participants' activity*. As the activity unfolds, the dynamics of the training group can impede with success, so you will need to be comfortable with *managing the group process*. In the middle of any activity, energy may begin to flag, and your task becomes one of *keeping participants involved*. Finally, at the activity's end, its meaning may be unclear. You now need to involve the participants in *processing the activity*.

Without the necessary skills in each of these areas, these mistakes commonly occur:

1. **Motivation:** Participants aren't invited to buy into the activity or sold on the benefits of joining in. Participants don't know what to expect during the exercise.
2. **Direction:** Instructions are lengthy and unclear. Participants cannot visualize what the trainer expects from them.
3. **Group process:** Subgroups are not composed effectively. Group formats are not changed to fit the requirements of each activity. Subgroups are left idle.
4. **Energy:** Activities move too slowly. Participants are sedentary. Activities are long or demanding when they need to be short or relaxed. Participants do not find the activity challenging.
5. **Processing:** Participants are confused and/or overwhelmed by the questions put to them. The trainer's questions don't promote the goals of the activity. The trainer shares his opinions before hearing the participants' views.

How can you avoid these mistakes? Many of the skills you need can be explained best in the context of a case situation. Imagine the following:

• You have been asked to create a two-day training program on interpersonal effectiveness. You have pulled together materials from other communication skills classes that you have taught previously and redesigned some key pieces to fit the group you expect. Today is the first time that you have tried out the newly designed program.

So far, the session is going very smoothly: there were no latecomers, and the total group comprises eleven participants—a comfortable number. Introductions were straightforward and the first activity, a needs assessment survey, was completed individually. You followed up the survey with a brief lecture that tied in the needs assessment to the overall learning goals for the course. It's now 9:45 and time for you to facilitate the first structured activity, a small group exercise called "Making Connections."

The exercise calls for the group to form trios and discuss questions that relate to interpersonal communication skills. After the first question, two of the three group members rotate to join new groups and discuss another question. The goals for this activity are for participants to learn more about each other as well as to practice opening up about themselves.

HOW WILL YOU INTRODUCE THE ACTIVITY TO THE GROUP?

Your participants need to be tempted before they will feel motivated to join in and take the exercise seriously. Getting participants to buy in to an activity is essential to the success of your planned exercise, especially if it involves risk or effort. Here are some ways to motivate participation:

1. Explain your objectives. Participants like to know what is going to happen and why. Don't assume that they know your objectives for the exercise—make sure they do.

> "Right now I'm going to ask you to take part in an activity called 'Making Connections.' This activity should help you to get to know other members of our group a bit more than you were able to during our brief introductions. In addition, this activity will allow you to practice opening up to people in new situations."

2. Sell the benefits. Tell participants what's in it for them. Explain what benefits they will derive back on the job as a result of the activity.

> "We often meet new people and introduce ourselves to each other. Usually, getting acquainted is somewhat anxiety provoking. This exercise should help you to feel more comfortable about getting to know someone."

3. Convey enthusiasm. If you sound motivated about seeing them involved in an activity, participants will internalize some of your enthusiasm.

> "This activity is a good one; I think that you are really going to enjoy some of the questions that I have planned for you to ask each other."

4. Connect the activity to previous activities. Explaining the relationship between activities helps participants to see the common thread in your program.

> "On the survey you just completed, many of you identified overcoming shyness as one of your goals. During our first exercise, you will get some immediate practice in conversation skills."

5. Share personal feelings with participants. Explain why you have found the activity (or one like it) valuable to you.

> "I know that I can be shy at times. It's nice to have a structured exercise designed to reduce the anxiety involved in meeting people."

6. Express confidence in participants. Tell participants that you think they'll do a good job with the activity or that they are now ready to tackle a new challenge.

> "Now that you've already met each other at least once, you should have no problems asking each other questions that are a bit more detailed. Let's go ahead and get started."

HOW WILL YOU HELP PARTICIPANTS KNOW WHAT THEY ARE EXPECTED TO DO?

Incomplete or unclear instructions can spell disaster for a structured activity. If you do not take the time to explain exactly how the exercise should be completed, participants may spend more time asking questions about what they are supposed to be doing than actually taking part in the activity. Although you need to be careful not to sound like a school teacher, don't be afraid of oversimplifying, for there is always someone who needs clarification and repetition. Here are four tips for making sure that the group understands your directions.

1. Speak slowly. Processing instructions for a complex activity is harder than listening to a lecture. Slow down so that participants can follow you.

> "Before we begin the exercise, I'd like to take a few minutes to explain exactly how this activity will take place. Please let me know if I am speaking too quickly."

2. Use visual backup. If appropriate, write directions on a handout or flip chart and allow participants to refer to this visual information as you orally explain it.

> "As you can see from this handout, I will be asking you to discuss four separate questions with other members of the class."

3. Define important terms. Don't take for granted that every participant will understand key words in your instructions in the same way as you. Explain important directions in more than one way.

> "As you can see, the first question is 'What are your strong points in communication?' In thinking how you'll respond to this question, remember that communication has two parts, the speaking end and the listening end. So, include your strong points in both of these areas."

"We will be forming new trios whenever there is a new question to be discussed. When I ask you to rotate out of your trios, I am, in effect, asking your group of three people to split up and for each one of you to join two other members of the class to form a new trio."

4. Demonstrate the activity. Sometimes it is important for participants to have a mental picture of what they are to do. Provide a brief sample of what the activity will look like. Use yourself and/or a few participants to illustrate the instructions.

"Now that the first question has been answered, we're ready to rotate. Each of you has been assigned a number—0, 1, or 2. The 0s will stay where they are but the 1s will advance one trio (clockwise) and the 2s will advance two trios (clockwise). Let's have a sample group try this out so that you understand what I mean. John, Kathleen, and Mary were together in a trio. Because he is a 0, John will stay where he is, while Kathleen will move one group over there [point] and Mary will move two groups over there [point]. Have I been clear?" [Avoid saying, "Do you understand?"]

When a trainer's directions are ineffective, a few basic flaws are generally responsible, singly or in combination. These and their associated solutions are described below.

Problem: It is not clear how the various parts of an exercise fit together.

Solution: Explain the big picture first, then describe each of the parts that form the whole activity.

Problem: Information is left out of either the oral or written directions.

Solution: Try out your instructions in advance on a colleague or friend. Ask the listener if anything seems unclear.

Problem: A confusing format makes written directions hard to find and decipher.

Solution: Redesign your handouts so that any written instructions are at the top of the page and printed in bold type.

Problem: There is no mention of special requirements/obstacles in the activity (such as the importance of a group timekeeper or leader, the need for felt-tip markers or paper, or pitfalls encountered by previous groups).

Solution: Take notes when facilitating an activity for the first time. Watch for any problems that come up and either alter the design or make the next group of participants aware of any pitfalls to be avoided or preparations to be made.

Problem: Separate parts of a complex activity are not clearly divided or differentiated.

Solution: Give the group detailed directions for one part at a time.

Clear, easily followed directions prepare your participants for the transition from trainer-led training to the independent learning that takes place in structured activities. Many trainers overlook the importance of verifying understanding before an activity begins only to find that the participants are confused, frustrated, or misguided. A design that you have worked hard to perfect on paper is worth a few extra moments spent on clear directions up front.

HOW WILL YOU MANAGE THE GROUP PROCESS DURING THIS ACTIVITY?

Most structured activities involve subgrouping. Small groups give participants an opportunity to discuss ideas and ask questions in greater detail than is possible in a large group format. Group movement also accommodates the diverse personal learning styles of your participants, many of whom may feel more comfortable speaking in a small group than they do when all of the participants are together.

Managing this process of forming and monitoring subgroups is difficult because you cannot control completely how participants behave in smaller units. Also, some participants may not be as comfortable, at least initially, in subgroups as they are when the full group is together. Here are some suggestions to maximize peer interaction and productive work.

1. Form groups in a variety of ways. In order to separate acquaintances or randomize group composition, assign numbers to participants after they have seated themselves and then form groups corresponding to those numbers. Or allow participants to choose their own partners when you want to encourage friends to work together. Or form the groups according to specific criteria (e.g., by sex, by department, etc.) when you want to achieve a certain composition.

• Count the number of participants as soon as you believe that you have full attendance. Then determine how large your subgroups will be by finding a number that easily divides into your total number of participants. Twelve is the easiest number of participants to work with—a group of this size can be divided into subgroups of two, three, or four members without you having to join the last group to make it even.

2. Mix teams and seat partners. Mixing up groupings offers the participants the chance to get a broad range of opinions and adds interesting variety to their discussions. Keep teams and seat partners together for long periods only when you need continuity.

• Set place cards in new locations in the training room to change seating patterns and create new seat partners.

3. Vary the number of people in any activity according to the exercise's specific requirements. The smaller the group, the more opportunities for each participant to contribute. Work with the number of participants in your course to create groups whose sizes fit your design's requirements. If possible, try to keep work groups to six people or fewer to maximize individual participation. Include yourself if subgroup adjustments have to be made.

• The "Making Connections" activity calls for trios, yet there are only eleven participants in the course. In this instance, you would join the participants as a contributor in order to form four groupings of three people each.

4. Divide participants into teams before giving further directions. Ask participants to move to their new locations first, and then describe the particulars of how to conduct the exercise. Many trainers have to repeat directions for an activity twice because the participants forget them by the time subgroups are formed.

• "Before I go over the directions for this exercise, I'd like you first to get settled in your project teams. So, please go to your tables now."

5. Ask for groups of five or more to elect a facilitator or timekeeper. Larger groups can be difficult to keep on track and on time. A facilitator for each group relieves you of that burden.

• "I'm going to ask one person in each group to volunteer to be timekeeper. We need to keep each round of discussions to just five minutes in order to stay on schedule today."

6. Give groups instructions separately in a multipart activity. Subgroups may finish their assignments at different times. Instead of waiting for all groups to finish one section of a multipart activity, quietly give the next set of directions to each subgroup when it is ready to move on.

- "I see that you have completed the first round of questions. For your next assignment, please complete this conversation skills rating questionnaire that we will be discussing as a whole group when everyone else is finished."

7. Keep people busy. If one subgroup finishes all its work well in advance of the other groups, find a task to keep its members focused and busy. You might ask participants to read material in the course manual or to complete an assignment that will be given to the other participants at another time.

- "You'll notice that I have included some information on assertive behaviors in your course handouts. Since you've finished the exercise, why don't you take a few minutes now to read through that information so that you are prepared for tomorrow's class."

8. Inform the subgroups how much time they have. State the time allotted for the entire activity and then announce periodically how much time remains. Visit subgroups to see how much they have accomplished. When you are about to stop a group activity, give the participants a warning.

- "You'll have ten minutes to do this activity. Make sure each person gets a two-minute turn. . . . You should be about halfway around the group by now. . . . There are two minutes left. . . . Please wrap up your discussions now so that we can get back together as a full group."

A trainer who quietly and smoothly manages group process is rarely noticed; the chaotic atmosphere of the training course will give away one who does so clumsily. For example, an activity that calls for participants to work together in pairs is awkwardly set up by the instructions, "Pair up with the person seated next to you" (on the left or right?). Such pairing can be facilitated gracefully by pointing out two participants at a time and saying, "You two are a pair, and you two, and you two. . ." It is simple moves like these that give the participants a clear indication of what to do.

HOW WILL YOU KEEP PARTICIPANTS INVOLVED IN THE ACTIVITY?

Your job is not over once the participants are organized into groups and begin working on a structured activity. You may find yourself redesigning an activity on the spot if it seems to be too long, short, simple, or complex for a particular situation. Altering a training design to fit the time of day and mood of your participants helps to keep the energy level of your training group up and active. Redesigning also adds interest and fun. Go with what is happening in the classroom if it meets your training goals. If an activity or exercise yields an unexpected surprise or draws an unusual response from your participants, make a training moment happen by weaving that surprise response into what you are trying to achieve educationally. The ability to be flexible within the design of a planned activity adds energy to the exercise for both you and your participants. Here are some other guidelines for sustaining group energy.

1. Keep the activity moving. Don't slow things down by speaking very slowly, endlessly recording participant contributions on flip charts, or letting a discussion drag on too long.

- Usually, more energy is generated when participants have to complete an activity within a specific time. Keep time frames short and move things along at a brisk pace.

2. Challenge the participants. There is more energy when activities create a moderate level of tension. If tasks are a snap, participants will get lethargic. Emphasize the importance of a challenging activity and encourage participants really to think about their answers or try out new behaviors.

- "Now, I've got a tough role-playing situation for you. After trying it out here within your training group, you'll be prepared for anything that might happen back home."

3. Reinforce participants for their involvement in the activity. Show interest in participants as they work. Don't stand off or busy yourself with other things. Give the impression that you are really interested in how they are doing and praise success.

- "I'm really impressed at the way you're going about this task. You're off to a great start!"

4. Build physical movement into the activity. Have participants move their chairs, stand up, or use their entire bodies during the activity as a way to wake them up.

- "Since you've been sitting for a long time, how about doing the next segment standing up. I'd like each trio to get up and find a spot in the room to discuss the next question."

5. Let your enthusiasm show. Genuine feelings of excitement and enjoyment about an activity will inspire like emotions in the participants. Your high energy level can lift up the energy level of the entire group.

- "I can't wait to see how you'll do on the next part of this activity. I think that you're really going to like it."

Behaviors that energize participants can easily be woven into your facilitation style. Once your active training designs are joined with these behaviors, you'll become both effective and believable as you reinforce participant involvement. Using these behaviors in the classroom will help you accomplish your educational objectives while maintaining high levels of energy and interest in your planned activities among participants.

HOW WILL YOU HELP PARTICIPANTS TO REFLECT ON THE SIGNIFICANCE AND IMPLICATIONS OF THE ACTIVITY?

When an activity has concluded, it's quite important for participants to process it—that is, to discuss any feelings that the activity elicited and to share their final reflections and insights. Processing questions help to complete the learning cycle by collating information gathered by the participants during the activity and applying that information within the context of the subject of the training program. Here are some tips to help you facilitate the processing portion of an activity.

1. Ask relevant questions. Often, trainers think they are processing activities when they ask participants questions such as "Did you like the activity?" or "Was it worthwhile?" Below are some examples of processing questions that encourage participants to go beyond simple answers and invite responses related to training goals. Be careful, however, not to ask too many processing questions at once. Usually one to three are all a group can handle at a time.

- How did you go about doing this activity?
- What were your concerns?
- On a scale from one to ten, how well did you think you did on this activity? What went well and what needs improvement?
- What helpful and not so helpful behaviors occurred in your group during this activity?
- Who else had the same experience? A different experience?
- What conclusions can you draw from this activity?
- How did this experience apply to your work/personal situation?
- What struck you while doing this activity?
- What do you understand better about yourself or your group as a result of this exercise?
- What skills can you transfer from this activity to your own work/home environment?
- As a result of this activity, what would you like to change?

2. Carefully structure the first processing experiences. A high percentage of activities invite processing in an active training program. Knowing this, it makes sense to train your participants early on to process activities. The first time that you process an activity with a group, ask only one or two simple questions and keep the discussion brief. It is probably a good idea to direct the processing as well. For example, you might present a question and then go around the group obtaining a short response from everyone. Later on, less direction will be necessary.

- One way to structure the processing of an activity is to use incomplete sentence stems (e.g., "One thing I thought worthwhile about this activity was . . .").

3. Observe how participants react during the processing. The most valuable and productive processing occurs when all participants feel comfortable expressing themselves. If participants begin to give responses that are personally critical of other members of the group, step in by modeling behaviorally specific information and deal with any personal confrontation in a positive manner. Through your own behavior, you can help the group to establish an open forum that promotes the expression of personal views without personal criticisms.

- "I didn't perceive Mark as being as hostile in this role play as some of you are suggesting. What I heard was a loud voice and some pointed feedback to the employee. I imagine that you were very annoyed with his procrastination. Is that true, Mark?"

4. Assist a subgroup that is having trouble processing an activity. If you have asked subgroups to process an activity and one group finishes well before the time you have allotted expires, it is likely that they have experienced difficulty processing and wrapped up their reactions too quickly, without probing below the surface. You can help them take a more in-depth look at the implications of an activity by asking them to share with you what they have discussed and then extending the discussion by probing further.

- "I see that your group has finished. Would you mind if I join in for a while? Tell me what some of your thoughts were."

5. Keep your own reactions to yourself until after you've heard from participants. Let the participants know that you respect them for their opinions. The processing time is primarily their opportunity to discover what can be learned from the activity. Your insights may be welcomed but save them for the end.

- "I noticed a number of interesting behaviors watching this project team at work. But, before I mention them, let me hear your reactions first."

Worksheet

FACILITATING A STRUCTURED ACTIVITY

Evaluate your effectiveness at facilitating a structured activity by responding to these questions the next time you are training. If you believe that the activity fell short of your expectations in any of the categories listed, work to improve those areas the next time that you present the same exercise to another training group.

1. **Motivation**
   a. Did you give the participants an overview of the activity before starting?
   b. Did you explain why you were doing the activity?
   c. Did you show how the activity connects with the other activities before it?

2. **Directions**
   a. Did you speak slowly and/or provide visual backup?
   b. Were the instructions understandable?
   c. If appropriate, was the activity demonstrated?

3. **Group Process**
   a. Did you divide participants into subgroups before giving further directions?
   b. Were changes in groupings managed smoothly?
   c. Did you keep idle groups busy?

4. **Energy**
   a. Did the design move at a good pace?
   b. Was there something challenging about the activity?
   c. Were participants reinforced for their involvement?

5. **Processing**
   a. Were the processing questions related to your training goals?
   b. Were the participants' reactions discussed before your own?
   c. Was the activity tied into the overall learning goals for the course?

CONCLUDING AND EVALUATING AN ACTIVE

TRAINING PROGRAM

15

Some trainers teach until the last moments of a program and then conclude by passing out an evaluation sheet for participants to fill out. An active training program should not end in such an impersonal and non-educational manner. Don't settle for an ordinary conclusion; there are many positive actions that you can take to bring your program to a meaningful close.

One of the many possible options is to leave plenty of time at the end of your program for reviewing **program content.** Another alternative is to invite participants to express any lingering **questions and concerns** about the course content. A third possibility is to engage them in some form of **self-assessment** of what they now know, what they now can do, and what attitudes they now hold. A fourth course of action is to focus the group on **back-home application.** A fifth approach is to provide an opportunity for participants to express their **sentiments** toward each other.

In this chapter, we will consider each of these steps. In addition, we will look at how you can build evaluation activities into the end of the program and also how you can obtain evaluative feedback during the program and several weeks after it.

REVIEWING PROGRAM CONTENT

Reviewing the program with participants can take many forms. On the simplest level, you can ask participants to **recall** the information and ideas that have been covered. If the program contained several experiences, you could encourage participants to **reminisce** about what they've been through together. You might also request that participants **rehearse** one more time the skills they've learned. Finally, you could call upon participants to **reconsider** their opinions about the training topic. Here are some tips on reviewing program content from these different angles.

1. Recall: Use games, exercises, quizzes, or tests that challenge participants to recall facts, concepts, and procedures they have learned. You might allow a study period in which participants could prepare for recall exercises individually or in groups. Utilize team competition to energize the review process.

- In advance of her final class, a trainer prepared a set of questions and their corresponding answers, putting each on a separate index card. The questions related to previously covered material. After shuffling all the cards together, the trainer dealt one card to each person then told the participants to walk around and match questions with answers. When the process was completed, the questions were read aloud, one at a time, for the group to answer. After each group response, the holder of the answer card would corroborate (or not) the answer.

2. Reminisce: Gather the group together to review memorable experiences that occurred in the training program. Ask them to share how these experiences affected them personally and professionally. Use an approach such as a fishbowl discussion or mental imagery exercise to add punch to the reminiscing.

- At the end of a five-day team-building program, participants were given a blank sheet of paper and told that it was time for their "final exam." The challenge was to write down, in order, the many activities they had experienced during the week. After each participant had finished, answers were compared until the correct list was jointly achieved. With the list in hand, participants were then asked to reminisce about these experiences, recalling moments of fun, cooperation, and insight. The discussion was an intimate exchange that brought about a wonderful, emotional closure to a special week.

3. Rehearse: Arrange an opportunity for participants to demonstrate all the skills they have learned in one final performance. Use methods such as role playing, simulations, written tasks, or projects as vehicles for rehearsing these skills.

- For a training program in family therapy techniques, four groups were each assigned a family type based on the circumplex model of family functioning taught by the trainer. Each group was given the task of role-playing a family of the type assigned to it that was coming to its first therapy session. The role play was to include a demonstration of techniques for beginning therapy with such a family. This assignment had the virtue of integrating all the cognitive and behavioral learning featured in the training program. The four therapy sessions created a powerful ending to the program.

4. Reconsider: At a program's conclusion, participants may have altered their views about many of the topics examined during the program. It can be useful, therefore, to allow time to discuss these shifts in perception. Use methods such as panel or case study discussions to allow participants to reconsider their opinions and attitudes.

- At the beginning of a workshop on delegation skills, managers were asked to write down on index cards one of their fears about delegating responsibilities to their employees. The cards were then passed around the group. Whenever a participant read an item that was true for himself, he was asked to make a check mark in the upper right-hand corner of the card. After circulating, each card was returned to its originator. At the end of the workshop, the cards checked most frequently were read aloud. The participants were then asked to reconsider their fears in light of the workshop. A discussion was held using a call-on-the-next-speaker format to allow the group to exchange opinions without prompting by the trainer. It was an enlightening way for participants to conclude the workshop.

OBTAINING FINAL QUESTIONS AND CONCERNS

When a program is about to conclude, participants are often reluctant to raise final questions or concerns because they don't want to appear to be delaying the program's end. This is unfortunate, since identifying these questions and concerns is a valuable closing exercise *even if there is little time left*. Leaving with some unanswered questions and concerns invites further reflection by participants after the program is over. Here are some techniques for your consideration.

1. Prepare a list of questions you would like the participants to take away with them. Clarify each question and then, if there is time, ask participants to select a few they want discussed before the program ends.

■ At the end of a seminar on the Myers-Briggs Type Indicator, the trainer distributed a final handout asking participants in what ways might each of the people in the following pairs differ when interacting with the other:

teacher	learner
salesperson	buyer
therapist	client
manager	employee
paid administrator	board president

2. Hold a final question-and-answer period. Hand out blank index cards and request that each participant write down a question. Then answer as many of these questions as time permits.

■ Using this approach, a trainer received the following questions at the end of a train-the-trainer program:

- "How much should I charge for one day of training?"

- "How can I handle questions about how qualified I am to conduct the training?"

- "How do I get participants to be comfortable with active learning processes when they are only familiar with a passive approach?"

- "How can I give directions without sounding like a teacher or boss?"

- "What do I do when no one wants to volunteer for a role-playing activity?"

- "Is there any way to perk up a group that is extremely tired?"

3. Write the following on a flip chart: *"One thing that still concerns me about [fill in the training topic] is . . ."* Using a whip format, ask each participant to complete the sentence. (Encourage participants to pass if they do not have something to share at that moment). Listen to the concerns without response.

■ At the end of a program on conflict management, participants supplied the following endings to the sentence stem, One thing that still concerns me is . . .

. . . how to handle a really aggressive person.

. . . whether I can listen effectively in the heat of a conflict.

. . . what to do if there is a complete stalemate.

. . . how to communicate that my intentions are cooperative.

. . . using role reversal techniques; they seem silly.

. . . how to pick the right time to confront someone.

4. Break participants into small groups and ask each group to record on newsprint its final questions and concerns. Display the items and request a volunteer to edit them into a final class list. Send the list to participants after the program is over.

■ Secretaries attending a half-day automated purchasing program split into groups of four and came up with several remaining questions. The secretaries then edited their subgroup contributions into this final list of questions:

• Can I still order supplies if the automated system is down?

• Where can I find a list of the item numbers for both stock and nonstock supplies?

• Who else besides my manager can approve entries for my department's cost code?

• What if the warehouse sends me the wrong supplies? How do I make sure that my department isn't charged for orders that are filled incorrectly?

• What if I have problems when I try using the system for the first time? Is there someone that I can call for help?

PROMOTING SELF-ASSESSMENT

If your program has been meaningful to participants, they have undergone some degree of affective, behavioral, and cognitive change. A fitting way to end a program is to engage participants in activities that allow them to evaluate their progress. The following suggestions may assist you in this process.

1. Ask participants to complete a questionnaire or test that provides feedback about their current functioning in areas related to the training.

- At both the beginning and the end of a bank platform training program, participants were given a self-scoring test on consumer lending products, business accounts, individual retirement accounts, and brokerage. Each participant was then asked to evaluate her results and assess areas of strength and weakness.

2. Design a way for fellow participants to give each other feedback and then ask them each to develop a personal profile based on the feedback they received.

- In a team-building program, participants filled out an index card for each member of their work teams describing their reactions toward this individual. Each participant was then given all the feedback cards commenting on his performance and asked to summarize the data and present it back to his team for clarification.

3. Using a physical continuum (i.e., a queue), ask participants to locate themselves on a particular dimension relative to other participants. Once the continuum has been formed, invite individuals to share why they placed themselves as they did and what changes they would like to make in the future.

- At the end of a train-the-trainer program, participants formed three continua in response to the questions, "As a trainer, are you more . . .

    . . . experiential or didactic?

    . . . challenging or nonthreatening?

    . . . spontaneous or well-prepared?"

4. Ask participants to write a short essay in response to the question: *"How do you see yourself now as a result of this program?"* Invite volunteers to read their essays or have participants exchange essays in small groups.

- At the end of a workshop on parenting adolescents, one parent shared the following:

    I am learning not to take my son's behavior so personally and not to blame myself for the unsettled nature of our relationship. He's going through a lot and so am I and that's to be expected. I think I'm now able to do a better job at sticking to the issue when we have conflicts and not getting sidetracked. I need to develop fewer but well chosen rules with clear, enforceable consequences. Perhaps I need to give up control over little things and accept behaviors that don't make a big difference at this stage such as what he eats for breakfast. I think I can make sure that my firmness doesn't cause him to "lose face." Finally, I now can share my feelings and opinions with him without lecturing or sermonizing. Once I started doing that, it was easier for us to talk. I think I've come a long way.

FOCUSING ON BACK-ON-THE-JOB OR BACK-HOME APPLICATION

In chapter 9, you were introduced to several activities—such as discussion of application obstacles, contracting, self-monitoring plans, and action planning—designed to support the transfer of training skills to real-life situations. These are excellent conclusions to a program because participants leave with an eye to the future. Unfortunately, however, participants are often weary near the end of a training program and so are reluctant to participate in such activities. Anticipating this, a trainer can take some steps to get past the obstacle of fatigue.

1. If possible, ask participants to prepare application ideas in advance. This way, you can use the last moments of the program to share plans rather than to create them.
2. Keep these activities brief and move at a quick pace. Don't dwell on your advice to participants. Make your final remarks memorable but to the point.
3. Lend some drama, inspiration, or excitement to the activities by the way you conduct them: bring participants together into a tight group huddle; invite participants to stand up and announce their plans; encourage applause when appropriate; have participants address envelopes to themselves so that contracts can be sent to them later as reminders; create a buddy system for later support and follow-up.

EXPRESSING FINAL SENTIMENTS

In many training programs, participants develop feelings of closeness for other group members. This is especially true if the participants have met for a long period of time and have taken part in extensive group work. They need to say goodbye to each other and express their appreciation for the support and encouragement they have received during the training program. There are many ways to help facilitate these final sentiments.

1. Assemble participants for a *group photograph*. As you are about to take the picture, express your own final sentiments. Then, invite one participant at a time to take a final picture of the group. As this is happening, applaud the participant for her contributions. Later, send each participant his own photograph of the group.

2. Develop an *artistic product* that affirms the value of the group and each individual member. Make a group collage, design a group shield, or assemble a booklet with a page devoted to each participant.

3. Create a *closing circle* and invite participants to express final sentiments sharing what they learned in the program, experiences they appreciated, and future intentions. Encourage participants to comment as the spirit moves them.

4. End with a *touch of humor*. Have participants design humorous awards for each member, compose symbolic toasts or wills, or present real or imaginary gag gifts.

EVALUATING THE PROGRAM

Although you may want to end the program with one or more of the creative strategies we have just illustrated, it is still important for you to gather data for evaluative purposes. Ideally, you should conduct any evaluation several days after the end of the program. If it is more practical to do it at the last session, try to create a clear separation between the end of the program and the time set aside for filling out any evaluation forms.

Actually, evaluation should not even wait till the end. You can design your active training program to provide for obtaining feedback and evaluation data on an ongoing basis so that you can make adjustments before it is too late. At the least, you might observe the behavior of the participants. Do they smile? Do they seem alert? Involved? Do they ask questions?

Behavioral cues are often good barometers; they can, however, give you incomplete feedback. You could fill in the gaps by guessing how participants think and feel. But, while these guesses might be accurate, more likely, they will be influenced by your fears (if you are anxious) or your ego (if you are too assured). Verifying your impressions is the only way to obtain accurate and detailed feedback.

There are two major ways (other than observation) to obtain ongoing group feedback: orally and in written reports. Obtaining oral feedback is a challenge. It can be time-consuming and threatening (both to the participants and the trainer). Obtaining written feedback is usually quicker and less threatening. However, you will not be able immediately to clarify the information you receive if you want to probe further. Both oral and written feedback activities must be well designed. Here are some of the best techniques.

1. Post-meeting reaction surveys. Create brief questionnaires and give them to participants at an appropriate moment. Items can be presented in different formats:

- *Short essay*

  Please respond in writing to the question, "What would you suggest to improve the session?"
- *Checklist*

  Check the words that describe your reactions to today's session:

  ____slow-moving

  ____illuminating

  ____overwhelming

  ____fun

  ____well-organized

  ____inappropriate
- *Sentence stems*

  Complete the sentence beginning, "Something I still am confused about is . . ."
- *Ratings*

  Use the scale below to rate how valuable you found today's session.

  (*high*)   5   4   3   2   1   (*low*)
- *Rankings*

  Rank each module by placing an *A* beside the one that was the most relevant to you, a *B* beside the next most relevant, and a *C* beside the least relevant.

  ____module 1

  ____module 2

  ____module 3

2. Anonymous remarks. Write a question on a blank flip-chart sheet or a blackboard, and ask participants to respond to it—on the flip chart, the board, or on blank index cards—during breaks. Possible questions are:

What one word best describes your reaction to today's session?

What will you remember from today?

What was the most important thing you learned today?

3. Oral survey. Survey reactions by asking participants to share out loud their feedback on the program. Ask for volunteers to contribute or go around the group if you want to hear from everyone. A good set of questions to pose is:

What would you like more of tomorrow?

What would you like less of?

What would you like to continue?

4. Informal interview. Casually solicit participant feedback during breaks and at lunch or schedule an evening rap session to discuss their feelings about the program in a relaxed manner. Ask questions such as:

Was the last segment helpful?

Am I relating this material enough to your situation?

Was anything unclear?

Are we ready to move on to new material?

5. Advisory group. Meet with a small representative group to obtain reactions. If appropriate, ask group members to interview some participants and report their feedback. Use questions similar to those above.

When your program has ended, you will naturally want to find out if the training met the participants' expectations. A final evaluation gives you a picture of participants' reactions to the training program as a whole as well as a sense of their response to the various parts. It should also allow participants to provide you with feedback for future use. Figure 15–1 presents the kind of form typically used to obtain these data quickly.

Figure 15–1. Program Evaluation Questionnaire

Course Title:

Date:

1. Circle the number that best represents your reaction to the program.

   a. I feel that I will be able to use what I have learned.
      (never)   1   2   3   4   5   *(often)*

   b. The program was presented in an interesting manner.
      (never)   1   2   3   4   5   *(often)*

   c. The training facilities met my needs.
      (never)   1   2   3   4   5   *(often)*

   d. The program covered the promised objectives.
      (never)   1   2   3   4   5   *(often)*

   e. The trainer encouraged participation and questions.
      (never)   1   2   3   4   5   *(often)*

2. What did you find most useful in the program?

4. What did you find least useful in the program?

5. Is there anything in this program that could be improved?

A less standard way to obtain participants' reactions is to use a semi-projective technique. Distribute to each participant a sheet of paper with the following instructions written on the top: *Imagine that a coworker (or friend) of yours was thinking about attending this program. He or she asked you: "What has this program been like for you?" How would you respond? Please take the next ten minutes to write your response below.*

The beauty of this technique is that you will usually obtain a deeper and more personal response than a questionnaire could elicit. The drawback, of course, is that it is much more difficult to quantify or summarize the results. The following is an example of one person's response to a program on counseling techniques:

This program provided me with a different look at what I had been doing. At first, I was bewildered. I was so much into crisis counseling—trying to solve the problem by applying Band-Aids without too much thought as to how I could help make a difference down the road. I will be different in the future. Now, I have some powerful techniques that, with practice, will remove the rush, the uncertainty, and, yes, the sometimes wishy-washy techniques I have occasionally used. This program helped to refresh a weary soldier!

Besides finding out how participants viewed the training program, you need to learn what attitudes, knowledge, and skills they acquired. Without this information, it is impossible to determine whether or not the training met its stated objectives. The simplest approach is to use a questionnaire or interview to ask participants such questions as:

1. What feelings do you have about the content of this program?
2. What tools/skills/ideas do you now have that you did not have at the beginning of this program?
3. What have you learned that you can put to immediate use?
4. What have you already practiced outside of class?
5. What intentions/plans do you have as a result of the program?
6. What do you want to learn next?

If possible, put these questions to participants not only at the end of a training program but also at a follow-up point a few months later. Ask them to report what they have done to implement the training they received. Don't forget to ask them what obstacles they have faced in their implementation efforts. A great idea is to summarize these reports and mail the results back to the participants.

In general, while the self-reports of participants may have value, there is every reason to confirm what changes have occurred. Post-training performance should be evaluated by testing participants' skills, observing their actual performance back on the job (or back home), or obtaining feedback from supervisors (or other key informants). A procedure recommended by Merwin (1981) combines participant self-report and supervisory feedback. She recommends asking participants at the end of a program to fill out a follow-up form containing statements as to how they plan to implement the training (see figure 15–2). In three to four weeks, they are sent follow-up instructions (see figure 15–3). Then, at each participant's option, the work statement and a supervisor's follow-up form (see figure 15–4) are sent to his or her supervisor for evaluation.

Figure 15–2. Work Statement Follow-Up Form

Describe situations in which you plan to apply this material and tell when and *how* you plan to apply it. Be specific.

Course Outline	Implementation Goals	(Do not write in this column)
I. _____	Situation: _____	
_____		
_____	My plan to apply: _____	A _____
	_____	B _____
	_____	C _____
II. _____	Situation: _____	
_____		
_____	My plan to apply: _____	A _____
	_____	B _____
	_____	C _____
III. _____	Situation: _____	
_____		
_____	My plan to apply: _____	A _____
	_____	B _____
	_____	C _____
IV. _____	Situation: _____	
_____		
_____	My plan to apply: _____	A _____
	_____	B _____
	_____	C _____

Please address the attached envelope to yourself; it will be returned to you in three to four weeks.

Figure 15–3. Follow-up Instructions

Please review the course content. Then review what you had planned to apply.

You may now place check marks in the third column of the work statement. If you were able to apply your plan successfully, check the "A" space. If you were partially able to apply your plan and are still working on the implementation, check "B." If you were not able to apply your plan successfully, check "C" and explain what obstacles stopped your application.

Figure 15–3. continued

Obstacles that stopped successful application:

Please feel free to make any additional comments about the workshop or yourself in the space provided below:

Figure 15–4. Supervisor's Follow-Up Form

[Name] was a participant in a workshop dealing with [subject]. During the last three to four weeks, s/he has attempted to implement the ideas or skills listed on the enclosed sheet labeled Work Statement. Please review what s/he has written. Did you observe any change? You should place check marks in the third column of the Work Statement. If you were able to note a change, any change, please check "A." If you were able to note some effort to change, check "B." If you were not able to note a change or an effort to change, check "C."

Were you able to offer your support to this person as s/he attempted to implement actions?

Please feel free to add any additional comments:

As you can see, any evaluation activity requires the same careful design as the training program it assesses. Attention must be paid to four central decisions:

1. **Focus:** *What elements are being evaluated?* Data can be gathered concerning any of the following:
   - Program content and design
   - Trainer's competence
   - Participants' knowledge, skills, attitudes
   - Training facilities
   - Organizational results
2. **Tools:** *What means are used to collect evaluative data?* Any of the following can be utilized:
   - Questionnaires
   - Observation
   - Tests
   - Reports
   - Interviews
3. **Timing:** *When is data collected?* Any of these times is possible:
   - Pretraining
   - During training
   - End of training
   - Follow-up period

Finally, it must be said that the evaluation of an active training program is not only about outcome but also about process. Evaluation efforts should address what is happening in a training program as much as whether it is making any difference. Why is process evaluation so important? Quite simply, *without good records of what happened during a training program, it is not always clear what needs changing if the outcome evaluation is disappointing.* Try to keep a log of the events in the program, how participants responded, and what your own reactions were as well. Or invite others to watch the proceedings and make observations of the program as it proceeds. By doing so, you, too, will be an active participant in your program.

Worksheet

CONCLUDING AND EVALUATING THE PROGRAM

Jot down ideas for concluding your training program under the categories below.

Concluding the Program

(reviewing program content, obtaining final questions and concerns, promoting self-assessment, focusing on back-on-the-job application, expressing final sentiments)

_____

_____

_____

_____

_____

_____

_____

_____

_____

_____

_____

_____

Evaluating the Program

(obtaining ongoing feedback, determining the focus, tools, and timing of evaluation activity, examining the process of the program)

_____

_____

_____

_____

_____

_____

_____

_____

_____

_____

_____

_____

INDEX TO CASE EXAMPLES

CHILD CARE
Opening exercise   45

COACHING AND COUNSELING SKILLS
Counseling interview case study   81
Training program outline   177

COLLEGE PLANNING
Participant questionnaire   11

COMMUNICATION SKILLS
Johari window   67
Defensive versus nondefensive communication demonstration   80
Manipulative communication role play   151
Interpersonal effectiveness activity   240

CONFLICT MEDIATION
Active listening in negotiations   153
Mediation skills role play   161
Participant final concerns   275

CREATIVE THINKING
Group brainstorming game   104
Creating a vision statement writing task   118

CULTURAL DIVERSITY
Indonesian/American group inquiry activity   86
Diversity in the workplace information search   89
Prejudice awareness activity   128
Peer consultation   165
Building cross-cultural rapport   198

CUSTOMER RELATIONS
Rating customer service   64
Irate customer role play   98
Customer service job explanation   153
Building rapport with customer service representatives   197

DEVELOPMENTAL DISABILITIES
Beliefs about disabled people questionnaire   48

MOTIVATION
Primary psychological motives exercise   71
Job-centered motivators lecture   73

FAMILY EDUCATION AND THERAPY
Opening exercise   45
Alcoholism and the family lecture   64
Family homeostasis lecture   70
Family proximity exercise   74
Family permeability demonstration   80
Obtaining support sequence   148
Roles in an alcoholic family closing activity   154
Family therapy techniques role play   255
Parenting adolescents essay   258

GROUP DYNAMICS
Task and maintenance roles learning goals   30
Task and maintenance roles lecture   70
Effective versus ineffective groups discussion   88
Intergroup competition activity   136

HEALTH CARE
Teaching patients to prepare for surgery   85
Team building in a hospital setting   112

INSURANCE
Work-related injury case problem   59
Accident claims questions   72
Irate customer role play   98

INTERVIEWING SKILLS
Hiring interviews lecture   72
Planning an interview   116

MEETING MANAGEMENT
Questionnaire   60
Five steps to effective meeting management   72
Improving meetings   92

MANAGEMENT TRAINING
Organizational change assessment   9
Management skills training objectives   37
Corrective action policies   44
History of leadership theory lecture   61
Supervisory styles   63
Management power visual   68
Delegation skills lecture   69
Why does an employee quit?   85

BIBLIOGRAPHY

Clark, Ruth Colvin. 1989. *Developing Technical Training*. Reading, Mass.: Addison-Wesley.

Mayo, G. Douglas, and Philip H. DuBois. 1987. *The Complete Book of Training: Theory, Principles, and Techniques*. San Diego, Calif.: University Associates.

Merwin, Sandra. 1981. *Effective Evaluation Strategies and Techniques: A Key to Successful Training*. San Diego, Calif.: University Associates.

Napier, Rodney W., and Matti K. Gershenfeld. 1983. *Making Groups Work: A Guide for Group Leaders*. Boston: Houghton Mifflin.

Pfeiffer, J. William, and Arlette C. Ballew. 1988. *Using Structured Experiences in Human Resource Development*. San Diego, Calif.: University Associates.

Pfeiffer, J. William, and John E. Jones. 1974. *A Handbook of Structured Experiences for Human Relations Training*. Vol 3. San Diego, Calif.: University Associates.

Pike, Robert W. 1989. *Creative Training Techniques Handbook*. Minneapolis, Minn.: Lakewood Books.

Repplier, Ann D. 1986. *A Study of Verbal Influence Strategies for Reducing Group Resistance in Consultation and Training*. Ph.D. diss., Temple University.

Spaid, Ora A. 1986. *The Consummate Trainer: A Practitioner's Perspective*. Englewood Cliffs, N.J.: Prentice Hall.

Thiagarajan, Sivasailam. 1989. "Instant Analysis." *Training and Development Journal* (June): 14–16.

Zemke, Ron, and Susan Zemke. 1981. "30 Things We Know For Sure About Adult Learning." *Training* (June).

INDEX

DR. MEL SILBERMAN is Professor of Adult and Organizational Development at Temple University, where he specializes in adult learning and training design. He is also president of Active Training (26 Linden Lane, Princeton, NJ 08540, 609-924–8157, mel@tigger.jvnc.net, http://www.activetraining.com), a consulting firm that provides courses on active training techniques, coaching, and team building. Dr. Silberman has conducted train-the-trainer programs as well as a variety of other courses for hundreds of corporate, governmental, educational, and human-service organizations. Among his recent clients have been:

ARCO Chemical
AT&T International
Automated Data Processing
Bristol-Myers Squibb
Franklin Quest
Hospital of the University of Pennsylvania
Johnson & Johnson
Meridian Bank
Merrill Lynch
Pennsylvania State University
Texas Instruments
United States Army

Dr. Silberman is a graduate of Brandeis University and holds an M.A. and a Ph.D. in educational psychology from the University of Chicago. He is the author and editor of fourteen books, including *101 Ways to Make Training Active* (Pfeiffer, 1995) and *20 Active Training Programs, Volumes I and II* (Pfeiffer, 1992, 1994).